# SNOW SQUALL

*The Last American Clipper Ship*

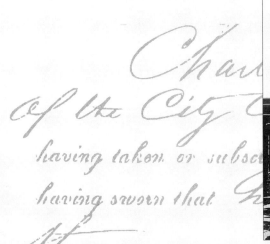

EXPEDITION ACCOUNTS
BY DAVID C. SWITZER

Tilbury House, Publishers  Gardiner, Maine

# SNOW SQUALL

## *The Last American Clipper Ship*

## NICHOLAS DEAN

*Maine Maritime Museum*  ⚓ Ⓜ  *Bath, Maine*

Tilbury House, Publishers
2 Mechanic Street
Gardiner, Maine 04345
800-582-1899
www.tilburyhouse.com

Maine Maritime Museum
243 Washington Street
Bath, Maine 04530
207-443-1319

First Printing: July 2001

10 9 8 7 6 5 4 3 2

Cataloging-in-Publication Data
Dean, Nicholas
    Snow Squall : the last American clipper ship / Nicholas Dean ; expedi-
tion accounts by David C. Switzer.
        p. cm
    Includes bibliographical references and index.
    ISBN 0-88448-231-6 (alk. paper)
    1. Snow Squall (Clipper ship)—History. 2, Excavations
(Archaeology—Falkland Islands. I Switzer, David C.  II. Title.
    VM311.S7 D43 2001
    387.2'24—dc21                                         2001027800

Jacket illustrations: Painting of the bark WARNER by James S. Buttersworth.
She was built at the Butler yard, and that may be her sister ship, SNOW
SQUALL in the background. Courtesy of Maine Maritime Museum, gift of
Elizabeth B. Noyce. The photograph of SNOW SQUALL's bow is by Fred
Yalouris. The screened-back drawing of SNOW SQUALL is also reproduced in
the text on page 62. It was drawn by William Bradford and is part of Hart
Nautical Collection at the Massachusetts Institute of Technology. The clip-
per card on the jacket front is courtesy of South Street Seaport Museum,
and the one on the back is courtesy of the Peabody Essex Museum. The
group photograph is by Dave Switzer.
Jacket and text designed on Crummett Mountain by Edith Allard,
Somerville, Maine.
Layout by Nina DeGraff, Basil Hill Graphics, Somerville, Maine.
Editing and production by Jennifer Elliott and Barbara Diamond.
Scanning and film by Integrated Composition Systems, Spokane, Washington.
Printing and binding by Maple-Vail, Kirkwood, New York.
Jacket printing by the John P. Pow Company, South Boston, Massachusetts.

# CONTENTS

# PROLOGUE:
## IN SEARCH OF THE LAST CLIPPER

*David C. Switzer*

IT WAS PITCH BLACK on February 2, 1983, when we landed at
Wide Awake Airbase on Ascension Island, a flyspeck on the
South Atlantic halfway between the mouth of the Congo River and
the point of Brazil. The blackness was punctuated periodically by
flashing lights, and the scene reminded me of the science-fiction
movie *Blade Runner.* Once we were on the tarmac, a disembodied
voice ordered us into groups of six, and six Mae West-type life
preservers were dumped at our feet. With our vests on, we were
led to a Wessex-type helicopter for a stomach-plunging lift to the
afterdeck of the liner CUNARD COUNTESS, which had been converted to a troopship for the Falklands conflict.

On board the COUNTESS were some four hundred soldiers
and officers, some journalists, a contingent of Falklanders returning home, and the six of us, the only Americans. It soon became
known that we were en route to carry out some sort of archaeological project, and we asked to provide entertainment for the
military personnel. Our impromptu lectures on nautical archaeology, the significance of the clipper era in nineteenth-century
maritime history, and the history of our quarry, the clipper ship
SNOW SQUALL, must have been viewed with some amusement.
We later heard everyone thought our archaeology business was a
cover-up, and we were actually CIA operatives keeping an eye on
British activities in the South Atlantic!

The voyage took over a week and had its surreal aspects.
British troops exercised and drilled on deck (and were sternly
warned that incapacity due to sunburn would be punished), while
we drank wine with dinner and were served impeccably by
Cunard stewards. After mostly sunny days and one severe storm,

the Falkland Islands appeared on the distant horizon, much the same as Captain James Dillingham must have seen them on SNOW SQUALL's fatal voyage in March 1864—bleak and foreboding.

A day after the troops were disembarked from the CUNARD COUNTESS at Port Stanley, it was the civilians' turn to descend to a lower deck loading port and climb aboard a landing craft to be ferried to the Stanley town jetty. As we approached the landing, the multi-hued houses of the town seemed hospitable, but a second look told us we were in what had recently been a war zone. Other troopships—some liners, some ferries—crowded the harbor. Overhead, large helicopters moved military supplies via containers and cargo nets. Close to the town jetty we passed the Falkland Islands Company (FIC) jetty, where the burned-out hulk of the landing ship RFA SIR TRISTRAM was moored. Bullet holes and explosion damage from Argentine air attacks were plain to see.

Just beyond lay SNOW SQUALL. This last surviving American-built clipper ship had ended up a hulk incorporated into the head of a Falkland Islands Company jetty more than a hundred years before. We were there to document her construction and to eventually bring part of her back to the United States for preservation.

The field of nautical archaeology has fairly recent beginnings. In 1972 a compendium of shipwreck sites that had been or were being archaeologically investigated was published by UNESCO. In the title was the editors' description of the then state of nautical archaeology—it was "a nascent discipline." With the exception of George Bass, Michael Katsev, and Peter Throckmorton, the new breed of archaeologists was mainly British, European, or Canadian.

The precursor to nautical archaeology in the United States began with the salvage of a Revolutionary War gundalow from Lake Champlain in the 1930s. The "real thing" got underway in the 1970s with the six-year excavation of the Revolutionary War privateer DEFENCE, in Maine's Penobscot Bay, which I directed. Somewhat simultaneously came the discovery and excavation of the scuttled Cornwallis fleet near Yorktown, Virginia, and the recovery of an eighteenth-century Brown's Ferry coastwise trader from

South Carolina's Black River. The later discovery, documentation, and partial recovery of the Ronson Ship from a New York City landfill site in 1982 brought the remains of an eighteenth-century American-built deepwater merchantman to light.

For years, sailing-ship enthusiasts knew that a number of nineteenth-century ships had ended up in the Falklands—and were still there. Articles about them would appear periodically, but it was not until the 1960s that British and American museum people (and those who felt that a "historic ship" might dress up a rejuvenated waterfront) began to give serious attention to these vessels. One of those spearheading the movement was San Francisco's Karl Kortum, who had brought the rusting hull of the British ship BALCLUTHA off the Sausalito mudflats, raised the money to have her restored, and turned her into a major exhibit at the San Francisco Maritime National Historical Park's Hyde Street Pier. Kortum had visited the Falklands in the 1960s and set his sights on two vessels there, the hulk of Isambard Kingdom Brunel's pioneering steamship, SS GREAT BRITAIN, then aground in Sparrow Cove in Stanley's outer harbor, and the British bark VICAR OF BRAY, which lay west of Stanley at Goose Green.

The beginning of the SNOW SQUALL Project occurred when professional photographer and maritime historian Nicholas Dean traveled to the Falklands in 1979 as part of a team surveying the VICAR OF BRAY for Kortum. While in the Falklands, Nick had a conversation with John Smith, a Falklander compiling a history of the many wrecks in and around Port Stanley, who mentioned that there was a Maine-built vessel in the waterfront complex of the Falkland Islands Company. It was SNOW SQUALL. Smith, somewhat truculently, asked Nick, "What are you Mainers going to do about her?"

Falklanders had become a bit protective of their wrecks. The VICAR was now owned by an American historical society which proposed to move her to San Francisco on a barge, following the successful salvage of SS GREAT BRITAIN, which was undergoing restoration in Bristol, England. The CHARLES COOPER, an American packet ship, then a hulk in Port Stanley, had been purchased by New York's South Street Seaport Museum, though exactly what they proposed to do with her was still uncertain. The iron bark FENNIA, the only one of the Falklands hulks still afloat, had been purchased by San Franciscans who hoped to turn her into a floating restaurant. They had her towed to Uruguay where they ran out of money, and she was scrapped in Montevideo. (One could buy a bitter reproduction of a watercolor, FENNIA Going Out, at local pubs.) In 1978 Peter Throckmorton had recovered forty feet of the Maine-built ship ST. MARY from a Falklands beach for the Maine State Museum. She was one of the last square-riggers launched in Maine, in 1890, and had come to grief in the Falklands on her maiden voyage.

Nick became determined to do something about retrieving SNOW SQUALL, since she was another significant piece of Maine's and the nation's maritime past. By then it was known that SNOW SQUALL's hull exhibited the fine lines of what were known as extreme clippers—and that the vessel that had rested forgotten under the Falkland Islands Company jetty for so many years was the last surviving example of an American-built clipper ship.

Nick enlisted the help of Fred Yalouris, then assistant director of the Harvard University Summer School, and in 1982 they made a reconnaissance trip to the Falklands. While Nick photographed SNOW SQUALL's bow from many angles, inside and out, Fred donned a wetsuit and, with scuba gear, examined the accessible submerged portion of the hull, recording many observations which, when boiled down, indicated that parts of the hull were worth rescuing. Important to what was soon to follow, Fred and Nick made many friends in Port Stanley, including the harbor master and members of the Falkland Islands Company. Particularly essential to the cause, as the adventure continued, would be the help provided by Billy Morrison, the FIC dockmaster.

Neither Fred nor Nick had an inkling that trouble was brewing between Argentina and Great Britain over ownership of the Falklands, and their departure from Port Stanley just preceded the outbreak of war. But soon after they were stateside, Fred began planning a second expedition to the Falklands to thoroughly document the hull structure both topside and underwater via photography and measured drawings, with a recovery effort to take place later. With each news broadcast, Nick and Fred fervently hoped that what was left of SNOW SQUALL would survive the war.

The war ended on June 14 with the Argentine surrender, and shortly thereafter John Smith sent word that SNOW SQUALL had survived but that she was in shaky condition after a runaway oil barge (though fortunately not a bomb) had slammed into her during the war. Whatever was going to be done should be done as soon as possible. So with the support of the Peabody Museum of Archaeology and Ethnology at Harvard University, Nick and Fred began putting together a team for a 1983 expedition. It consisted of Fred Yalouris, director; Nick Dean, photographer/historian; Sheli Smith, nautical archaeologist and draftsperson; Fred Feyling, engineer; Huston Dodge, master carpenter; and myself as nautical archaeologist.

Every archaeological experience is an adventure of sorts. For those of us who became caught up in it, the SNOW SQUALL Project was definitely the adventure of a lifetime. But the story of SNOW SQUALL herself is also an extraordinary adventure, almost a maritime detective story as Nick pieces it together with information gleaned from shipping lists, newspaper accounts, disaster books, and diaries. Her world is a fascinating one, from the laying of her keel in Maine at the Butler yard in Cape Elizabeth (later South Portland) in 1851; to her captain's problems with storms, unruly crews, rebellions in China, and attempted piracy; her owners' attempts to keep her profitable when news of her markets thousands of miles away was months old and her cargo wouldn't be delivered until months later; and her last captain's heroic efforts to repair his badly damaged ship after going aground near Cape Horn in 1864. Here is SNOW SQUALL's story, told by Nick Dean. We'll rejoin the expedition afterwards.

# PREFACE

As my friend and Snow Squall Project colleague Dave Switzer has outlined, the return of the bow of the last remaining American clipper ship hinged on a number of "what ifs." Had there been no expression of interest in South Portland when a recovery was first tentatively proposed in 1979, the whole far-fetched idea would undoubtedly have died on the spot. The tragic 1982 Anglo-Argentine conflict injured several good Falklands friends and killed two more, yet its aftermath brought the Falklands swiftly and brutally from a nineteenth-century-style colonial backwater to the twentieth century. We have speculated often what the nature of the recovery would have been had we not received incredibly generous assistance from Her Majesty's forces in the Falklands, and it has crossed our minds more than once that without that help a recovery might not have taken place at all. And had my mother not suggested that my godfather, Albert H. Gordon, might be interested in the project, it very well might have ended in dismal failure. Indeed, he was more than "interested." He became one of our staunchest and most enthusiastic team members.

When I set out on the adventure which became the Snow Squall Project a book such as this was about the last thing on my mind. However, if one is going to tackle a maritime archaeology project it is incumbent to find out as much as possible about its object. At the risk of oversimplification, scholarship demands trying to find the "life history" of the object to whatever extent possible and then to place it in some sort of context. In addition, when one is trying to drum up support for a project to "rescue" a piece of a vessel from eight thousand miles away it certainly does not hurt to be able to tell a good story about it when one goes on the lecture circuit.

When the Snow Squall Project began to "jell" in late 1981 I had already begun compiling a dossier on Snow Squall based on published reports in such works as Howe and Matthews's

*American Clipper Ships* and Carl Cutler's *Greyhounds of the Sea,* which are classics. I was well along on research for a book on another Maine ship and was fortunate in having been indoctrinated at the National Archives by the late Kenneth Hall, who had assisted Cutler in his research back in the thirties. I could not have had better basic training for chasing archival paper trails.

However, I almost immediately found out that these clipper-ship histories of the first quarter of this century, good reading though they were, for my purposes had two major flaws. They would speak of a "fast" passage of so many days between one port and another in a certain year, but they often lacked specific dates and never mentioned the cargo. This meant falling back on the pre-computer-literate researcher's old tool, a card file, with the hope of filling in the blanks one by one from reading the shipping news.

A photocopy of the file cards, blanks and all, accompanied me from archive to archive, as did a list of every name that had turned up in my research. It was at the University of California at Berkeley's wonderful Bancroft Library that a search of their card file turned up the Albert Dibblee Papers, and without their riches the story of SNOW SQUALL's last voyage would have been much the poorer. It was at the Baker Library at Harvard's Graduate School of Business Administration that key documents which illuminated the workings of the nineteenth-century maritime world came to light.

Since SNOW SQUALL's home port was New York, I followed the late Robert G. Albion's excellent advice in his *The Rise of New York Port* and read the shipping news in the *New York Herald* diligently and to great profit. My source for *Herald*s dealing with SNOW SQUALL's early career was the American Antiquarian Society in Worcester, Massachusetts; for her later career, I found bound volumes of the *Herald* in a local college library—until, at a crucial juncture, its librarian "deaccessioned" them as a so-called "fire hazard," so I began traveling to Worcester again. Fortunately, a generous donation to Maine Maritime Museum brought microfilms of the *New York Shipping and Commercial List* to Bath, and while that paper isn't as "newsy" as the *Herald*, and occasionally has inexplicable omissions, it provided useful details of a number of SNOW SQUALL's cargoes as well as the movements of her owner's other vessels. The *Boston Shipping List* at Mystic Seaport's G. W. Blunt White Library was invaluable for that port of call, and the San Francisco *Alta California* at the National Maritime Museum Library at Fort Mason filled in details there. An Australian colleague, the late Vaughan Evans, provided incoming cargo lists from the Sydney and Melbourne newspapers, while the Harvard-Yenching Library and the Phillips Library at the Peabody Essex Museum contained extremely useful information on Shanghai.

I mention this long list of institutions because putting together the details of SNOW SQUALL's career was something like doing a crossword puzzle, with a clue here that matched up with a clue there. To give just one specific example, a Boston insurance company "risk book" at Harvard's Baker Library listed a SNOW SQUALL voyage to New Orleans between certain dates. It just happened that my friend, Cathy Gates, had been researching vessel movements at New Orleans and tipped me off to the fact that unexpectedly the University of Maine's Fogler Library had microfilms of the *New Orleans Bee,* which the indefatigable Brenda Madore at our local Skidompha Public Library obtained on interlibrary loan. Indeed, all through my research Brenda found me one useful book after another, never failing me once!

Dave Switzer predicted early on, only half tongue in cheek, that as this long research project dragged on I was going to run up the longest list ever of people who needed to be thanked, which may well be true. I am grateful to all those who have been generous with assistance, encouragement, the odd key nugget of information which filled a gap, and hospitality as I worked in libraries and archives. One outstanding example of a "key nugget" is certainly Erik A. R. Ronnberg, Jr.'s finding of the only known contemporary drawing of SNOW SQUALL in the Hart Nautical Collections at M.I.T. Another is Steven Nitch's generosity in sharing the Edmund Rice SNOW SQUALL diary.

In the Falklands I am particularly grateful to John and Veronica Fowler for incredible just-postwar hospitality and good cheer; to Terry and Joan Spruce for access to old photographs and the Falkland Islands Company archives and for rescuing me from error; to Jane Cameron, Falkland Islands government archivist, and to the late Sydney Miller who first allowed me access to those archives; to John Smith, curator of the Falkland Islands Museum; and to the late Miss Madge Biggs, who produced amazing material from her archives.

In Great Britain, Dr. Basil Greenhill, former director of the National Maritime Museum, and Michael K. Stammers, keeper of the Merseyside Maritime, provided critical "missing links." Professor Aled Eames of the University of Wales kindly advised me on where not to bother looking. My oldest friends of nearly fifty years, Derek and Diana Phillips, were unfailingly generous and delightful hosts, and I gained a deep respect for the English Channel crewing for Derek aboard his sailboat in a frigid June off the Bill of Portland.

Steffen Tunge and Maryan Kohler, with whom I sailed in a pampero off East Falkland on the Norwegian ketch CAPRICORNUS in 1979, kindly looked at nineteenth-century Singapore newspapers.

In the United States, my great thanks to the librarians, archivists, and individuals who have been unfailingly helpful. At the National Archives, John and Angie VanDereedt and Milton Gustafson and the unknown archivist at Archives II who, when I was about ready to "come back later" after three exhausting days of reading State Department microfilm, insisted that I get printouts and "read them on the plane." Thanks also to Scott and Dottie Odell for their hospitality.

Many thanks to the following individuals: at the Peabody Essex Museum, librarians Will LaMoy and John Koza; at the Boston Public Library, Sinclair Hitchings; at the Nahant Historical Society, Mrs. Calantha Sears; at Mystic Seaport Museum, Paul O'Pecko and Douglas Stein; at South Street Seaport Museum, Norman Brouwer; at the New York Public Library, Warren C.

Platt; at the Union Club, Helen M. Allen; and at Maine Historical Society, Bill Barry and Nicholas Noyes, not to mention the informal right-hand side of the library mantelpiece, whereon messages and goodies may be placed (such as those from Bill Jordan), much as nineteenth-century captains did on Pacific Islands. Other invaluable Maine colleagues were the knowledgeable and friendly staffs of the Maine State Archives and Maine State Library; John Arrison at the Penobscot Marine Museum; Nathan Lipfert at Maine Maritime Museum; Tom Gaffney of the Portland Public Library's Portland Room; and fellow maritime researcher John Chesebro.

Two of my Maine neighbors, Carol Jaeger and Warren Riess, were instrumental in dragging me into the computer era and being remarkably patient with me in the process. Another neighbor, Jim Stevens, was patient as I repeatedly invaded his library in search of lists of merchant vessels. Hallowell antiquarian bookseller John Merrill, Wiscasset's Elliott Healy, and Frank McQuaid of the Edgecomb Book Barn came up with treasures about which I probably might not have known had they not phoned. Billie Todd, Georgetown, Maine's historical wonder, and Ada Haggett, her Phippsburg counterpart, were both prescient and generous.

In San Francisco, thanks to the National Maritime Museum Library's David Hull, Irene Stachura, Bill Kooiman, and darkroom technician Steve Danford, who brought forth an image of SNOW SQUALL's figurehead as a detail from a century-old photograph by arcane means beyond my comprehension. The late Dr. Albert Shumate kept mailing me excerpts from Caspar Hopkins's testy memoirs, and I cherish the memory of a lunch at the Pacific Union Club with Dr. Shumate and Albert Dibblee's great-grandsons. Sue Lemmon, late of the Mare Island Navy Yard, provided essential details. Old friends Ted and Arlene Miles and Bob and Becky Tracy (an easy walk to the Bancroft Library) made Bay Area research fun and feasible.

It is just plain impossible to thank adequately and individually each person who has contributed a fact here, or a lead there. Suffice it to say that I am enormously grateful to all of them.

Indeed, I can say that not once in the course of research was anyone ungenerous.

Thanks to John Rousmaniere, Captain Roger Duncan, and Captain W. J. Lewis Parker for having read and usefully commented upon my manuscript as it evolved, and to my editor Jennifer Elliott for her ability to cope with both my computer-software problems and lapses of proper usage. However, the real heroine in all of this has been my long-suffering wife, Zibette, who put up with my absences in the Falklands while she shoveled Maine snow, has been supportive all the way, and is the best (and most rigorous) copy editor I know.

Nicholas Dean
Edgecomb, Maine

To my godfather
Albert H. Gordon

ASIA

Shanghai

Amoy
Hong Kong

Penang

Manila

Singapore

Sunda Strait

Anjer

Batavia

AUSTRALIA

Melbourne

Sydney

Honolulu

San Francisco

NORTH
AMERICA

New Orleans

Portland
Boston

New York

Richmond

SOUTH
AMERICA

Rio de Janeiro

Montevideo

Falkland Islands

Le Maire Strait

Cape Horn

# MAP OF SNOW SQUALL'S VOYAGES

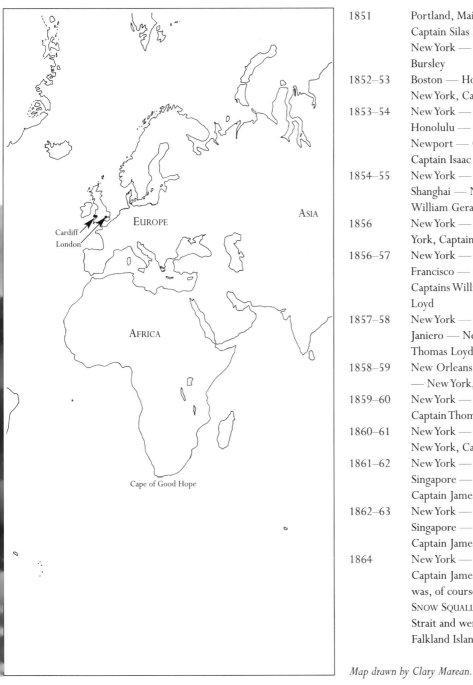

| | |
|---|---|
| 1851 | Portland, Maine — New York, Captain Silas D. Gregg |
| | New York — Boston, Captain Isaac Bursley |
| 1852–53 | Boston — Honolulu — Shanghai — New York, Captain Isaac Bursley |
| 1853–54 | New York — San Francisco — Honolulu — Shanghai — London — Newport — Cardiff — New York, Captain Isaac Bursley |
| 1854–55 | New York — Sydney — Batavia — Shanghai — New York, Captain William Gerard |
| 1856 | New York — Rio de Janiero — New York, Captain William Gerard |
| 1856–57 | New York — Montevideo — San Francisco — Manila — New York, Captains William Gerard and Thomas Loyd |
| 1857–58 | New York — Richmond — Rio de Janiero — New Orleans, Captain Thomas Loyd |
| 1858–59 | New Orleans — Boston — Shanghai — New York, Captain Thomas Loyd |
| 1859–60 | New York — Shanghai — New York, Captain Thomas Loyd |
| 1860–61 | New York — Shanghai — Amoy — New York, Captain Thomas Loyd |
| 1861–62 | New York — Melbourne — Singapore — Penang — New York, Captain James S. Dillingham, Jr. |
| 1862–63 | New York — Melbourne — Singapore — Penang — New York, Captain James S. Dillingham, Jr. |
| 1864 | New York — for San Francisco, Captain James S. Dillingham, Jr. This was, of course, terminated when SNOW SQUALL ran aground in le Maire Strait and went to Stanley in the Falkland Islands in hope of repairs. |

*Map drawn by Clary Marean.*

*Observe a ship at sea! Mark the majestic form of her hull as she rushes through the water...the leap of her bows, the symmetry and rich tracery of her spars and rigging, and those grand wind muscles, her sails.... What Academy of Design, what research of connoisseurship, what imitation of the Greeks produced this marvel of construction?*
—HORATIO GREENOUGH, 1893[1]

WITH THE POSSIBLE EXCEPTIONS of Spanish treasure galleons and the maiden voyage of the doomed liner TITANIC, perhaps no other deepwater vessels have so captured the public imagination over the years as have the "clippers" of the nineteenth century. They conjure up a vision beloved by bank calendar artists—vessels carrying veritable Everests of white sail over a white-capped sea under a lapis lazuli blue sky. The popular nineteenth-century American printmakers Currier and Ives produced hand-colored lithographs which were as sought after in the nineteenth century as rock star posters are today. One of their maritime prints shows the "clipper" packet ship DREAD-NOUGHT approaching New York in boisterous seas after a nineteen-day passage from Liverpool; another depicts the Maine-built clipper RED JACKET beset by impossibly turreted icebergs off Cape Horn on an 1854 voyage from Australia to Liverpool, her passage observed by penguins.

In the literature of the American clippers much has been made of their speed under sail. One historian, Carl Cutler, called

# THE WHITE-WINGED
# CHARIOTS OF COMMERCE

them the "greyhounds of the sea." Others, such as Samuel Eliot Morison, have compared them to Greek temples or Gothic cathedrals, while nineteenth-century sculptor Horatio Greenough (he who depicted a larger-than-life George Washington in a toga) wondered, "What Academy of Design, what research of connoisseurship, what imitation of the Greeks produced this marvel of construction?" While it is certainly true that a square-rigged vessel under sail is a stirring sight—as witness the crowds of spectators who flock to seaport shorelines during Operation Sail to watch the "Tall Ships" enter and depart—in truth the career of a vessel depended on engineering, economics, seamanship, and a good deal of luck both good and bad, rather than aesthetics.

"Clippers" evoke thoughts of the exotic, of the odors of teas and spices, the rustle of fine silks, or the sheen of intricately carved oriental furniture—the stuffs of the "China trade." My maternal grandparents were born just as the American clipper ships were vanishing from the seas, one by one, in the third quarter of the nineteenth century, but their family china was blue and white

"Canton," and my grandmother always had to hand a supply of crystallized ginger in a gray, raffia-wrapped Chinese jar. In John Masefield's rousing novel *Bird of Dawning,* one can read as good a sea yarn as ever was written, the climax of which is the finish of a "tea race" between the later big British "composite" clippers (wood-on-iron frames as opposed to American oak) up the English Channel towards the Port of London.

If one takes a Thames excursion today downriver from Tower Bridge, approaching Greenwich one gets a first glimpse of the masts of the last British clipper, CUTTY SARK, in her drydock berth. Or at the Peabody Essex Museum in Salem, Massachusetts, one can view some of the luxuries that came into Derby Wharf, a few minutes' stroll from the museum, in the few years before the American clippers forsook Salem for the waterfronts of Boston and New York. It must be remembered, however, that exciting and glamorous as all this was, and though the China trade made huge profits for a handful of merchants, what kept America's balance of trade solidly in the black during this period was the export of agricultural products, particularly cotton, and this was a trade in which the fine-lined clippers took no part.

But what, exactly, *was* a "clipper"? It was a vessel built and operated with speed under sail as its primary objective, and not great, or even efficient, hull cargo capacity. To call a vessel a "clipper" generally was to praise its sailing qualities without getting too specific as to details, though in general the type had a very sharp, concave bow, in contrast to most generally bluff-bowed merchant vessels. The hull was often quite narrow in relation to its length.[2] Some hard-driving captains set enormous areas of sail, often to the detriment of both crew and rig. But the bottom line was that the term "clipper" was usually more of an admiring adjective than a precise definition, just as today we throw around the terms "sports car" or "jumbo jet." In describing vessel "models," surveyors for *American Lloyd's Register*, which began annual publication of its vessel lists in 1857, used the letters "F, M, S, and C" to designate "full, medium, sharp, and clipper." However, as far as it can be determined, Lloyd's never published a set of definitions, so the surveyor relied on his subjective judgment, presumably by means of the rule of his exquisitely calibrated thumb.

The so-called American "Clipper Era" lasted from about the middle 1840s to the middle 1850s. Much folklore to the contrary, it is impossible to designate a particular vessel as the "first" American clipper just as it is to define the last of the breed. The prototypes, more or less, were fast Baltimore-built vessels in the China trade. Historically, Baltimore vessels capable of an excellent turn of speed had been popular since early in the century. These so-called "Baltimore clippers" were generally topsail schooners, moderately spoon-bowed, very deep aft, and carrying a fore-and-aft rig with a pronounced rake. They were efficient privateers during the War of 1812. When slave-running became a capital crime in the United States in May 1820, the Baltimore type was popular for its ability to outrun the law, though not renowned for its seaworthiness.

However, using the Baltimore clipper hull form as a starting point, by the 1830s Baltimore was producing fast, seaworthy ships which found their way into the China trade. It had long been assumed that the ship Ann McKim, built in Baltimore in 1832, could be called the "first American clipper ship," but when she made the 1843 record-breaking voyage back from Canton, there was at least one similar ship which sailed ahead of her. It is of course a matter of record that on the McKim's triumphant return to New York, her owners, Messrs. Howland and Aspinwall, commissioned John Willis Griffiths to design them a larger, and if possible faster, ship for the China trade, and this turned out to be Rainbow, launched in late 1844. However, while Rainbow was building and her nervous owners getting second opinions about what they considered too lofty a rig (concerns proving accurate when she was dismasted on her maiden voyage), the New York firm of A. A. Low & Bros. had commissioned another clipper, Houqua. Built in an amazing four months, she was as different from Rainbow as chalk from cheese. Griffiths had his own opinions on hull form, based on tank testing of models. These included the now familiar sharp, hollow entry and a great deal of deadrise, i.e., a V-shaped hull cross section. HOUQUA, presaging what would be a more typical design later on, was boxier amidships though still sharp forward.

Griffiths was extremely vocal about his theories, perhaps to the extent of being something of a crank. HOUQUA's designer, Captain Nathaniel Palmer, an experienced Connecticut captain (Palmer Land in the Antarctic is named for him), had his own theories on hull design and these included minimum deadrise. HOUQUA was a smashing success, and by the time he developed the lines for what would prove his masterpiece, the 1846 SEA WITCH, even the abrasive Griffiths had eaten a little quiet crow. SEA WITCH had RAINBOW's sharp bow and HOUQUA's cross section.

At the same time, neither Griffiths nor Palmer could claim a monopoly on innovation. Eckford Webb's New York shipyard, where Griffiths had gotten his start, could also boast as alumni Boston's Donald McKay, and Eckford's son, William, who was probably New York's most successful shipbuilder. There was plenty of talent floating around, including Samuel Hartt Pook, whose 1853 Rockland, Maine-built RED JACKET promptly shattered the transatlantic speed record (and that with a supposedly "indifferent" crew) with a New York-to-Liverpool run of thirteen days, one hour, and twenty-five minutes before going into the England-to-Australia emigrant trade.

There is one quite wonderful RED JACKET yarn which symbolizes the "hype" of the clipper era. In his 1915 memoir *Sea Yarns,* Cape Cod captain Joshua N. Taylor recalled shipping out "in his teens" for a round-trip voyage to Cape Town in the Boston bark SEA BIRD. SEA BIRD was no "greyhound," just an ordinary merchant vessel, and nearing the equator, outward bound, she was swiftly overtaken by what proved to be RED JACKET, her deck crowded with Melbourne-bound passengers, all canvas set including the port studding sails. "She soon came up to us, going very fast and sailing at least two feet to our one. Instead of passing us under our lea [*sic*], as is the custom, she hove down her wheel and shot across our port quarter, taking the wind out of our sails, which almost becalmed us." As RED JACKET headed towards the horizon after this seagoing practical joke, the ship's band struck up *The Girl I Left Behind Me*. SEA BIRD's captain, Taylor recalled, "continued to rave and swear about the 'damned lime-juicer' as long as she was in sight."[3] Abominable maritime manners on the part of RED JACKET's captain, of course, but what a nifty tale for her passengers to tell on arrival in Australia!

During the decade of American clipper building the major shipyards turning them out were in New York City, Medford and East Boston, Massachusetts, the rivers and estuaries around Portsmouth, New Hampshire, and the Maine coast, though some clippers were built in places like Cape Cod. Granting that the parameters are extremely vague, how many American clippers might there have been? The best estimate, admittedly a guess, would be between three and four hundred, with about ninety coming from Maine shipyards. The peak construction year appears to have been 1853 when somewhere between ninety and just over a hundred went overboard. By 1855 the boom California market was drying up as the West Coast became increasingly self-sufficient, and in 1857 there was a severe, though short-lived, bank panic and depression, brought on by wild speculation in western American real estate. Venture capital dried up as banks called in their loans.

Perhaps the most illustrative (if possibly apocryphal) anecdote concerning the approaching end of America's "Clipper Era" concerns the brilliant—and prescient—New York designer and shipbuilder William Webb. Before abandoning sail for steamships Webb built his last clipper, YOUNG AMERICA, in 1853. He is supposed to have told the chief mate just before the beginning of the new ship's maiden voyage, "Take good care of her, mister. When she's gone there will be no more like her." Webb saw the future more clearly than did his Boston competitor, Donald McKay, who continued building clippers long after they were economically viable. Webb died rich enough to endow the institute of naval

Clipper ship CHALLENGE, built
at New York by William
Webb. Launched in May
1851, CHALLENGE was 224
feet in length, 2,006 tons,
with three decks.
*GLEASON'S PICTORIAL DRAWING ROOM
COMPANION,* AUTHOR'S COLLECTION

Clipper ship STAFFORDSHIRE, built at East Boston, Massachusetts, by Donald McKay. Launched in June 1851, STAFFORDSHIRE was 228 feet in length, 1,817 tons. Though she was of the clipper type, she was intended as a packet ship on Train's line in the Liverpool run.

GLEASON'S PICTORIAL DRAWING ROOM COMPANION, AUTHOR'S COLLECTION architecture which still bears his name and pay for a lavishly printed two-volume edition of the lines of his hundred favorite productions. McKay died in respectable near-poverty.

The focus of our present story, the little clipper SNOW SQUALL, was built at Cape Elizabeth, Maine, in 1851, about midway in the decade of clipper popularity. She was never as famous as CHALLENGE, FLYING CLOUD, or SEA WITCH, but she made a few notable passages and once outsailed a Confederate commerce raider. SNOW SQUALL was both a China and a California clipper, sometimes calling at both in the course of a round-the-world voyage by way of Cape Horn, or sometimes bringing cargo to Australia by way of the Cape of Good Hope on her way out to the Orient. On the colorful (if not gaudy) pasteboard cards handed out along the New York waterfront to advertise her California voyages she was billed as "celebrated," "extreme," "famous," and so on, but she sailed at a time when P. T. Barnum's museum-cum-sideshow was the darling of New York and patent medicines were hawked as cures for everything from catarrh to cancer with an abandon which today would solicit the wrath of government regulators.

Although SNOW SQUALL and her sisters made some splendid passages under sail, it cannot be stressed too heavily that that is but one part of the story. The American clipper, for a good part of her voyage, was what today we would call a "tramp" freighter, proceeding to the first port of call under charter and at subsequent ports dependent on the vagaries of market conditions. The clippers were not packets like those in the famous transatlantic Black Ball Line, which ran regularly between two ports, whether full or not. There were periods when SNOW SQUALL was "laid up," awaiting a profitable run.

But there was excitement, too: perilous storms, crew desertions, deaths and illness at sea, dodging pirates and Confederate raiders, the challenge of gauging a long-distance market, uprisings in foreign ports, and more. It is unfortunate that none of SNOW SQUALL's logbooks have turned up and only a miniscule portion of her owner's correspondence—and that dealing with just one voyage. But by piecing together her story from far-ranging sources—from old copies of the *North China Herald* to shipping and tax records from her various ports to the tattered journals of the ship's "boys"—we have a wonderful window into the mid-nineteenth-century American mercantile marine world. SNOW SQUALL herself ended up in a maritime backwater, "frozen" by events that passed her by. Her remains are the last tangible relic of the graceful ships that continue to captivate our imagination.

---

NOTES

[1] Henry T. Tuckerman, *A Memorial of Horatio Greenough, consisting of a memoir, selections from his writings, and tributes to his genius* (New York, G. P. Putnam & Co., 1853), pp. 124–25. Published the year after Greenough's death at the age of forty-seven.

[2] SNOW SQUALL had a breadth to length ratio of 1:4.9, just slightly beamier than the American clipper average of about 1:5.

[3] Joshua N. Taylor, *Sea Yarns* (Orleans, MA: Orleans Historical Society reprint, 1981), pp. 12–13.

SNOW SQUALL was built in 1851, the year the "low black schooner" AMERICA won the yachting cup that now bears her name by outsailing her competitors off England's Isle of Wight. It was the year of publication of Herman Melville's *Moby Dick,* and the popularity of American products was burgeoning, from Samuel Colt's revolvers to Hiram Powers's marble *Greek Slave* at London's Crystal Palace. The rail line from Boston now ran near the Cape Elizabeth, Maine, shipyard that built SNOW SQUALL across to the steamboat wharves in Portland. (The north half of Cape Elizabeth would become South Portland in 1895.) The California and Australian gold fields attracted adventurers and would play a major role in SNOW SQUALL's career as she brought freight to San Francisco, Sydney, and Melbourne. Not quite thirty years earlier, Maine had become a state under the Missouri Compromise, but the tensions that brought on the American Civil War were still a few years away from reaching fever pitch. Gambling on their ability to build a clipper ship at a profit, sometime in the spring of 1851 Alford and Cornelius Butler began work on SNOW SQUALL.

# 2

# THE BROTHERS BUTLER
# BUILD A SHIP

Construction progressed over the spring and early summer. Over the weekend of July 12–13, 1851, there was a partial eclipse of the moon. As the moonlight dimmed and the fireflies twinkled along the marshy shore, on the northwest corner of Turner's Island could dimly be seen the bulk of the new ship, painted white for her maiden voyage, and all but ready for her launching on the noon high tide on Monday.

Monday sunrise was at 4:30 but even before that Cornelius Butler's yard hands had begun the driving-up process that transferred the vessel's weight from the keelblocks, on which it had rested during construction, to the launching ways. As the sun rose over Munjoy Hill at Portland's east end, where the tall, brown-shingled tower of the Observatory signaled the arrival of incoming vessels, Butler's dozen workers, joined by others, swung their mauls in unison, pausing occasionally for a breather. In the air was the acid tang of chips from freshly adzed oak framing timbers, mixing with the sweeter smell of resin from the southern hard pine hull planking and the pine tar on the standing rigging.

1859 U.S. Coast and Geodetic Survey chart of Portland Harbor. Turner's Island, site of the Cornelius Butler shipyard in the section of Cape Elizabeth that became South Portland, is in the center. As the yard was on the northwest corner of the island, west of the railroad bridge, it is possible that the dark rectangle with a jetty behind it may be one of the Butler yard buildings. The yard almost certainly had a large mould loft where patterns for framing timbers were laid out on the wood floor. Such a mould loft can be seen today at the Percy & Small shipyard at Maine Maritime Museum in Bath.

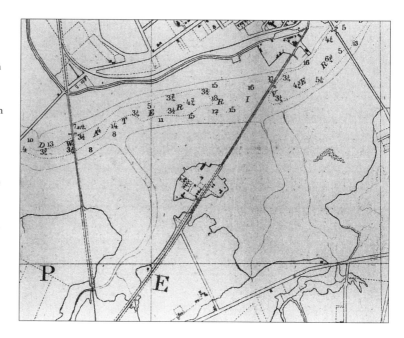

Along the gunwales of the white hull ran a gay red-orange stripe.

As the noon high tide—an unusually high "spring" tide because of the phase of the moon—approached, the Fore River began to lap at the lower ends of the shipways, already slathered with a coating of tallow. On the stroke of twelve the ship SNOW SQUALL slid smoothly down the ways. Unlike launchings further Down East on the majestic Kennebec River, there was no option of waiting for the slack just after full tide. The Fore River estuary is very shallow, and at 157 feet, 742 register tons, SNOW SQUALL was a large vessel for the area—the largest Butler had built or ever would build. No sponsor broke a bottle of champagne across the clipper's knife-like bow, and if the launching was celebrated with a tot of grog, it was on the sly. Portland Quaker reformer Neal Dow's Maine prohibition law was in effect.

A few weeks later SNOW SQUALL lay at Portland's Custom House Wharf for her final touches. The Portland firm of Charles A. Donnell on Fore Street, at the head of the wharf, had provided some hardware during construction, everything from brass screws to a hundred or so "hatch plates" to sheet lead and pipe. As SNOW SQUALL prepared for sea under the eagle eye of Cape Elizabeth native Captain Silas D. Gregg, a reporter from the Portland *Advertiser,* the city's Whig newspaper, visited her and liked what he saw.

"This fine, clipper-built vessel…is well worth the inspection of connoisseurs in naval architecture," his story began. He described her as "mainly built of white oak," (a slight exaggeration, as it turned out), gave her beam as 32 feet and her depth of hold (the distance from the underside of the main deckbeams to the top of the floor timber next to the keelson) as 18 ½ feet. "She is very sharp at the bows, with a lean, but handsomely graduated run, but from her great breadth of beam, and fullness of bulge [*sic*], will be enabled to carry well, while at the same time she cannot fail of being a fast sailer." Her masts and spars were "very long," the height of the main truck being 142 feet and the length of the

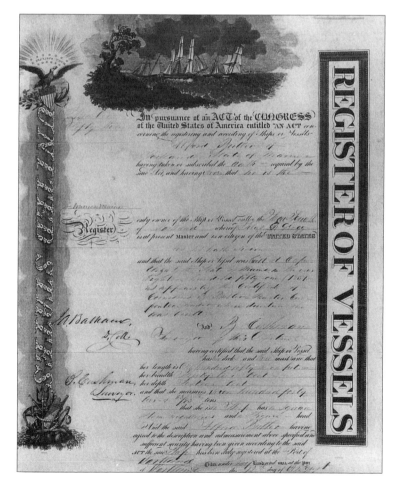

SNOW SQUALL's certificate of register, issued at Portland, Maine, August 12, 1851, shortly before she sailed for New York. Alford Butler took out a register, which was valid for overseas voyages, rather than a coastwise enrollment, so that if he was unable to sell the ship in New York she could be "put up for freight or charter."
U.S. NATIONAL ARCHIVES

main yard 65 feet. She carried "standing skysail poles and yards," supposedly the first vessel in the Portland-Falmouth customs district to do so. When under a full press of sail, she would "remind one of a snow cloud, if not a Snow Squall," the writer predicted. The accommodations aft came in for special praise. "Her cabin is furnished with polished mahogany, rose and satin wood, with coving, and caps and bases to the pilasters of burnished guild [*sic*]; the floor is carpeted with rich tapestry carpeting, and the cabin furniture is to be of a style in keeping. Between decks she is finished in better style than it was formerly the practice to finish the cabins of most of our shipping." The *Advertiser*'s reporter noted that SNOW SQUALL's white hull boasted "a vermilion streak along her gunwales."[3] There was no mention of SNOW SQUALL's grinning dragon figurehead.

Portland, Maine, in the 1850s, as seen from the Cape Elizabeth shore. The railroad bridge, which was near the Butler shipyard, can be seen at the far left. Custom House Wharf, where SNOW SQUALL received her final touches, is roughly in the center.
*THE ILLUSTRATED LONDON NEWS*, AUTHOR'S COLLECTION

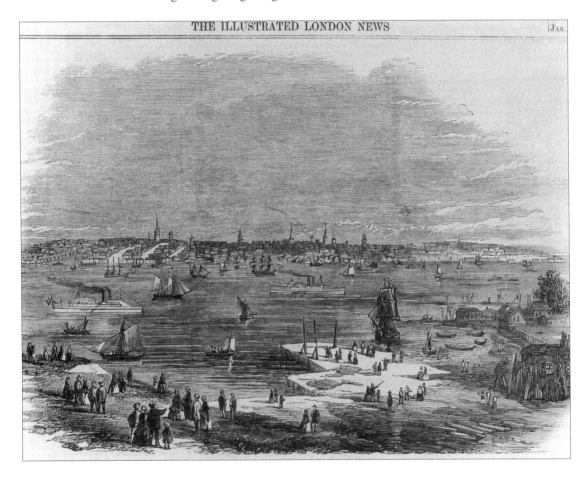

THE ILLUSTRATED LONDON NEWS [JAN.

16   *Snow Squall*

Captain Silas D. Gregg, SNOW SQUALL's captain on the voyage from Portland to New York. A native of Cape Elizabeth, Maine, Gregg had also been the first (and only) captain of the Butler ship-yard's first vessel, the BUTLER of 1850, which was wrecked later that year in Argentina. Captain Gregg and his family made it back to Maine safely.

COURTESY OF MR. AND MRS. HENRY GREGG SMALL, JR.

Eight days after the first story appeared, the *Advertiser* re-ported on SNOW SQUALL again. At noon on August 15, with a light northwest wind, she sailed for New York. In spite of the fitful breeze, she "slipped through the water rapidly and was 'hull down' in the offing, in the course of an hour."[4] She arrived in New York on August 19.[5] In late September, just over a month after her arrival, as SNOW SQUALL awaited a buyer, the *New York Herald* pub-lished a feature on "The Yachts of America." "While on the subject of fast sailers," the story ran, "we may as well append a list of our clipper ships and fast running ocean steamers, that have sprung into being, almost like a work of magic, within the last three years." Not surprisingly the list of thirty-eight vessels included such well-known clippers as STAG HOUND, CHALLENGE, and FLYING CLOUD, but it also included two Butler-built vessels, BLACK SQUALL and SNOW SQUALL.[6] In November the Portland *Advertiser* ran its final SNOW SQUALL story. She had been sold in New York "for a sum not far from $40,000."[7]

The Butler shipyard's first production had been the 445-ton ship BUTLER, apparently launched in early January 1850, though the event was not reported in the local newspapers. Her owner, Portland merchant Captain Charles Richardson, promptly advertised the BUTLER for sale: "For sale, a new ship of the following dimensions: 123 feet on deck, breadth 28 feet, depth $18^{6}/_{12}$ feet, built of the best materials, thoroughly fastened, with a poop and a forward house. Can be fitted for sea in about 3 weeks."[8] The BUTLER sailed for New York near the end of February.[9] In July, just before she was to sail for San Francisco under the same Silas Gregg who would be SNOW SQUALL's delivery captain, ownership of the BUTLER was divided between Charles Richardson and three New Yorkers.[10] On her way south towards Cape Horn the BUTLER went ashore in a fog at Cape San Antonio near the mouth of the River Plate in Argentina. Eventually Captain Gregg and his family reached Buenos Aires and headed back to Maine.[11] Without citing his authority Maine historian Robert Applebee claimed that the BUTLER "was one of the early ship models often termed 'near clippers' because they sailed so well," adding that the Butlers "did their own designing."[12] The BUTLER, however, had a brief and fairly ignominious career and no picture of her has yet turned up.

Fortunately for the curious, the building of the Butler brothers' first vessel took place in a census year and 1850 saw the compilation of the inaugural *Products of Industry,* as well as demographics. It was also the first year in which not just "heads of households" were tallied but the individual inhabitants of each dwelling as well. The initial industrial compilation is a highly flawed document because, if the census taker is to be believed, there were but two shipyards in Cape Elizabeth. *Products of Industry* failed, for example, to mention the huge Turner and Cahoon shipyard complex at Ferry Village, with its steam sawmill and company housing. We can only be grateful that the enumerator, likely a political hack, managed to get to the Butler yard at all before quitting at the end of what was most likely a hot Maine summer day, not to return to finish up.

However, before examining the census data, with its interesting "snapshot" of 1850 Portland and Cape Elizabeth that included Cornelius and Alford Butler, their operations, and their home life, we must attempt to answer the questions of how Alford Butler, who had been in business for himself for only about two years at the end of 1848, scraped together the capital to purchase the shipyard property and set up his younger brother to build his first vessel. No other names appear on the shipyard deed, hence the only possibility is that he had a "silent partner" or received enough of an advance on his first vessel to buy the property, assemble the needed materials, and begin construction of the Butler. Whether that seed money stemmed from faith in Alford's business acumen or in Cornelius's presumed abilities as a designer and shipwright is an interesting question.

Portland's First Ward was at the eastern end of the city below Munjoy Hill and in it were born in 1822 and 1823 Alford and Cornelius, the oldest of Samuel and Abigail Warner Butler's six children. Samuel was a pump and block maker and eventually moved to 2 Bradbury's Court, a narrow alley running off waterfront Fore Street near the corner of India, conveniently near the Clay Cove shipyards which would have been his customers. Nothing is known of Alford and Cornelius's early years. Alford married Caroline Partridge in 1843,[13] went to work in Harris Dresser's clothing store at 179 Fore Street sometime prior to 1846,[14] and by the following year had apparently taken over the business and was living up the street at number 25.[15] We must assume, based on what happened later, that Cornelius, still living at home in 1847, worked in one of the nearby shipyards, as his occupation is listed as "ship carpenter."[16] The following year Cornelius married Catharine Cobb.[17]

In December 1848, Alford paid six hundred dollars to one Samuel Dyer, "ship carpenter" of the neighboring town of Westbrook, for an acre and a half of land with a half interest in "all the buildings, wharf and all other improvements," the tide flats to the low water mark, and a "right of way to the mainc [sic] road" on low-lying Turner's Island across the Fore River in Cape Elizabeth.[18] The Butler brothers had acquired the site where they would build four vessels between 1850 and the end of 1851, including the clipper ship SNOW SQUALL.

Alford Butler is a complex and slightly shady character. His 1858 R. G. Dun and Company credit report called him a "slippery customer," adding that, "people used to think him hardly honest, but we never saw anything against him."[19] This somewhat less than glowing assessment may have stemmed from an incident the year before, when Butler got himself into deep financial difficulty. In January 1856 he signed a note for $518.08, payable in a year to Moses G. Palmer, a Middle Street, Portland, supplier of fabric trimmings. The interest, though not specified in the note, must have been a usurious 93 percent per year, for by February 1857 Butler owed Palmer a thousand dollars, and Palmer took him to court. (Under current Maine law there is a cap of 18 percent annual interest on most loans.) On March 2, 1857, Cumberland County Sheriff Henry Pennell turned up at Butler's factory and seized a fairly long list of goods to the value of $1,000.21—including the cast iron office safe valued at sixty dollars.[20]

And in the past Butler had had some "interesting" associates. In October 1846, about the time he was setting up on his own, one Phillip Quinn of Portland came up before Judge Fitch on several charges of "retailing," i.e., selling liquor without a license (Prohibition was not yet law). Judge Fitch convicted Quinn on both counts and under the law made him give a bond that he "would not retail for 6 months from date [of conviction]." Alford Butler and another went surety for his bond.[21]

On the other hand, by 1850 Butler was running an apparently thriving clothing factory on Portland's Fore Street. According to the census, he had seven male and sixty female employees, used twenty-five thousand yards of cloth (worth just over a dollar a yard) annually, and between June 1849 and June 1850 produced goods worth $39,500. His seamstresses made about 35 cents a day, while his seven male employees, presumably supervisors, made a dollar. It is not known if the factory made use of Elias Howe's recently patented lockstitch foot treadle sewing machines. All "motive power" in Butler's factory was "hand."[22] An intriguing advertisement, suggesting that some of Butler's seamstresses may have taken work home, appeared in the *Eastern Argus* late in 1849 and early in 1850:

> *Lost:* In the upper part of the city, Saturday eve, a pair of pants, unmade. The finder shall be suitably rewarded by leaving the same at No 179 Fore Street. Alford Butler[23]

In any case, it seems extremely probable that Alford Butler had help from some backer in late 1848. The most likely candidate, though it cannot be proven, is Captain Charles Richardson, owner both of the BUTLER and of the yard's second vessel, the clipper bark BLACK SQUALL. Richardson was a native of Bath, Maine, and after an early and successful career as a sea captain had become a partner in Lyman and Richardson, ship chandlers, with premises at 118 Fore Street at the head of Portland's Custom House Wharf. In addition to hard pine from Georgia and Florida, Lyman and Richardson dealt in marine hardware such as Waterman and Russell's "Patent Iron Strap'd Blocks." Whether or not Richardson bankrolled Alford Butler or advanced credit for lumber and hardware, it would well have been in his interests to do so.

The 1850 census also provides details on the building of the BUTLER and shipwright turned designer and shipyard proprietor Cornelius Butler. The Butlers had $1,500 invested in the shipyard, which employed twelve hands and paid about a dollar and a half for the newly legislated ten-hour day. (This was slightly above the local average of $1.25.) There was no powered machinery and all work such as sawing was done by hand. Work in a yard such as Butler's could be hazardous. The mark of the ship carpenter was often a "four-fingered hand," and the din of the wooden mallets driving caulking into seams soon affected the caulkers' hearing. Death or serious injury from falling or being fallen on by objects from above was all too common.

Into the BUTLER went two hundred tons of timber, worth $1,800, sixteen thousand feet of plank at $304, eleven tons of iron at $605, and an unspecified amount of copper at $750 for a total cost of materials of $3,459. The BUTLER's "value" when completed was $15,575.[24] This calculates to thirty-five dollars per ton, slightly below the New England average.[25] Whether this figure represented the Butler yard's total investment in the BUTLER before making a profit or her actual selling price is unclear. Beyond the figures given in the census the Butlers would have had to pay for rigging, caulking, painting, mast and spar making, sailmaking, and so on, all items generally contracted out to itinerant work gangs by most nineteenth-century Maine shipyards. The BUTLER supposedly was sold in New York for $24,000.[26] This last, unsubstantiated, assertion raises two interesting questions. What was the Butlers' actual profit on the ship, and what was Charles Richardson's profit when he sold a half interest in her?

The 1850 census data also gives a flickering glimpse into the condition of Cornelius Butler himself. He lived in Cape Elizabeth with his wife Catharine and their one-year-old daughter Ann. Catharine's maiden name was Cobb, and also living in the house was fourteen-year-old Benjamin Cobb, possibly Catharine's younger brother, or at least a relative. Also in the household were George H. Gray, twenty, "ship carpenter," George Millikin, twenty-one, George Stoddard, thirty-two, and Charles McLellan, forty-two, "born Nova Scotia." Though there is no record of this in the Cumberland County deeds, Cornelius was supposed to have owned real estate worth a thousand dollars.[27] Meanwhile, Alford and Caroline Butler lived on Fore Street a few blocks from the clothing factory with their two children, Alford, four, and Caroline, a year old. Alford's real estate was said to be worth $3,500.[28]

In the fall of 1850 the Butler yard launched its second vessel, the "clipper bark" BLACK SQUALL, which attracted a good deal more attention in the Portland papers than had the BUTLER. In any case, in October 1850, after having essentially ignored the Butler shipyard's BUTLER, Portland's newspapers felt that their next vessel was worthy of notice. The *Eastern Argus* announced on October 21 that, "to be launched this day about 10 o'clock, from the yard of C. B. Butler, Cape Elizabeth, western end of Railroad Bridge, clipper Bark BLACK SQUALL, about 400 tons, elegantly built of best materials."[29] A few weeks later the *Argus*'s rival newspaper, the *Advertiser,* fairly rhapsodized over the new vessel:

> LOOK OUT FOR A "SQUALL!" We learn that the new clipper barque—the "Black Squall"—will sail this forenoon for New York, weather permitting. There is considerable curiosity among our nautical men, to see this craft get under-weigh [*sic*]. For sailing qualities, it is supposed she will eclipse anything that ever sailed from this port. The great increase of shipments to California, via Cape Horn, is bringing into use a new

United States Census, 1850, *Products of Industry* return for the Butler shipyard. These figures would be for the ship BUTLER, launched that year. The $1,500 figure is for investment in the yard. The next three columns show materials used and their value. "Manual" refers to power used at the yard, i.e., no steam-powered saws. There were twelve hands employed at an average monthly total wage of $468. The WARNER was 445 tons. The final column, with a figure of $15,575, is the "value of goods produced." SNOW SQUALL, at not quite double the tonnage of the WARNER, sold for just over $30,000.

class of vessels, namely large clippers; for their passages are so much shorter than ordinary vessels, that they command nearly double the rates of freight. Although the "Black Squall is not so large as some of the China clippers, (being 420 tons) yet, as her accommodations are all on deck, she will carry with her great breadth of beam, a good cargo; and we think she will prove that while Maine keeps up her rank as the first state in quality of tonnage built, she can also keep up with the times in style, strength, and beauty of finish."[30]

The only sad occurrence regarding the new vessel was that in November, during her final fitting-out, the spanker boom fell, fracturing the skull of fifty-year-old rigger Simon Stanforth, who died a few hours later. Riggers were intinerant contractors who

United States Census, 1850, *Products of Industry* return for Alford Butler's clothing factory in Portland. Butler's sixty female employees made about thirty-five cents a day, while his male employees made a dollar. Using 25,000 yards of cloth, valued at about a dollar a yard, Butler's factory's annual output was worth $39,500, an impressive sum in 1850.

moved from yard to yard, and Stanforth had just returned from working east of Portland on a job. He was described as "an industrious, hard working man" who "left a large family, that was dependant [sic] on his daily exertions for a livelihood."[31]

BLACK SQUALL, owned by Captain John Codman of Boston and New York, apparently was a reasonably successful vessel in the New York to Rio and San Francisco runs. On one occasion, in 1852, she made a near-record passage from Rio to New York of twenty-six days. Her register was surrendered in New York at the end of 1853 when she was "sold to foreigners."[32] The details of her career under the American flag are sketchy, and unfortunately, as with the BUTLER, no painting of her has turned up, so we are left with her description in the *Advertiser,* such as it may be.

Work on the Butlers' third vessel, the clipper ship SNOW SQUALL, probably began early in 1851. And here let us detail the probable building of this 742-ton, 157-foot ship, the largest vessel the yard ever built. Most of us have a mental picture of a twentieth-century shipyard, with its large permanent launching ways, and the adjacent machine and woodworking shops with their bedlam of power tools. As the information in *Products of Industry,* mentioned earlier, attests, everything at the nineteenth-century Butler yard was done by hand. There very likely was a primitive wooden derrick, known as a "gin pole," with a boom for lifting heavy timbers, and the shipyard may well have had a draft horse or horses for dragging timber about and for supplying—literally—some horsepower for the gin pole. The sawing of planking and framing timbers would have been done with a two-man pit saw which liberally showered the sawyer below with sawdust. The lower sawyer wore a cloth mask to keep the worst of the sawdust out of his eyes and nose, but it was a most unpleasant job. The wooden treenails (pronounced "trunnels"), which fastened frame sections together and planking to frames, would have been shaped by hand on rainy days.

There would have had to have been a good-sized building with a smooth wood floor, a mould loft, on which the patterns for frames were "moulded," or drawn, working from the carved wooden half model that showed the hull's three-dimensional shape. (Captain Nat Palmer carved such a model for his HOUQUA on a maddeningly slow voyage home from China.) There are many such half models surviving today, but they may well be more decorative than accurate. The specific hull forms on which a clipper builder's reputation depended were guarded with the same zeal as those of an AMERICA's Cup contender. While a beautifully finished half model might decorate a shipowner's office wall, famed builder Donald McKay's grandson, Richard, recalled that no builder possessed of his senses ever let a really accurate model pass through the shipyard gate!

Which brings us to the questions of who designed SNOW SQUALL and what may have influenced the process. The most likely candidate is Cornelius Butler, since an advertisement for his next, and last, production, the 500-ton bark WARNER, launched at the

The Charles V. Minott shipyard on the Kennebec River in Phippsburg, Maine, about 1900. Hull framing sections were assembled flat on the ground, then hoisted into place. Each section consisted of two rows of timbers called futtocks, which were assembled with staggered ends, then treenailed together. COURTESY OF ADA M. HAGGETT

end of 1851, lists her as "modelled by the builders of the clipper ship Snow Squall."[33] However, on several occasions during 1850, advertisements appeared in Portland's *Eastern Argus* for "a superior model and set of moulds for a ship of 750 tons, made by Donald McKay, East Boston," as well as "a set of floor timbers" (the lowest frames running athwart the keel), both offered for sale by one J. L. Farmer at Portland's Widgery's Wharf.[34] Farmer was a successful Portland businessman with diverse interests ranging from railroads to the sugar trade. How and where he acquired the McKay model is a complete mystery. At the time the advertisements appeared, Cornelius Butler had either begun to work on or was about to commence the relatively small BLACK SQUALL of 420 tons, but SNOW SQUALL's register tonnage was 742, intriguingly close to the advertised figure. It would not have been out of the question for a designer-builder such as Butler to have taken the train to Boston to attend a launching and to observe details of hull form.

Compare this circa 1900 image of the Charles M. Minott shipyard with the view (following page) of the William Webb shipyard in New York in the 1860s. Little had changed in the way of wooden shipbuilding technology in the intervening years; indeed, seventeenth-century British diarist Samuel Pepys would have felt perfectly at home.
COURTESY OF ADA M. HAGGETT

In any case, as the design process went on and the subtleties of form became refined in the model (whoever may have been its author), the task of assembling materials had to begin, which by 1851 was becoming complicated and often frustrating in Maine and other New England shipbuilding centers. There were two interrelated problems. First, most iron used in shipbuilding was imported. This included the tons of iron fastenings used in hull construction, including the cast iron "dagger knees" which helped to support the 'tween-deck beams near SNOW SQUALL's bow. There were the anchors and their chains, and so on down the shopping list. A builder such as Butler had to calculate carefully the quantities and specifics needed and order them from a dealer who imported them, generally from England. Portland possessed the industrial capacity to fabricate some iron, whether by forging or casting, but first it had to be imported, generally from Liverpool or Cardiff. Earlier in the century Portland merchants such as Asa Clapp had imported a good deal of Swedish iron, but by mid-

William Webb's New York shipyard in the 1860s. Like the Minott yard, though Webb had teams of horses to move heavy timbers (the two-wheeled rig in the right foreground was called "big wheels" or a "timber arch"), most of the heavy lifting, such as the gang in the upper left, was manual.

*HARPER'S WEEKLY,* AUTHOR'S COLLECTION

century coal-poor Sweden was running low on the wood needed to make the charcoal essential for smelting. At the middle of the nineteenth century the American iron industry was a long way from the giant it would become a few years later; in 1851 entrepreneurial America's attention was engaged in a frenzy of railroad building.

Second, the builder had to estimate the various types and quantities of timber required, and this was becoming a logistical nightmare, as readily available local timber grew more and more scarce, distant, and difficult to transport. No Butler shipyard records have come to light, but in the summer of 1851, though white oak was the theoretically favored timber for ship framing, the records of the Clark and Sewall shipyard at Bath, Maine, show that one James Lightbody agreed to deliver to the Sewalls' wharf by the following January, "48 floor & rising timbers @ $7/ton, ninety navel timbers @ $7/ton, ninety futtocks @ $7/ton, the above all of good hard wood Birch, maple & Beack [beech] wood."[35] Maine shipbuilders coped with the realities of supply: they built with what was available. The best that can be surmised is that while white oak, and its equally useful botanical cousin, "burr oak," were reasonably common in the southern two-thirds of Maine and the preferred wood for ship framing timbers, in practice a shipyard built with what came in through the shipyard gate in time to keep construction going. As long as it was a reasonable choice, the master carpenter refused to quibble.

Although the diversity of hardwoods in SNOW SQUALL's framing belies the newspaper description of her as "mainly built of white oak,"[36] a master wooden shipbuilder, the late Norman ("Sonny") Hodgdon of East Boothbay, Maine, reviewed the analysis of the wood types in her construction after her recovery and concluded that they had been used appropriately. A modern anecdote illuminates the timber problem. During the Korean War of the 1950s, various Maine shipyards contracted to build wooden minesweepers for the U.S. Navy. The specifications sent Down East from Washington demanded white oak. Harassed

Maine shipbuilders, faced with severe shortages of that material and over-eager young officers from the Bureau of Ships, dryly pointed out that "white" oak came in a variety of shades. There was "pink" white oak, "grey" white oak, and so on. The mine-sweepers were built and delivered.[37] One was still in use as a marine sciences training vessel well into the 1980s, a thoroughly respectable lifespan.

For the mid-nineteenth-century Maine shipbuilder another of the most serious shortages, for which there was no easy solution, was good quality pine for masts and spars. Portland, Maine, mast- and spar-maker John Bradford, interviewed in 1893, explained his difficulties:

> In the beginning of his business, back in the [eighteen] thirties, he procured his timber in the forests surrounding this city. In the next decade he began to look to Canada for a supply and before the [Civil] war he sent to Pennsylvania after the Susquehanna masts, so called.[38]

But the quality of later supplies was inferior. In the early days, Bradford recalled, "if one of the great white pine masts that grew in Maine or Canada, began to rot after ten years of service, it would have been declared rotten when first placed in the vessel." He had seen "many 15 years old as sound as when felled in the forest." The Susquehanna masts, however, "frequently had to be replaced after four years."[39]

By the time construction on SNOW SQUALL began, Cornelius Butler had already launched two vessels, hence it is unlikely that major modifications were needed. Mid-nineteenth-century ship-ways were sturdy but relatively simple affairs, the lower ways spiked or treenailed to heavy bed logs which functioned like the ties on railroad tracks. Modern shipways have a pitch of about $9/16$ inches per foot. On Maine's Kennebunk River in the 1850s the pitch was somewhat greater, $1\frac{1}{8}$ inches per foot.[40] First the keel-blocks, which supported the ship during construction, were laid down, then the keel, resting on a false keel or "worm shoe," set on top of them. The hull frames, fabricated in pairs treenailed together, were each made up of the floor timber, which sat athwart the keel, first futtock, second futtock, the butts staggered between the sister frames for plenty of overlap, and so on up to the top timbers. These were assembled flat on the ground, then hoisted and propped into a vertical position. At the bow and stern, where it was not possible to extend the frames all the way down to the keel, shorter, diagonal pieces known as "cant frames" filled in the spaces. As there were crews working on each side of the hull, occasionally one side might end up with an extra cant frame, just to close a gap![41]

Ideally the framing lumber had a natural crook. Some shipyards sent gangs of sawyers into the woods in New England, Georgia, and the Carolinas, armed with the wooden moulds which had been worked out on the loft floor. The framing timbers they cut, each numbered to correspond to the mould that had served as its pattern, were brought to the shipyard site over the winter or in early spring for spring assembly. Alternatively, the frames and other structures, such as the deck hooks and breast hooks—horizontal, roughly triangular assemblies which functioned much like a wishbone—might be fabricated at the yard from whatever timber could be procured. In SNOW SQUALL's case, for example, the 'tween-deck deck hook is not "natural crook" but built up from a number of pieces spiked together. The outer edges are symmetrical; the internal components are not.

Once the frames were in place work began on the real backbone of the ship: the massive fore and aft keelson, in SNOW SQUALL's case a stick of southern hard pine 14 inches high by 12 inches wide, topped by rider keelsons and flanked by sister keelsons (a massive structure 2 feet 6½ inches tall, all told), went on top of the floor timbers and was secured into place with long iron or bronze "drifts." The stem and sternposts were likewise prefabricated, lifted up, and supported temporarily. At this point, heavy as all these timbers were, the hull still had about as much structural strength as a nest of jackstraws. Only the hull planking would bind the whole thing together, and to attach these planks of Georgia or Florida hard pine, ranging in thickness from 4 to 6 inches, some of them 40 feet or so long, required bending and torturing wood into curves it stalwartly resisted—unless placed in the hell of the steambox. Stoking the steambox boiler was a youngster's job: tossing in the wood chips which lay nearly a foot thick on the ground around the hull and keeping a watchful eye on the steam and water gauges.

Many years after he worked in an 1850s local shipyard, an elderly resident of Georgetown, Maine, whose name, unfortunately, has been forgotten, recalled the process: "The planks that formed the outer coatin' of a vessel at the bow and stern…had to be bent. They couldn't be put on dry. Had to be steamed till they was red hot, almost…. They put in [the steambox] only one or two plank to a time—never more than three—and left 'em there till they was steamed sufficient—about an hour, as a general thing."[42] The planking was manhandled up a wooden ramp with wooden cleats. In the case of the Georgetown shipyard, "The plank was 4 inches thick and 8 or 10 inches wide and some of 'em was 40 foot long. Sometimes it took fifteen men on an end. But a short man didn't need to lift more than he was a mind to: the tall men got it!"[43] Frames had to be dubbed or "trued" with adzes to insure the most perfect fit possible, and once the planking had been treenailed in place and the plank ends secured with square bronze spikes, the planking itself was dubbed to a smooth surface. To give some idea of the brute force required to build a hull such as SNOW SQUALL's, it must be remembered that along the length of each 35- to 40-foot plank, at each set of frames, set about 15 inches apart, Butler's workers had to drill—by hand—a hole just over an inch in diameter through roughly 4-inch-thick hard pine and into the hardwood frame, then drive the treenail and wedge the end, exactly as a hammer or axe handle is wedged. The whole process was repeated inside the hull for the ceiling planking that sheathed it. Not every treenail actually connected with its intended frame. Not every frame was as perfectly dressed as a

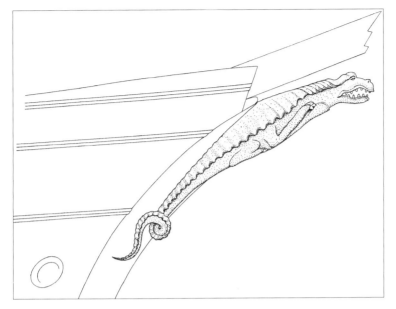

A reconstruction of SNOW SQUALL's figurehead. The dragon was a popular figurehead motif. The one newspaper description of SNOW SQUALL fails to mention her figurehead and its carver is unknown.

DRAWING BY RYAN M. COOPER

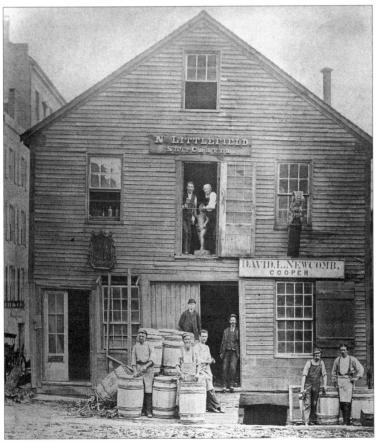

Portland, Maine, shipcarver's shop, circa 1875. Increasingly, the less expensive billethead, seen in front of the second-floor window on the right, began to replace more elaborate figure-heads, such as SNOW SQUALL's fanciful dragon.

MAINE HISTORIC PRESERVATION COMMISSION

*The Brothers Butler Build a Ship*    *33*

marine surveyor might have wished, had he inspected it before it was covered up, yet in her career SNOW SQUALL weathered brutal Cape Horn gales, and in an era when the average useful life of a wooden vessel was reckoned at eight to ten years, with a maximum of about two decades, she was nearing that mark when she met with her fatal accident.[44] It is easy to quibble after the fact, but the Butler yard produced a remarkably staunch vessel.

Hull planking and ceiling in place, there was much yet to do. SNOW SQUALL was a two-decked vessel, unlike some of the larger clippers, which had three. Both the main and 'tween-deck were carried by beams supported in their centers by stanchions and strengthened at their outer ends by natural crook oak knees, both vertical hanging knees, like an upside-down letter "L," and lodging knees in the horizontal plane. The steps for her masts on top of the top rider keelson were ingenious. In a modern yacht the tenons at the butts of the mast or masts are stepped into a mor-

*A Sail-Loft Down in Maine.* Note the stove hung from the ceiling. MAINE MARITIME MUSEUM

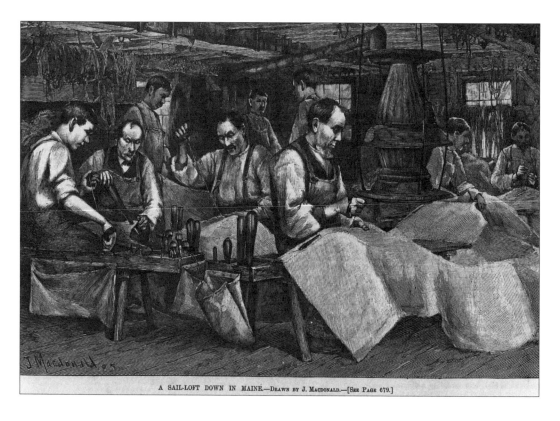

A SAIL-LOFT DOWN IN MAINE.—DRAWN BY J. MACDONALD.—[SEE PAGE 679.]

tise. SNOW SQUALL's masts were slotted and fitted over an iron tenon securely bolted to the keelson. This arrangement not only lessened the torque on the hull, but meant that there was no possibility of standing water to rot the mast butt.

If the practices of other mid-nineteenth-century Maine shipyards are any guide, specialized gangs of workers, operating under contract, performed such tasks as caulking, rigging, and painting. In her later career we know that SNOW SQUALL carried imported English Muntz metal sheathing on her hull as anti-fouling, anti-marine worm protection. These overlapping sheets, fourteen inches high by four feet long, fastened over a layer of tarred felt with six nails on the short edges and twenty-seven on the long, were a 60-percent copper, 40-percent zinc alloy whose anti-fouling properties depended on a slow but steady corrosion over the sheathing's expected useful life of forty months. There were advertisements for Colonel Muntz's patent "yellow sheathing

The bark WARNER, oil on canvas by James S. Buttersworth. The WARNER was launched from the Cornelius Butler shipyard on December 12, 1851. At 138 feet, 500 register tons, the WARNER was somewhat smaller than SNOW SQUALL. The second vessel in the painting does not appear to be another view of the WARNER, as the rig is different, since she carries skysails, which the WARNER apparently did not. However, as launched, SNOW SQUALL carried "standing skysail poles and yards," so the possibility exists that the second vessel might be SNOW SQUALL.
MAINE MARITIME MUSEUM, GIFT OF ELIZABETH B. NOYCE

metal" in the Portland paper, but it is not known with certainty if SNOW SQUALL was first metaled before her launching. However, Butler's next and last production at Turner's Island, the clipper bark WARNER (Warner was the Butlers' mother's maiden name), was advertised as metaled when brand new so it seems likely that this was the case with SNOW SQUALL.

SNOW SQUALL, then, represented many aspects of nineteenth-century American wooden shipbuilding technology and of the complexities of obtaining labor and raw materials, but she also was the product of a particular Maine community at the beginning of the second half of the nineteenth century. A few years after the building of the WARNER, Alford Butler moved his clothing business to Boston and apparently became moderately prosperous. Cornelius Butler worked for a few years as a "ship carpenter" and then vanished from the Portland–Cape Elizabeth scene. We do not know what became of him. No trace of his shipyard remains today.

## NOTES

1 John Greenleaf Whittier, *The PoeticalWorks* (Boston: Houghton Mifflin, 1892), p. 87.

2 Henry Hall, *Report on the Ship-Building Industry of the United States* (Washington: Government Printing Office, 1884), p. 128.

3 *Portland Evening Advertiser,* August 6, 1851.

4 Ibid., August 15, 1851.

5 Boston *Shipping List,* August 23, 1851.

6 *New York Herald,* September 20, 1851.

7 *Portland Evening Advertiser,* November 21, 1851. The exact sale price was reported as $30,410 by O. T. Howe and F. C. Matthews in their *American Clipper Ships* (Salem: Marine Research Society, 1927), p. 582, but it has not been possible to verify this. In his *American Maritime Industries and Public Policy* (Cambridge: Harvard University Press, 1941), pp. 280–81, John G. B. Hutchins gives vessel prices for the period as ranging from $60 to $70 per ton at New York and from $45 to $65 per ton in Maine in the "mid-fifties." SNOW SQUALL's register tonnage was 742. If Howe and Matthews's figure is correct she sold for about $50 per ton. However, in citing his figures Hutchins cautions that "it is not clear what outfits, if any, are included, and whether the builder's profit or loss is added in" (p. 280).

8 *Portland Eastern Argus,* January 2, 1850.

9 Ibid., February 22, 1850.

10 Certificates of Register Nos. 416 and 417, New York, July 24, 1850. Records of the Bureau of Marine Inspection and Navigation. Record Group 41. National Archives, Washington, DC.

11 *Portland Christian Mirror,* March 27, 1851.

12 Robert B. Applebee, *200 Sailing Vessels of the Portland–Falmouth Customs District and the Builders,* compiled 1942. Typescript mss. Phillips Library, Penobscot Marine Museum, Searsport, ME, p. 3.

13 Portland, Maine, Vital Records, Maine State Archives, Augusta.

14 S. B. Beckett, *The Portland Reference Book and City Directory for 1846* (Portland: Thurston, Fenly & Co., 1846), pp. 134, 149.

15 S. B. Beckett, *The Portland Reference Book and City Directory for 1847–48* (Portland: Thurston & Co., 1847), p. 26.

16 Ibid.

17 Vital Records.

18 Cumberland County Deeds, Book 214, p. 104, December 19, 1848.

19 Maine, vol. 14, p. 249, R. G. Dun & Co. Collection, Baker Library, Harvard Business School.

20 Cumberland County Supreme Judicial Court, January term, 1858, Writ #624, vol. 30, p. 539. Maine State Archives, Augusta.

[21] *Portland Washingtonian Journal,* November 4, 1846.

[22] 1850 Federal Census: *Products of Industry,* Original mss. at Maine State Archives, Augusta. Calculation of the approximate daily wage is based on an assumption of twenty-five working days per month, though they could have ranged a day either side of that. I am grateful to Professor John F. Battick of the University of Maine for assistance in this calculation.

[23] *Portland Eastern Argus,* January 2, 1850.

[24] 1850 Population Census, Cape Elizabeth. *Products of Industry.*

[25] The *First Annual Report of the Commissioner of Navigation,* (Washington: Government Printing Office, 1884) cites a national average of $45 to $48 per ton (p. 24), while John G. B. Hutchins in *American Maritime Industries and Public Policy* says that prices in New York and Boston yards in the early 1850s ranged from $55 to $100 per ton. However, as he points out, it is difficult to determine from published figures if these were builders' costs or actual sale prices.

[26] Applebee, pp. 17–18.

[27] 1850 Population Census, Cape Elizabeth, microfilm, Maine State Archives.

[28] Ibid.

[29] *Portland Eastern Argus,* October 21, 1850.

[30] *Portland Evening Advertiser,* November 12, 1850.

[31] *Portland Eastern Argus,* November 8, 1850. S. B. Beckett, *The Portland Reference Book and City Directory* (Portland: Brown, Thurston, 1852), p. 216. There is a bit of confusion over which vessel Stanforth was actually working on, hence both references. Beckett, in general, seems to be reasonably accurate.

[32] Letter from National Archives, November 1, 1983. Washington, DC.

[33] *Boston Daily Advertiser,* January 3, 1852.

[34] *Portland Eastern Argus,* February 23, 1850, for example.

[35] Memorandum of Agreement, August 26, 1851. Sewall Family Papers, Maine Maritime Museum, Bath, MS-22, Box 10, Folder 12.

[36] *Portland Eastern Argus,* August 17, 1851.

[37] On a timber cruise in the 1980s in Newcastle, Maine, up to our shins in snow in search of white oak, the shipwright involved, who shall be nameless, failed to find the reputed oak but brought forth this anecdote.

[38] *Portland Transcript,* September 6, 1893.

[39] Ibid.

[40] William E. Barry, *Sketch of an Old River* (West Kennebunk, ME: Phoenix Publishing, 1993), reprint of 1888 edition, p. 42.

[41] Author's personal experience from 1979 survey of 1841 British bark VICAR OF BRAY.

[42] Roy Newman interview, *The Georgetown* (ME) *Tide,* November–December 1984, p. 5. Unfortunately Newman did not record the name of the worker he interviewed.

[43] Ibid, p. 6.

[44] *Causes of the Reduction of American Tonnage* (Washington: Government Printing Office, 1870, the so-called *Lynch Report*), pp. 10 and 140. At the congressional hearings Ambrose Snow of the New York Ship-owners' Association "mentioned…that the life of a wooden ship is usually considered as ten years, although by extensive repairs they are sometimes made to last twenty years." Cyrus F. Sargent of Yarmouth, Maine, in answer to the question, "What is the average life of American ships?" testified that he believed that the insurance underwriters "state it at about eight years."

S NOW SQUALL arrived in New York on August 19, three days from Portland,[2] but in spite of the glowing September story in the *New York Herald* which listed her among the "yachts of America," her sale in New York apparently took until late November. She had lain at a Brooklyn wharf or anchorage in the interim. Shortly before Christmas she left New York for Boston to begin loading cargo for her maiden overseas voyage to Honolulu under the watchful eye of veteran Captain Isaac Bursley. SNOW SQUALL's new certificate of register, a requirement when a vessel's ownership or home port changed, was issued at New York's Greek-columned customhouse on downtown Wall Street on December 10, 1851, and listed Charles R. Green of New York as her sole owner, with Bursley as master.[3]

Charles Reynolds Green, who would own SNOW SQUALL for her entire career, was born in Malden, Massachusetts, in 1810, the youngest of four children of the Reverend Aaron and Eunice. The Greens were an old Malden family, which went back to 1647, when one James Green, who had emigrated from England, settled in Mystic Fields, the hamlet that became Malden, and was admit-

# 3

## THE SHIPOWNER

ted as a "freeman" of the town.[4] By the annual Malden Town
Meeting of 1695, at which (as in many small New England communities today) all village affairs for the coming year were voted
on, the moderator and town clerk were Greens, as were four of
the selectmen. As Malden historian Deloraine Corey wrote dryly
in 1899, "This family has great preponderance in the early period
of Malden history."[5] In other words, the Greens were a good,
solid, respectable North Shore line, and by the eighteenth century
they were prosperous enough to send some of their sons to Harvard College. Charles's father, Aaron, was Harvard Class of 1781
and became the minister of Malden's First (Congregational)
Parish, while his Uncle Ezra, Class of 1765, became a physician,
served with distinction in a New Hampshire regiment in the siege
of Boston during the American Revolution, and made one cruise
in English waters with (and had the temerity to disagree with)
John Paul Jones aboard RANGER.

Unlike his father and uncle, Charles Green apparently did
not attend Harvard, but instead, as he recalled about fifty years
later, was "brought up in the office of Peter C. Brooks of Boston

SNOW SQUALL's certificate of register number 529, issued at New York on December 10, 1851, showing Charles R. Green as "only owner." She is described as having a "square stern" and a "figure head." Captain Isaac Bursley was "at present Master."

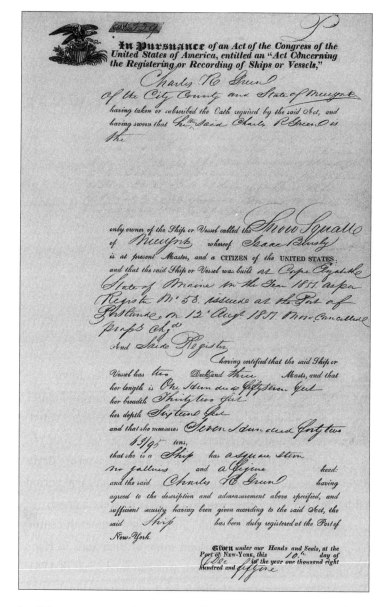

[and] later went into business at the south for sd. Brooks."[6] Peter Chardon Brooks (1767–1849), was a native of Yarmouth, Maine, who had grown up in genteel poverty in Medford, next door to Malden. On Brooks's father's death in 1781, the fourteen-year-old boy was apprenticed to a Boston merchant. By 1789 he had set himself up in the marine insurance business and was spectacularly successful. Brooks family tradition has it that the key to that success was that Brooks was extremely choosy about which vessels he

would insure. Any shipowner taking out a policy had to maintain and operate his vessel to Brooks's exceedingly high standards, thus cutting his potential losses. He also invested shrewdly in the East India spice trade, and at his death was reputed to be the richest man in New England. It would be difficult to imagine a better role model for young Charles Green.

Green and Brooks came from remarkably similar backgrounds. Brooks's father, the Reverend Edward Brooks, was like Aaron Green, a Congregational minister and a Harvard graduate (Class of 1737). Ordained at Yarmouth, Maine, some years later in 1764, he was honored by his new congregation at an ordination dinner "which has never been equalled since in its profusion and cost."[7] But to Brooks's conservative Maine parishioners, he soon began to seem "dangerously liberal," even "an opening wedge" for the heresy of Unitarianism (or at the very least, unorthodoxy) then regarded as serious theological threats. In 1769 Brooks resigned under pressure and returned to Medford.[8] The Reverend Aaron Green's relationship with Malden's "Society of Congregational Christians" seems also to have gotten off to a promising start. Under his leadership, in January 1803 the Congregationalists had dedicated a "new and elegant brick church," with a bell donated by Newburyport's wealthy and eccentric merchant, "Lord" Timothy Dexter.[9] However, by 1827 relations between Green and his flock appear to have soured. In 1827 or 1828 Green was either dismissed or resigned. Charles was in his late teens when his father left Malden for Andover, some eighteen miles to the northwest, though by that time he may well have been in Peter Brooks's office for some time.

We don't know how old Charles Green was when he entered Brooks's office. Boston's Robert Bennet Forbes, who made and lost and made several fortunes in the China trade in the nineteenth century, began clerking when he was twelve, after his father, too, had fallen on hard times. His duties were "to sweep out, make the fires, close and open the store, copy letters into a book in a very indifferent manner, collect wharfage bills, [and] run errands."[10] Captain Charles P. Low later recalled going to work for a wholesale jobber of dry goods in New York, at age fourteen, with no pay for his first year on the job and fifty dollars the second. The workday was from six in the morning to eight at night, though occasionally, in a rush period, it lasted until two in the morning, "when we lay down on the counters till daylight." The young clerks, Low remembered, "were allowed a shilling (twelve and a half cents) for our meals, when so kept from our homes."[11]

At some point Charles's older brother, George, nine years his senior, had joined other ambitious Yankees in New Orleans. In the twenty years or so after the Louisiana Purchase, a stream of northerners migrated south to the bustling, growing, cosmopolitan port city upstream from the delta of that great avenue of commerce, the Mississippi River. By 1822, at age twenty-one, George, with an office on Conti Street, was the southern agent for the Regular Line of packets between Boston and New Orleans.[12] If this seems a tender age for such responsibility, by modern standards it may have been, but in the period before the Panic of 1837, opportunity awaited a "typical" New Englander arrived in bustling New Orleans in his late teens or early twenties, "without money but possessing a skill and the all-important letters of introduction." The rise from clerk to junior partner to senior partner or sole owner "took, on the average, from ten to twelve years."[13] By 1855, according to *DeBow's Review,* "nearly one-fourth of all free, white native-born Americans in New Orleans were Yankees."[14] The "letter of introduction" may well have been a key factor in Charles Green's eventual move south to join his brother, for Peter Brooks and his son-in-law, Rezin D. Shepherd, had strong New Orleans ties, particularly with merchant and philanthropist Judah Touro.[15]

In 1839 Charles Green, "merchant, of New Orleans," then twenty-nine years old, married Charlotte Augusta Coolidge of Boston, two years his junior.[16] Charlotte's father, Samuel, was a Boston merchant and "auctioneer" who lived on lower Chestnut Street, near the bottom of Beacon Hill. He was a partner in the firm of Coolidge and Haskell, then located on Kilby Street, a few blocks south of the long granite buildings of Quincy Market, built in the previous decade by filling in the heads of the wharves. Nearby was brick Faneuil Hall, made famous by the orations that took place there but given by Peter Faneuil to the city as a market. In the early years of the nineteenth century auctioneers like Samuel Coolidge played a vital role in Boston's commerce, selling off a good proportion of incoming cargoes at wholesale. By the time Charles Green married into the family, however, the seaport of Boston was steadily losing its market share to New York, to which even Bostonians such as Russell and Company more often sent their cargoes from China. Boston money flowed into the enterprises of railroads, banking, and mills, while increasingly New England-built and -owned ocean-going vessels seldom visited the home ports painted in white letters on their sterns. Ambitious New Englanders, such as the Green brothers, headed for developing markets elsewhere.

In New Orleans the young Charles Greens lived on Canal Street at the western edge of the French Quarter, at that time a street of three- and four-story brick houses with a plank-covered canal down the middle, dominated by the tall spires of the Cathedral of St. Louis at the head of the Place des Armes to the south. The offices of the firm of George Green and Brother were by then on Gravier Street, several blocks away. By 1842 Charles was part-owner of his first vessel, the 432-ton ship AUGUSTA, built at Bowdoinham, Maine, in 1831 He and his co-owner John Hughes sold her "abroad" at the end of 1846.[17] Apparently Charles's older brother George died about this time. The first credit report on Green's firm, written in July 1847, lists him as "the surviving brother."[18] Shortly before disposing of the AUGUSTA he bought shares in the 218-ton brig CZARINA of Boston, built at Newburyport in 1829, selling her in the spring of 1851.[19] Both of these were relatively small vessels, and neither was exactly new. Green Brothers' R. G. Dun and Company credit reports described the firm as a "house of long standing," "large importers of Rio Coffee," and "regarded as extremely solvent."[20] Charles Green was beginning to use the profits from the coffee trade to diversify his investment.

However, much could go wrong in the coffee trade. In February 1847 Green Brothers brought the owners of the brig CHERAMUS before a special committee of the New Orleans Chamber of Commerce, alleging that 251 bags of coffee, out of a cargo of 3,604 loaded at Rio, were damaged because "the brig was in an unseaworthy condition when she took her cargo on board, and that she encountered no perils of the sea which will warrant [the owners] having recourse on their underwriters."[21] The captain, on behalf of the owners, denied the charge, claiming that he had had his vessel caulked in Rio. This denial began to fall apart when the committee examined the logbook. On the voyage from Cadiz to Rio, loaded with Spanish salt, with "fresh breezes and pleasant weather," CHERAMUS leaked so badly that on most days the crew had to pump every half hour.[22] Five days out of Rio, bound for New Orleans, the crew was pumping every fifteen minutes. The committee concluded that the brig "was not fit to go to sea with a cargo on board; every page of her logbook shows it," and awarded damages, with the costs of arbitration, to Green Brothers.[23]

The following year, 1848, Green's agent, Reed Schwartz, secured a New Orleans register for the 218-ton, Newburyport-built brig CZARINA.[24] Green was to hold onto CZARINA for five years, selling her back to Boston interests in 1851.[25] At the end of 1849 he made his first substantial long-term ship investment when he bought a ten-sixteenths interest in the brand-new ship GEORGE GREEN, built at Medford, Massachusetts, by one of that shipbuilding city's major builders, Jotham Stetson, who built about thirty vessels there between 1822 and 1876. Green's co-owners were builder Stetson, with three-sixteenths, and St. Croix Redman of Medford, who became her master, with another three-sixteenths. The GREEN received her New Orleans register early in 1850.[26] She was a substantial ship, 171 feet in length, 33 feet beam, and 23 feet depth, 866 $\frac{40}{95}$ tons. Green owned her until she was lost with all twenty-six hands on the Devon coast in the English Channel in January 1877. The only body recovered was that of her captain, Calvin Wilcox's wife, Amelia.

By 1850 there were three children in the Green family, ten-year-old Charles, who unfortunately was "deaf and dumb," seven-year-old Sarah, and four-year-old John.[27] At about this time Charles Green decided to move with his family to New York. He may have done so gradually between 1850, when he appears in the New Orleans census and in the city directory, and 1853 when *Dun's Reports* lists Green Brothers as "out of business—closed up."[28] He first appears in New York City directories in the early 1850s as living on Fifth Avenue with a Wall Street office. His first New York credit report is dated 1855 and states that he moved there in 1849. By 1853 he was well enough established in New York that one S. C. Marsh, seconded by Samuel Nicholson, nominated him for membership in the prestigious Union Club on 69th Street, to which he was duly elected on November 2.[29] The 1855 New York municipal census, taken in July 1855, lists him as having been "4 years resident in N.Y.," occupation, "merchant," owner of a brick house and land worth $30,000, presumably at his city directory address of Fifth Avenue at Twelfth Street. There were six servants (four Welsh females and an Irish coachman and "waiter") and three "boarders," one Sara Jones, a native of Wales in her late thirties, and two teen-aged Jones boys, most likely Sarah's sons. The Greens had one child, Jessie Jane, then aged one and a half.[30] Did Green's other three children die in New Orleans of cholera or yellow fever, as well they might have?

Not one of the popular, gossipy volumes listing "prominent" merchants or businessmen of Manhattan of this period mentions Green, though by the end of the Civil War his wealth was estimated at over half a million dollars.[31] This may stem, in part, from snobbery in that Green's fortune was very much "new," as opposed to "old," New York money, but in trying to review the historical record one also senses that Green was an intensely private person. The last entry for him in *Dun's Reports,* dated October 26, 1877, says that he "has never given a note in his life or put his name to paper obligation & does not propose to do so. Declines giving any information as to his means for the reason that he does not ask for credit." *Dun's* added that, "We find that he has borne for years the reputation of being a prudent & successful merchant of large means. Safe & good for all he undertakes."[32]

Green opened his New York office at 82 Wall Street, on the north side of the street, a few minutes' walk from the custom-house to the west at the corner of Wall and Nassau. (This hand-some Greek revival building, later the U.S. Sub-Treasury, survives today.) The Merchants' Exchange was practically across the street. If he turned left, Sutton and Company, who were SNOW SQUALL's agents for her first voyage to San Francisco in 1853, had their offices at 84 Wall Street, and she received her cargo at Pier 16, at the foot of the street. Other brokers with whom Green dealt were W. C. Annan at 94 Wall Street, and Cornelius Comstock at number 96. SNOW SQUALL occasionally lay across the East River in Brooklyn between voyages, and beginning in 1853 the Wall Street ferries MONTAGUE, EXCHANGE, and METROPOLIS began service to Brooklyn between elegant new two-story Italianate terminals on each shore. This area of several blocks was Charles R. Green's

The Old Merchants' Exchange at 55 Wall Street, which became the Custom House in 1863. It was just a short walk from Charles R. Green's office at 82 Wall Street.
*VALENTINE'S MANUAL*, AUTHOR'S COLLECTION

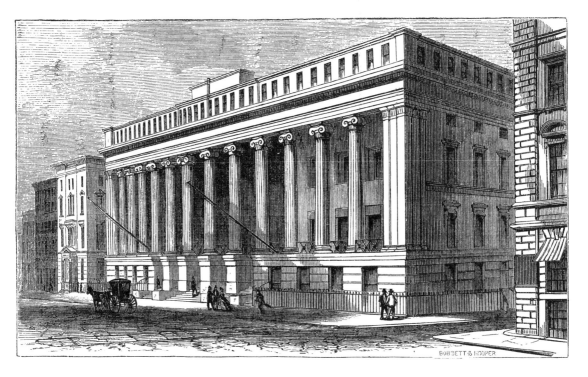

day-to-day working world, to which he presumably was driven each day by his coachman. By 1869 he had moved his business several doors to the east, to 88 Wall Street.

When Charles Green bought SNOW SQUALL at the end of 1851, he had been operating the GEORGE GREEN, with St. Croix Redman in command, for several years as a packet out of New Orleans. His new ship made a logical complement to his older one. Whether Charles Green freighted cotton on his own account, for other New Orleans commission merchants—or both—is unclear. In either case the voyages enabled Green to secure bills of exchange on London bankers. These could be used to purchase goods on Green's account as part of the GEORGE GREEN's return cargo, or, perhaps more important to his operations, since SNOW SQUALL generally ran out to Shanghai in ballast after discharging cargo at an intermediate port, the London bills could be sold there to raise the capital for Green's share of a cargo back to New York. In modern financial terminology, one ship acted as a "cash cow" for the other.

This was the New York Custom House at 26 Wall Street for most of SNOW SQUALL's career. Built in 1842, it became the U.S. Sub-treasury in 1863 when the Custom House moved to the former Merchants' Exchange. Renamed Federal Hall, it is now a museum.
*VALENTINE'S MANUAL*, AUTHOR'S COLLECTION

As we have seen, Green sold the brig CZARINA roughly six months before he bought SNOW SQUALL. In January 1853, not quite two weeks before SNOW SQUALL returned from her maiden voyage, Green bought the bark SAONE, 292 tons, with Randolph Schwartz of New Orleans. She had been built at Bath, Maine, in 1846 and Green retained an interest in her only for about three years. Judging from her half model, now at the Smithsonian Institution in Washington, she was, quite literally, a "tub."[33] Extremely "kettle-bottomed," the 112-foot vessel fell over sideways at her launching instead of gliding gracefully into the Kennebec River, and went through three owners in four years before Green and Schwartz took a chance on her. (One suspects that the price was probably right.) They sold her in 1856, and after several more owners, over twenty years after her launching, she was the MARIQUITA of Buenos Aires.

At the end of 1855, Green bought a three-quarters share and St. Croix Redman one-quarter in the brand new ship HARRY BLUFF, also built by Jotham Stetson, who had moved his operations downriver from Medford to Chelsea. Stetson had named his new ship with the pen name used by oceanographer Matthew Fontaine Maury in his series of articles in the Richmond, Virginia, *Whig* in which, among other things, he advocated establishment of a naval academy. She was a substantial vessel: 186 feet in length, 1,197 tons.[34] An article, probably from the Boston *Atlas* for Christmas Day, described her figurehead as "the full figure of a tar, represented in the act of lifting his hat, when homeward bound, to the first pretty girl he meets."[35] More important, the article describes her color scheme. The HARRY BLUFF had a black hull but "inside, she is buff color, her between decks white, and their standing strakes and waterways blue," giving some idea of the appearance of a packet "designed for the New Orleans and European trade."[36] The HARRY BLUFF is included in some modern lists of "clippers," but no such claim was made for her in 1855. She had a very long poop, extending forward to the mainmast, the forward end of which was "designed for the stowage of light cargo or if required could easily be converted into a second cabin for the accommodation of passengers."[37] Captain Redman personally oversaw her construction and selected her gear. "Deacon" Jotham Stetson (1794–1876) had just turned fifty-nine and had been building vessels since about 1822. In 1855 he pronounced the HARRY BLUFF "the best ship he ever built."[38] She soon cleared from Boston's Commercial Wharf in the Dispatch Line for New Orleans, which seems to have been her only run as a coastwise packet. Charles Green owned her first with Captain Redman and after 1856 wholly. She was abandoned on Nantucket Island's South Shoal in March 1869, bound from Cadiz to Boston with a cargo of salt and wine, and was a total loss, with two of her crew drowned and two frozen to death.

Later in 1855 Green purchased the last ship he would own in concert with SNOW SQUALL, the "clipper" DICTATOR, built earlier that year by James W. Cox at Robbinston, near Maine's eastern Canadian border. Cox sold her at auction to William Train of Medford for a reported $51,720.[39] On her arrival at Boston ownership passed to Samuel Train, who in November sold her to Green, with her master, John W. Shaw of Quincy, Massachusetts, taking a one-eighth share. DICTATOR was the largest vessel Green had yet owned, 189 feet in length and 1,292 tons register.[40] With one exception she seems to have had a relatively uneventful career under Green's red and blue house flag and rates but brief mentions in the literature on American clippers. Cox had built her after the earlier passion for extremely sharp vessels was pretty well spent, and it is more than likely that the "clipper" label notwithstanding DICTATOR was closer to the type of square-rigged vessel which came to be known as "downeasters" because so many of them came from Maine shipyards such as James Cox's. Apparently Green ran her out to the Pacific. She arrived at Hong Kong from San Francisco in October 1859, then in January 1860 sailed for Java.[41] The following year Green insured her for a voyage from Hong Kong to San Francisco.[42] In March 1863 he prudently took out a policy on her for a voyage from Liverpool to Hong Kong.[43]

On April 24 she was captured and burned by the Confederate raider CSS GEORGIA off the coast of Africa, a fate which, as we shall see, SNOW SQUALL narrowly escaped a few months later.

None of Green's day-to-day business records have come to light, but by examining the shipping news in the New York *Shipping and Commercial List* for one year it is possible to obtain a "snapshot" of his operations from the reports brought back from various ports. Admittedly this is likely an incomplete picture, but from it can be gained at least some idea of Green's operations. We'll look at the year 1860 because it was long enough after the bank panic of 1857 for market conditions to have stabilized once again, and because it was just before the disruption of the American Civil War. It must be remembered, however, that the modern historian has a perspective which Charles Green did not. For example, by reading the New York *Shipping and Commercial List* in January Green could learn that three months earlier SNOW SQUALL, which had left New York in July 1859, had passed by Anjer in the Sunda Strait on October 6, and was in port at Shanghai on November 7.[44] When SNOW SQUALL arrived back in New York on March 21, an enterprising reporter for James Gordon Bennett's *Herald* would have boarded her for the tow up the harbor and readers of that paper next morning could learn of what other vessels she brought news. In 1860 a transatlantic cable had been laid three years earlier—and had promptly failed. News from California took about a month by steamer. Hence Green and other shipowners avidly read these detailed shipping news columns because they were their essential source of information. Sometimes that information was slightly contradictory. SNOW SQUALL was also reported as having arrived at Shanghai on November 10, not the seventh. By the end of the year SNOW SQUALL was once again reported in the Sunda Strait in late September.[45]

As to the other vessels in Green's fleet, his GEORGE GREEN cleared New Orleans for Havre on February 21 under Captain Fairbanks, arriving April 14. She apparently returned to New Orleans before clearing for Genoa on July 27,[46] while the HARRY

BLUFF, under Captain Redman, arrived at Havre from Key West on March 31, at Mobile from Havre on August 11, sailed again for Havre on October 2, and arrived on November 17.[47] As has been mentioned, DICTATOR was in China and Java. From his office at 82 Wall Street, then, Charles Green was operating a fleet of four square-rigged tramp freighters all over the globe, only one of which, SNOW SQUALL, actually returned to her home port during the year 1860. As maritime historian Robert Albion commented, with only sketchy knowledge of what conditions one's far-flung vessels might be encountering, there was little a shipowner like Green "could do to secure his interests except to take out more insurance."[48] As with DICTATOR, previously mentioned, this Green did with his vessels, according to the "risk book" of the Mercantile Marine Insurance Company of Boston. It is more than likely that he insured with more than one company, but since none of his vessels came to any grief during 1860, they do not turn up in those great compendiums of marine disasters, the Atlantic Mutual Insurance Company's "disaster books," for that period. In the case of SNOW SQUALL, we have some knowledge of who some of Green's agents were at her ports of call, but a detailed study of his overall operations—who, for example, handled the HARRY BLUFF's affairs at Key West, Havre, and Mobile—is simply beyond the scope of this study. It is enough to know that Green's small shipping empire was far-flung, complex, and apparently highly profitable.

The Greens apparently began summering at Nahant, on Boston's North Shore, around 1853, in one of Cornelius Coolidge's two-story mansard-roofed stone and wood cottages, wrapped with a wide veranda, on Vernon Street on the west side of the peninsula, with a fine view of sunsets over the waters of Joseph's Cove. Charlotte Coolidge Green must have blessed the summertimes at Nahant after the Greens' sojourn in New Orleans. Her Uncle Cornelius was an enterprising (though not always successful) Beacon Hill architect, real estate speculator, and developer. If he did not build Charlotte Green's father Samuel's Boston house, Cornelius Coolidge may very well have designed it. He was also actively

Next pages: One of the hazards of Yankee shipowning during the Civil War was depredations by Confederate warships, which were denounced in the northern press as "pirates." Here the caption in *Harper's Weekly* reads, "Destruction of the Clipper Ship 'Jacob Bell' by the British Pirate 'Florida.'" Flying the Confederate flag, the CSS FLORIDA had been built in a British shipyard over the strenuous protests of the American ambassador. In the summer of 1863 Charles Green's ship DICTATOR was burned by the CSS GEORGIA and it was only the superb seamanship of Captain Dillingham that got SNOW SQUALL away from the CSS TUSCALOOSA. Dillingham would encounter the FLORIDA in his efforts to get home from the Falklands in 1864, and lose all his books, charts, and navigational instruments as a result. *HARPER'S WEEKLY*, AUTHOR'S COLLECTION

engaged in developing the fledgling summer colony of Nahant, and built the cottage in which the Charles Greens would eventually summer. Coolidge, unfortunately, never really reaped the full benefits of his far-sighted real estate development. The bank panics of 1829 and 1837 wiped him out, and when he died broke in 1844, he apparently had no estate worth filing for probate.

The pioneering rusticators at Nahant, such as wealthy and thoroughly eccentric Frederick Tudor, who had made his fortune shipping drink-chilling New England ice to outposts such as Bombay, sneered at Coolidge's "miserable" summer cottages. As an architect Coolidge was no Bulfinch, but his rustic, salt spray-drenched retreats, if no masterpieces, were apparently well built. Not for these northern Yankees were the effete palaces of Newport. The affectionately self-mocking term, "Cold Roast Boston," was coined by a Nahant summer resident. It was a high-powered community financially and intellectually. The Greens' near neighbor, Henry Wadsworth Longfellow, wrote part of *The Song of Hiawatha* while summering there, while naturalist Louis Agassiz, whose cottage lay across Nahant to the north, wrote up his travels in Brazil, and John Lothrop Motley worked on his *Rise of the Dutch Republic*. The nearest railroad connections from Boston to Nahant were at nearby Lynn, but Nahant's summer residents apparently preferred to come by steamer, coming ashore at the wharf at the north end of Curlew Beach below one of the Tudor cottages. By August 1855 the 300-ton NELLY BAKER, prudently equipped with two "forcing pumps," 200 feet of hose, 25 buckets, and a lifeboat, was in service.[49]

Like many other New England seaside summer communities, Nahant had a non-denominational chapel, officially known as The Nahant Church but locally as the "Boston" or "Union" Church. Its first structure was a Greek revival temple, built on a lot donated by Cornelius Coolidge and dedicated in 1832. Charles Green's early mentor, Peter C. Brooks, who summered at Nahant in the 1830s before switching to Newport, was one of its founding "proprietors." The church was replaced by a new edifice in 1868, and in 1873, 1874, and 1875 Charles Green served as one of its two wardens. His 1874 co-warden was Henry Cabot Lodge.[50]

In 1877 Charles Green, then aged sixty-seven, seems to have begun to divest himself of his fleet, perhaps prompted by the tragic loss of his first ship, the GEORGE GREEN, early in the year. He was ready to enjoy a well-earned retirement with winters in New York and summers at fashionable Nahant.

Back home in New York, the Greens were listed in the first edition of the *Social Register* in 1887. Nor did the Greens neglect Nahant's summer social life. In 1889 Charles Green was one of the founding members of the Nahant Club, which leased Frederick Tudor's old but imposing "cottage" and installed a bowling alley, pool table, and "other amusements as may appear practicable."[51] Dues were thirty dollars a year and women were welcome—in their places, which were "the ball room, ladies' parlor and piazzas adjacent thereto, the dining room, the ladies' dressing room, and on Sundays, the Committee room." They were not permitted to play cards on Sundays.[52] At the meeting at Boston's Parker House in the spring of 1889 which established the Nahant Club's by-laws and rules it was firmly established that this was a club for what Nahant historians Paterson and Seaburg term "'blue-bloods' not 'squatters.'"[53] At age seventy-nine and retired from active business, Charles Green could watch the young people play tennis and listen as "every minute speck of gossip was retold half a dozen times lest any one of the select hundred who made up Nahant society should have missed it."[54]

But the Greens' Nahant Shangri-La would come to an abrupt end in the dry spring of 1896. Apparently Longfellow's old cottage, still in the family, caught fire on May 18 with a strong wind blowing. The fire spread to the Green cottage's laundry, a separate building, then to the house itself. Before firemen from Nahant and Lynn could get things under control, five cottages burned. Green's was valued at $12,000. Four years later, on April 2, 1900, Charles Green, by then widowed and apparently frail, died in a New York hotel of pneumonia. He is buried in Mount Auburn Cemetery in Cambridge, Massachusetts, in the same plot as his father and his brother George.

# NOTES

1 I. R. Butts, *The Shipper's and Carrier's Assistant* (Boston: I. R. Butts, 1848), p. 24.

2 *New York Herald,* August 20, 1851.

3 New York Register No. 529, December 10, 1851, Records of the Bureau of Marine Inspection and Navigation, Record Group 41. National Archives, Washington, DC.

4 Deloraine P. Corey, *The History of Malden* (Malden: Published by the author, 1899), p. 234.

5 Ibid.

6 Charles R. Green Credit Report, October 26, 1877, New York, vol. 345, p. 538. R. G. Dun & Co. Collection, Baker Library, Harvard Business School. (Henceforth *Dun's,* New York.)

7 William H. Rowe, *Ancient North Yarmouth and Yarmouth, Maine* (Somersworth, NH: New England History Press, 1980), p. 133.

8 Ibid., pp. 133–34.

9 *The Register of the Malden, Massachusetts, Historical Society* (Malden: No. 2, 1911–1912), p. 53.

10 Robert Bennet Forbes, *Personal Reminiscences* (Boston: Little, Brown & Co., 1892), pp. 27–28.

11 Charles P. Low, *Some Recollections* (Boston: Geo. H. Ellis Co., 1905), pp. 6–7.

12 Carl Cutler, *Queens of the Western Ocean* (Annapolis: Naval Institute Press, 1961), p. 444.

13 William W. Chenault and Robert C. Reinders, "The Northern-Born Community of New Orleans in the 1850s," *Journal of American History,* vol. 51, September 1964, pp. 233–34.

14 *DeBow's Review,* September 1855.

15 For example, later on the Shepherd-owned packet, JAMES H. SHEPHERD, built at Medford, Massachusetts, in 1838, ran in the Regular Line between Boston and New Orleans and in 1839 her captain was thirty-four-year-old St. Croix Redman, a Medford native who would later become a part-owner and captain of several vessels in association with Charles Green. Two years later Redman was elected a member of the prestigious Boston Marine Society, a singular honor for a relatively young captain.

16 Emma Downing Coolidge, *Descendants of John and Mary Coolidge of Watertown, 1630* (Boston: 1930), pp. 320–21.

17 New Orleans Registers No. 17, February 10, 1842; No. 79, October 11, 1845. Register surrendered November 15, 1846. Record Group 41. National Archives.

18 George Green & Brother Credit Report, July 13, 1847, Louisiana, vol. 9, p. 81 (New Orleans). R. G. Dun & Co. Collection, Baker Library, Harvard Business School. (Henceforth *Dun's,* New Orleans.)

19 Boston Register October 21, 1846; New Orleans Register July 6, 1848; Boston Register March 1, 1851. Record Group 41. National Archives.

20 *Dun's,* New Orleans, June 1849.

21 *Decisions of the New Orleans Chamber of Commerce from its Formation in 1843 to August 4th, 1856* (New Orleans: c. 1857),

p. 266.

[22] Ibid., p. 267.

[23] Ibid., pp. 268–69.

[24] Boston Register No. 269, October 21, 1846; New Orleans Register No. 116, July 6, 1848.Records Group 41. National Archives.

[25] Boston Register No. 72, March 1, 1851. Record Group 41. National Archives.

[26] Boston Register No. 551, December 13, 1848; New Orleans register No. 28, February 16, 1850. Record Group 41. National Archives.

[27] 1850 Population Census, Parish of New Orleans, reel No. 235, p. 11.

[28] Dun's, New Orleans, July 1853.

[29] Letter to author from Union Club Librarian Helen M. Allen, November 24, 1993.

[30] New York City Census, 1855. Doggett's City Directories, 1854–55 to 1858–59.

[31] Dun's, New York, August 31, 1870.

[32] Dun's, New York City, October 26, 1877.

[33] National Watercraft Collection, No. 76071, Smithsonian negative No. 873C.

[34] Boston Register No. 13, January 7, 1856. Record Group 41. National Archives.

[35] Unidentified clipping at the Peabody Essex Museum. The typeface and general style are similar to articles appearing in the Atlas during the 1850s describing new vessels.

[36] Ibid.

[37] Ibid.

[38] Ibid.

[39] Portland Eastern Argus, May 22, 1855.

[40] Boston Registers Nos. 116, June 8, 1855, and 188, June 11, 1855; New York Registers Nos. 709, November 13, 1855, and 710, November 13, 1855. Record Group 41. National Archives.

[41] New York Shipping and Commercial List, January 1 and March 3, 1860. (Henceforth S&CL.)

[42] Risk Book, June 7, 1861, Policy No. 15994, Mercantile Marine Insurance Company of Boston. Baker Library, Harvard Business School.

[43] Ibid., March 26, 1863, Policy No. 16341.

[44] S&CL, January 7 and 21, 1860.

[45] Ibid., December 1, 1860.

[46] Ibid., February 21, May 2, August 4, 1860.

[47] Ibid., April 21, August 18, October 20, November 24, 1860.

[48] Robert G. Albion, Business History Review, Spring 1964, pp. 132–33.

[49] Gleason's Pictorial Drawing Room Companion, July 28, 1855.

[50] Andrew P. Peabody, A Sermon Preached in Commemoration of the Founders of the Nahant Church (Cambridge: John Wilson and Son, 1892), p. 41.

[51] Stanley C. Paterson and Carl G. Seaburg, Nahant on the Rocks (Nahant: Nahant Historical Society, 1991), p. 194. Constitution and By-laws and List of Members of the Nahant Club, 1889 (Boston: J. L. Fairbanks & Co., 1889).

[52] Ibid.

[53] Ibid.

[54] James Phillips, quoted in Paterson and Seaburg, p. 195.

*During long periods the ship was beyond the owner's direct control…for months at a time there was little that the most agitated of owners could do to secure his interests except to take out more insurance. The greatest problem of management, indeed, can be put in a nutshell: to find a paragon to be master, rescue him if he turned out a fool, and restrain him if he turned out a scoundrel.*

—Robert G. Albion[1]

*We are all accustomed to accord the highest mark of mercantile greatness to the merchant who owns his own ship, loads her with silver, ginseng, lead and sterling bills and starts her off on a voyage of a year…and to come back a wooden island of spicy perfumes, equal to any from Araby the blessed, as he lies at anchor in the North or East River, loaded with teas of all classes, with silks, nankeens, cassia, and a thousand other things that come from China.*

—Walter Barrett[2]

SNOW SQUALL cleared New York on December 10 on the first leg of her maiden overseas voyage,[3] and arrived in Boston on December 14, 1851, under the command of Isaac Bursley.[4] He was an experienced captain. Born in Barnstable, Massachusetts, on September 27, 1806,[5] he came from a Cape Cod family that followed the sea; his older brothers Ira and Alleyn were also captains. Isaac had been a captain in packet lines between New York and New Orleans in the late 1840s, and it is possible that shipowner Green knew him from his New Orleans period.

After her arrival, SNOW SQUALL lay at Central Wharf awaiting her cargo and passengers for Honolulu, the first port of call on her maiden round-the-world voyage via Shanghai. SNOW SQUALL's Boston agents were "commission merchants" Cunningham Brothers with their offices a stroll away on Central Wharf, and A. A. Frazar at the Merchants' Exchange. With her rose- and satinwood-panelled cabin SNOW SQUALL offered "very superior accommodations" for passengers and was scheduled to sail on

# 4

# MAIDEN VOYAGE: 1852

January 15, though as things turned out she did not clear from Boston until two days after that.[6] Her Honolulu cargo was varied, and much of it was bulk such as lumber, probably loaded through the small square "lumber ports" in her 'tween-decks aft of the foremast. These openings, about four feet square, allowed the loading of long sticks without having to jockey them through the hatches on deck. After loading was complete, under the watchful eye of the chief mate, the ports were sealed with covers set flush with the outer hull planking, secured tightly in place, and thoroughly caulked.

SNOW SQUALL had loaded 120,000 feet of lumber, 137,500 shingles, 21,725 pickets, and 10,500 clapboards. Other items included a carriage and a buggy (and a pair of shafts), twenty cases of crackers, and eleven boxes of "miscellaneous goods."[7] Some of these miscellaneous items were, as we shall see, very much luxury goods. Meanwhile, in the same issues of the Boston *Advertiser* that solicited cargo, Alford Butler advertised his new bark WARNER.

A New Clipper Bark For Sale—If applied for soon. The new clipper bark, now at Portland, Me., built and modelled by the builders of the clipper ship Snow Squall, with a full poop, veneered cabin..., Sheathed with copper up to 15 feet, very heavily fastened, and calculated to compete with any of the clippers afloat.[8]

This, as mentioned previously, was the clipper bark WARNER, which had a short career, going missing on a voyage from New York to Dunkirk about two years later.

It has not been possible to determine the freight rates from Boston to Honolulu in late 1851 and early 1852 from published sources, but the bloom was definitely off the rose in the California trade. In 1849 no fewer than 151 vessels had cleared Boston for San Francisco and in 1850, 166—but by 1851 clearances had

Drawing of SNOW SQUALL, probably made in Boston in late 1851 or early 1852. The artist is William Bradford (1823–92), a New Bedford, Massachusetts, artist.
HART NAUTICAL COLLECTION, MASSACHUSETTS INSTITUTE OF TECHNOLOGY

dropped dramatically to but 35. The California boom was over. Boston's maritime newspaper, the Boston *Shipping List*, said that the numbers "will show at a glance the falling off in this trade."[9] There were reports that the San Francisco market was completely glutted with unsaleable shoes, for instance, and San Franciscans taunted East Coast entrepreneurs in letters reprinted in East Coast papers. "The sooner the merchants of the Atlantic States learn that California cannot absorb ten times the amount of goods her population require, the better for themselves," said a writer in the San Francisco *Herald*, quoted in the Portand, Maine, *Eastern Argus*.[10] No doubt on the advice of his Boston agents, owner Green decided that a China voyage by way of Honolulu was a better way to start recouping his investments in his new clipper ship.

Freights from Boston to San Francisco in late 1851 were quoted as twenty dollars per ton for "heavy goods" and "measurement goods," i.e., boxes, crates, and barrels, at fifty to sixty cents per cubic foot.[11] A cargo ton was forty cubic feet, simply a convenient unit of measure based on the old measurement of the space taken up by a large cask or "tun" of wine. It was, it must be emphasized, a measure of volume, rather than actual weight, and also had little relation to a vessel's customhouse "tonnage." Vessel admeasurement for tonnage, which was used in determining such things as port dues, *attempted* a rough approximation of cargo capacity through a complicated formula but fell rather short of real accuracy. SNOW SQUALL's "customhouse register" tonnage was 742 gross tons of 95 cubic feet each, but her actual carrying capacity (presumably discovered through experience) was advertised repeatedly as about 900 tons. Though her cargo on this voyage varied considerably in sizes, shapes, and weights one can think of it as roughly equivalent to nine hundred cubes, each just shy of three and a half feet on a side.

On this maiden voyage there were three passengers, a "Mr. Pratt," listed only as a "merchant," and the Reverend and Mrs. Albert Sturges, missionaries in their early thirties, travelling out to the Pacific under the auspices of the Boston-based American Board of Foreign Missions.[12] The Sturges went on to long and distinguished careers on Ponape (modern Pohnpei in the Federation of Micronesia). It is said that at one point the missionaries wondered aloud why they could not have been sent out to the Pacific by the much shorter route over the Panama isthmus rather than around Cape Horn. The response, evidently, from their New England Calvinist sponsors was that they needed "the discipline of a voyage around the Horn." These missionaries became known by the islanders as "The Boston Men," but the records of the Board of Missions are very skimpy regarding the Sturgeses. (The label "Boston Men" was also applied to Yankees in the Pacific Northwest fur trade but does not seem to have been widespread elsewhere.) The possibility exists that shipowner Green, son of a Congregational minister, assisted the Sturgeses on the first leg of their voyage to Micronesia.

SNOW SQUALL cleared and sailed from Boston on January 17, 1852, and was described in the Boston *Shipping List* as one of the "East India Fleet."[13] Normally a vessel bound from Boston or New York to the Orient went out by way of the Cape of Good Hope, across the Indian Ocean, through Java's Sunda Strait, and into the South China Sea. A voyage to Hawaii or California meant going around Cape Horn at the southern tip of South America.

But getting to Cape Horn, or to the Cape of Good Hope, for that matter, was not a simple matter of just sailing towards it along a relatively straight line, avoiding continental bulges and dangerous shoals en route. The oceans have bands of prevailing winds with which a sailing captain must cope or for whose aid he must plan, and currents such as the well-known Gulf Stream, which may aid or hinder depending on the desired objective. Headed from New York via either route meant first sailing east nearly to the Azores to get to windward of the northeast trade winds, then altering course to the south to clear the eastern tip of Brazil in about 28 or 29 degrees south latitude, then either heading towards Africa or around into the Pacific by way of Cape Horn.

Once past Brazil's Cape St. Roque the strategy on the Cape Horn run was to pass east of Cape St. Blanco in about 47 degrees south latitude, then run west of the Falkland Islands, and, if possible (weather and tide permitting), to take the inside passage through the Strait of le Maire between Staten Island and the larger island of Tierra del Fuego in Patagonia. This shortcut could shave about a day's sailing off the voyage. According to the *South America Pilot,* "Ships bound to the Pacific will find it advantageous to keep within 100 miles of the coast of Eastern Patagonia…to avoid the heavy sea that is raised by the westerly gales…. Having once made the land…it will be desirable to keep it topping on the horizon, until the entrance of the Strait of Magellan be passed." As to the merits and demerits of the le Maire passage, the *Pilot* quoted co-author Robert FitzRoy (who had surveyed the Strait aboard HMS BEAGLE some thirty years earlier) as opining that generally there was "neither difficulty or risk in passing through it."[14]

It must be appreciated that getting to the latitude of the Azores or setting a course for Cape St. Roque was not merely a matter of pointing the ship's bow in that direction. A modern fore-and-aft rigged yacht (i.e., with sails set more or less along the long axis of the hull) can sail about 39 degrees "off" or into the the wind, while a square-rigger such as SNOW SQUALL (with the major sails set more or less at right angles to the axis) can only point about 70 degrees off the wind. Any sailing craft, unless the wind is from astern, proceeds in a series of tacks, zig-zagging along the desired course. Once through le Maire and around Cape Horn a vessel headed for the Pacific still had to battle the westerly winds and deal with ocean currents. To get to San Francisco was not just to set a course north past Cape Horn; it was necessary to sail nearly to Hawaii to pick up a decent westerly—and to avoid the current which sets strongly southward along the California coast.

In the 1840s the U.S. Navy's Matthew Fontaine Maury began the Herculean task of analyzing sailing vessel logbooks stored in Washington to determine where and when favorable (or adverse) winds blew and currents ran along the world's major sailing routes. By 1847 Maury had published the first of his wind and current charts based on that data, and the following year he put out the first of a series of *Sailing Directions* to accompany the charts.

Captains could obtain these without charge by sending Maury a filled-out copy of the blank logbooks he provided, to add to his ongoing research. As far as can be determined, however, none of SNOW SQUALL's captains ever participated.

On June 2, 1852, after picking up the pilot, Captain Bursley left looming landmark Diamond Head to starboard and picked his tide carefully to enter Honolulu, or as some charts called it into the 1860s, "Honoruru." His ship drew 16 feet and at low water there were reportedly only 20 feet over the 300-foot-wide smooth coral harbor bar, with white breakers foaming like sharks' teeth on either side, though there was plenty of water just inside up the channel. Up she eased into a harbor which could easily contain seventy to eighty vessels.[15] She was consigned to J. C. Spalding, who had begun his Honolulu career as a ship chandler and now lived in one of the town's more elegant houses, very likely with a

Detail from chart, *North Pacific*. The widely used Imray charts were known as "bluebacks" from their dark blue paper backing. JAMES IMRAY AND SON, LONDON, 1869. AUTHOR'S COLLECTION

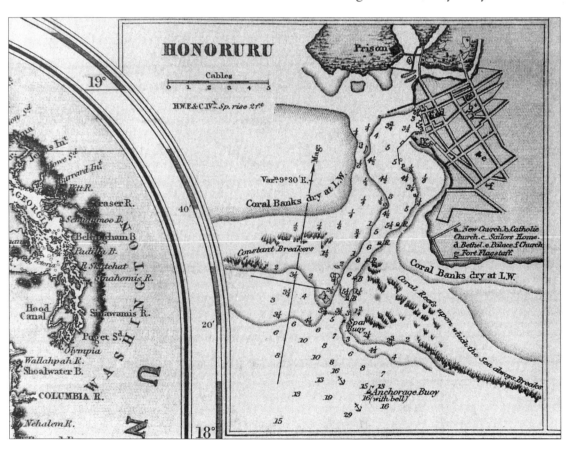

small garden of exotic plants. It had been a rough 135-day passage from Boston around Cape Horn with "adverse wind and weather conditions throughout."[16]

Pilotage fees were twenty-eight dollars, a sum calculated from SNOW SQUALL's draft.[17] The United States Consulate reported that she had arrived with a cargo of "merchandise and lumber, value $50,000," with an incoming crew of "15 American, 5 foreign."[18] Clearly the "foreignisation" of American vessels' crews was underway.

Two days later Honolulu diarist Captain Stephen Reynolds remarked on her white hull as, on a "beautiful morning," SNOW SQUALL began discharging cargo.[19] On June 12 J. C. Spalding advertised "Pilot and navy Bread, just received per 'Snow Squall.'"[20] In the early 1850s Honolulu was really a fair-sized but rapidly growing small town with a population of 6,000 or so. It straggled along the waterfront and extended about a quarter of a mile inland, and was described as "one good street, with a number of narrow, irregular alleys."[21] In 1853, the year after SNOW SQUALL's first visit, 154 merchant vessels arrived, but by far the greater volume of harbor traffic was the 256 whalers which called to reprovision.[22]

View of Honolulu in an 1857 lithograph by G. H. Burgess. This vista is probably little changed from SNOW SQUALL's visits in 1852 and 1853.
HAWAII STATE ARCHIVES

Between farming and servicing the whaling fleet, Honolulu was something of a boom town, though in another twenty years or so the whalers would vanish. There was a demand in Honolulu not just for shingles and house lumber but for luxuries. Among the "rare and valuable works just received per 'Snow Squall,'" Henry M. Whitney offered a "superbly bound" illuminated Bible for thirty dollars—a considerable sum of money in 1853—and apparently less exotically bound editions of Prescott's *Conquest of Peru* and *Conquest of Mexico* with more modest price tags. A. P. Everett had just unpacked his shipment of bridles, horse collars, saddlery, whips, and girths.[23]

However there was some trouble brewing on the Honolulu waterfront. On Friday, June 25, one Captain Weissenhorn appeared in police court "on suspicion of attempting to take off some of the crew of the Snow Squall," and though two of the crew gave testimony, all of the evidence against Weissenhorn appeared to be circumstantial. The following day Weissenhorn was back in court with Captain Reynolds defending him against the charge of "aiding deserters." Once again there seemed to be no hard evidence, but Weissenhorn had to post an appearance bond of a hundred dollars.[24] Under the law then in effect, no non-Hawaiian sailor could be discharged in Honolulu without the written consent of the authorities. Many whalers discharged at least part of their crew there, and there was a constant demand for American seamen as apparently (perhaps due to lack of experience) native Hawaiians were not highly sought after as replacements. In any case, the Weissenhorn affair ended when SNOW SQUALL cleared for Shanghai on June 28. That Monday morning Weissenhorn's accusers simply failed to appear in court.[25] SNOW SQUALL's outward-bound crew consisted of ten "Americans" and fourteen "foreigners," a radical shift in composition showing that nearly half of her Americans had deserted in Honolulu.[26]

On this next leg of her voyage, headed out in ballast and drawing four feet less than when she had come in,[27] SNOW SQUALL carried one passenger, a Mr. Cunningham. It is unclear what this gentleman's relation was to the Cunninghams of Russell and Company, to whom SNOW SQUALL was consigned at Shanghai. Edward Cunningham of Boston had arrived in China in 1845, was admitted as a partner in the Russell firm in 1850, and served as the American vice-consul from 1850 to 1854. But the Cunninghams had been one of SNOW SQUALL's Boston agents. In any case, on this passage SNOW SQUALL had the benefit of the southwest monsoon, which blows from about May to September in the western Pacific, and she arrived at Shanghai on August 1, apparently without incident.[28] By contrast, the experience of the clipper HOOGLY, which left Boston for Shanghai by way of San Francisco the day after SNOW SQUALL's departure, points up the things that could go wrong in the trade to China around Cape Horn.

En route to San Francisco Captain Chadwick had to bring the HOOGLY into Rio for repairs after having lost fore and main topmasts, and arrived in San Francisco on May 28, just before SNOW SQUALL arrived in Honolulu.[29] It is worth noting here, and will become apparent later on in SNOW SQUALL's career, that the violent weather that sent the HOOGLY into Rio could have missed SNOW SQUALL by a few hours or a few miles. In other words, the difference between a good, mediocre, or just plain terrible passage was a mixture of the sailing qualities of a particular vessel, her captain's judgment on the information available, and a certain amount of pure, unadulterated luck.

The HOOGLY passed Taiwan and apparently approached the mouth of the Yangtze from the southeast, as the eyewitness account of what happened next mentions sighting the Saddle Islands and the tiny islet of Gutzlaff.[30] The south entrance to the river hugs the shore, but it was fairly narrow and surrounded by shoals. By 1847 there was a government beacon at Yangtze Cape, but on August 20, as the HOOGLY groped towards the river, the weather had deteriorated into low clouds, rain, and a "fair gale." There were what were considered to be excellent charts of the China coast, drawn up from British Admiralty surveys, though sailing directions urged careful attention to taking soundings. But here

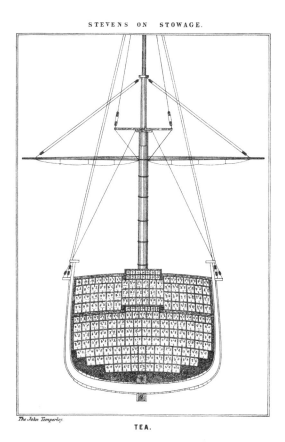

The John Temperley.

TEA.

Stowage of tea chests. Every usable cranny of space was filled with chests of varying sizes, kept from contact with water in the bilge by a layer of dunnage. The illustration is from *Stevens on Stowage*, one of the standard works on the subject.
AUTHOR'S COLLECTION

Captain Chadwick, who had never before attempted this landfall, made a fatal mistake. One of his passengers claimed to be an "Old China Hand" and familiar with these waters. This "Mr. Woodbury," recalled Chief Mate Candage, "thought the ship was too near the coast, so he at once changed her course and when the water shoaled he changed it still more. In a few minutes we struck with a whack." The crew stayed with the wreck as long as they dared, finally made it ashore, and eventually reached Shanghai safely. It should be noted that when a vessel wrecked or simply went aground in those parts it was not exactly prudent for her crew to linger in the vicinity. The China coast had been infamous for its pirates for centuries and these brigands regarded a few throats cut as part of the normal "salvage" process.

SNOW SQUALL sailed for New York on September 6 with a "cargo [of] teas &c., dispatched by Russell & Co."[31] and the HOOGLY's third mate. This was just before the start of the new tea season in October, and the tea was likely last year's crop. Black teas apparently did not "lose much by being a year old, except their freshness of smell."[32] Teas were packed in chests lined with metal foil, and Chinese stevedores were skilled at stowing the chests of varying sizes, which ranged in weight from just over a hundred pounds to about twenty-four pounds. According to one shipping manual, "when stowing the last chest in an early tier, a Chinaman, rather than strike it with any hard instrument, walks off to a distance, and running back jumps into the air and falls in a sitting posture on the chest, which is thus sent uninjured into its place."[33]

Even before the ship had left New York, owner Green could only hope that Captain Bursley was indeed a "paragon," as the

China trade was both complicated and chancy. Shanghai was one of the "treaty ports" opened up as a result of the Anglo-Chinese Opium War of 1841–42. In 1844 the United States and China signed the Treaty of Wanghia, which opened these ports to American flag vessels on the same basis as the British and allowed American merchants to set up year-round headquarters ashore. Under the pre-Opium War system, foreigners were allowed at Canton—Guangzhou—only seasonally. As Shanghai was nearer the sources of supply for tea and silk, it almost immediately flourished and soon eclipsed Canton, but mid-nineteenth-century Shanghai was not the most pleasant place to do business.

First, doing business was complicated. There was no guarantee, of course, that an arriving vessel could obtain a cargo speedily. It was a matter of how many vessels were in port, and with the Taiping Rebellion raging ashore, shipments from China's interior might be delayed. Russell and Company employed a Chinese "comprador" (a Portuguese word for a house purchaser) who juggled his duties as business agent, ship chandler, interpreter, and general factotum. While the comprador could, and often did, become wealthy himself, he did not stand high in the Chinese social pecking order, as being "in trade" was judged to be considerably inferior to being a scholar.

Second, trade was expensive. The comprador expected a "cumshaw" or present of two or three hundred Spanish silver dollars, depending on the size of a vessel's crew. The interpreter, whose talents apparently could vary wildly, expected a fee of 216 silver dollars plus his boat hire. The cumshaw to the Emperor was 1,950 taels (about $2,778 U.S.) plus a tonnage duty of from five to eight hundred taels at the rate of about $1.39 per tael.[34]

Finally, though the foreign quarter of Shanghai was on its way to developing into the westernized enclave it became, with imposing offices and warehouses along the Bund, the climate remained unpleasant: hot and humid in summer; cold, drizzly, and raw in winter. Disease was always a threat, whether malaria in summer or cholera from the squalid Chinese walled city with its primitive or nonexistent sanitation. Provisioning a vessel for the homeward voyage was tricky. As late as 1884 Captain Charles Bullock reported that "Shanghai water is very impure and sometimes brackish, containing a large quantity of organic matter, and its use is a fertile source of sickness to the crews of vessels." Due to the use of human waste as a fertilizer, local vegetables were regarded as "unsafe," and Bullock recommended rice "as the best substitute for vegetable diet."[35]

At least by 1847 British and American pilots were working out of Shanghai. Pilotage was $4.00 per foot of a vessel's draft from the lightship and $3.00 from Wusung up to Shanghai. *The China Pilot,* published in London, noted dryly that "it would be imprudent for a stranger to enter the Wusung without a pilot, who is always in attendance at the entrance, for the banks within are constantly undergoing change from the alluvial deposits."[36]

On August 7 and 14, 1852, Russell and Company advertised SNOW SQUALL's impending homeward voyage. "Having fine accommodations, [she] will take passengers." She left Shanghai on September 6 with the Russells in New York as "consignees."[37] Her cargo was "teas &c," and there was no mention of passengers. She arrived at New York on either January 22 or 23, 1853, probably stopping at Anjer in the Strait of Sunda for decent water and fresh provisions. As reported in New York's *Shipping and Commercial List*, her cargo was:

> Teas 1,740 pkgs, T. W. Ward—silk 14 cases, tea 990 pkg, E. King & Co—368 do. Manton & Hallet—438 do. Gordon & Talbot—230 do, Fogg Brothers—4,563 do. Brown Brothers & Co.—silk 3 cases, A. A. Low & Brother—mdse 1 box, Middleton & Co—1 case, J. A. Cunningham—teas 1,528 pkgs, raw silk 50 bxs, mdse 4 do. Order [i.e., to Charles Green].[38]

Tea, "in American vessels from place of growth," such as SNOW SQUALL carried, was admitted free of duty, but there was a tariff on silk which ranged from about 25 to 30 percent of its value. For years such cargoes had been sold at auction in New York, and a tax on these auctions had helped finance the Erie Canal. By 1853 there were still a few auctions but the bulk of imports went directly to the jobbers around Pearl Street, who sold to retailers. Wholesale prices for teas ranged from 20 to 80 cents per pound, depending on the variety and quality.[39] Unfortunately, no information was published in the New York shipping news on the specifics of SNOW SQUALL's tea cargo.

While the American travelling salesman flourished later in the century, bringing samples to outlying shopkeepers or selling door-to-door by horse and buggy (and later by automobile), in the 1850s country merchants visited New York themselves to obtain their merchandise on credit and departed for home with it by train, steamboat, or coastwise packet. Along New York's Broadway the new-fangled department stores such as Lord and Taylor offered imported luxuries to a growing middle class. Historian Robert G. Albion describes their elegant male "ribbon clerks" who "could murmur most delightfully to their feminine customers over the sheen of a bolt of silk."[40]

As SNOW SQUALL arrived in New York, Charles Green awaited word of market conditions in San Francisco. Mail travelled from San Francisco by steamer to the Pacific side of the Isthmus of Panama. During the dry season from December to April it was possible to take a river boat the 39½ miles up the Chagres River to Gorgona, the head of navigation, traverse the twenty miles to the Atlantic by mule (the railroad across the Isthmus would not be in operation until 1855), then go by steamer again from Panama to New York. It generally took about a month for mail from California to reach New York and by the end of January word arrived that the market for provisions in California might be favorable.

On January 29, the New York *Shipping and Commercial List* published news from San Francisco: "December 31, 1852. Since the last mail, business has been extremely depressed. We have had almost continual rains.... The stocks of provisions are all but

Next pages: Taking a Sandy Hook pilot off New York Harbor. The pilot schooners (identifiable by the numbers on their mainsails) cruised offshore in nearly any kind of weather. SNOW SQUALL ended her maiden voyage at New York in January 1853, so this wintry scene might have been what she encountered on her arrival.
*HARPER'S WEEKLY*, 1877, AUTHOR'S COLLECTION

South Street waterfront, New York, 1865. The packet ship DREADNOUGHT, also with a dragon figurehead, is in the foreground.

SAN FRANCISCO MARITIME NATIONAL HISTORICAL PARK, NEGATIVE NO. I 2.331

exhausted, and the roads are impassable."[41] Of course this report of a hungry market was no guarantee of what conditions might be in San Francisco when a cargo arrived roughly four months later from New York. A consignee might have been burned out in one of that city's frequent fires or simply have gone bankrupt. One visitor to San Francisco during the 1850s reported an overstock of pianos being used to fill a rain-washed gully. It is not clear just when Charles Green made the decision to send SNOW SQUALL around to San Francisco, but by February 5 she was reported as "nearly full," to sail in Sutton and Company's "Despatch Line."

# NOTES

[1] Robert G. Albion, *Business History Review,* Spring 1964, pp. 132–33.

[2] Walter Barrett, *The Old Merchants of New York City* (New York: Joseph A. Scoville, 1870), p. 292.

[3] New York *Shipping and Commercial List* (henceforth *S&CL*), December 13, 1851.

[4] *Boston Atlas,* December 15, 1851.

[5] Barnstable County "genealogy notes," Sturges Library, Barnstable, MA, vol. 6.

[6] *Boston Daily Advertiser,* January 3, 1852.

[7] Boston *Shipping List,* January 21, 1852. Though SNOW SQUALL was not mentioned specifically by name in "foreign exports to Honolulu," she was the only vessel which cleared Boston for Honolulu during the reporting period.

[8] *Boston Daily Advertiser,* January 3, 1852.

[9] Boston *Shipping List,* January 3, 1852.

[10] *San Francisco Herald,* May 1852, quoted in the Portland, Maine, *Eastern Argus,* June 13, 1852.

[11] Boston *Shipping List,* December 17, 1851.

[12] Harbormaster's Records, Port of Honolulu, June 3, 1852. Hawaii State Archives.

[13] Boston *Shipping List,* January 21, 1852.

[14] Captains Phillip Parker King and Robert Fitzroy, *The South America Pilot* (London: Hydrographic Office, Admiralty, 1860), p. 209–10.

[15] *Lippincott's Pronouncing Gazetteer* (Philadelphia: J.B. Lippincott & Co., 1873), page 868.

[16] *The Friend* (Honolulu), July 1852. Captain Stephen Reynolds journal, vol. VIII, June 2, 1852, Phillips Library, Peabody Essex Museum. Octavious T. Howe and Frederick C. Matthews, *American Clipper Ships* (Salem: Marine Research Society, 1927), p. 582. It has not been possible to verify Howe and Matthews's statement about the voyage from other sources.

[17] Collector General, Customs Accounts, 1852–53, Entries and Clearances of the Harbor Master, June 3, 1853. Hawaii State Archives. (Henceforth "Entries and Clearances.")

[18] Records of the Foreign Service Posts of the Department of State, Register of Arrivals and Departures, Consulate of the USA, Honolulu, June 3, 1853. Record Group 84. National Archives, Washington DC. (Henceforth "Arrivals and Departures.")

[19] Reynolds Journal, vol. VIII, June 1852.

[20] *The Polynesian* (Honolulu), June 12, 1852.

[21] *Lippincott's Pronouncing Gazetteer.*

[22] Ibid.

[23] *The Polynesian* (Honolulu), June 12, 1852.

[24] Reynolds Journal, June 25 and 26, 1852.

[25] Ibid., June 28, 1852.

26 "Arrivals and Departures."

27 "Entries and Clearances," June 28, 1852.

28 *North China Herald* (Shanghai), August 7, 1852.

29 Carl. C. Cutler, *Greyhounds of the Sea* (New York: Halcyon House, 1930), p. 482.

30 Captain R. G. F. Candage, "The Last Voyage of the Hoogly," in Clarissa M. Silitche, ed., *The Perilous Sea* (Dublin, NH: Yankee Books, 1985), pp. 21–30.

31 *North China Herald* (Shanghai), September 11, 1852.

32 Joseph Blunt, *The Shipmaster's Assistant and Commercial Digest* (New York: Harper & Brothers, 1853), p. 590.

33 Charles H. Hillcoat, *Notes on the Stowage of Ships* (London: Imray, Norie & Wilson, 1918), pp. 223–24.

34 Blunt, pp. 590–91.

35 Charles Bullock, *The China Sea Directory* (London: Hydrographic Office, 1884), p. 198.

36 John W. King, *The China Pilot* (London: Hydrographic Office, 1861), pp. 198–99.

37 *North China Herald* (Shanghai), August 7 and 14, September 11, 1852.

38 *S&CL,* January 26, 1853.

39 Ibid.

40 Robert G. Albion, *The Rise of New York Port* (New York: Charles Scribner's Sons, 1939), p. 282.

41 *S&CL,* January 29, 1853.

SNOW SQUALL's second Pacific voyage in 1853, again by way
of Cape Horn, was a calculated gamble. Owner Green and
Captain Bursley knew from her previous run that she could
be expected to arrive off Cape Horn about two months out of
New York, just after the "equinoctial gales," which according to
tradition or superstition—take your pick—blew around the third
week in March. "The winds are then strong, but may not always
be expected on the exact day of the [spring] equinox," reported
the Royal Navy's Captain Becher.[3]

As SNOW SQUALL prepared for departure, New York's South
Street waterfront was all abustle with the California trade. On February 2 New York's *Shipping and Commercial List* reported that there
was "a good deal going and Clippers fill up readily, often engaging a
full cargo before they are ready to begin to load—the ordinary rate
is 70 to 75 cents per [cubic] foot...up to 90 to 100 per foot when

# 5

## SECOND VOYAGE:
## CALIFORNIA, CHINA, AND
## ENGLAND (BY WAY OF HAWAII)

finishing off."[4] The explanation for the jump in rates towards the end of loading can be explained by the old principle of "last in: first out." In a market as volatile as San Francisco's it was worth a premium to get goods ashore before the market was glutted. By February 5 Snow Squall was "engaged nearly full at 70 to 75 cents."[5]

A week later her agents, Sutton and Company, placed an advertisement in New York's *Shipping and Commercial List*. They were a well-established firm of "commission merchants," a few doors away from shipowner Green's office, and specialized in loading West Coast-bound cargo out of New York and Philadelphia for a percentage of the freight money. Many years and several mergers later, the firm became part of the American-Hawaiian Steamship Company. The ad is typical of the hyperbole of the 1850s, which was, after all, a time when patent medicines were touted as curing nearly any ailment known, and one Phineas T. ("there's a sucker born every minute") Barnum was running a "museum" of "curiosities" both real and fabricated, in New York.

DESPATCH LINE

FOR SAN FRANCISCO

The Splendid and Favorite Clipper Ship

SNOW SQUALL

CAPT. BURSLEY

(only 700 tons)

Is now loading at the foot of Wall Street, ER [East River] and having the most of her cargo engaged, will have unprecedented dispatch.

This beautiful vessel is of the extreme sharp clipper model, being 700 tons register, and carrying only 800 tons cargo, has made but one voyage, and proved herself of unsurpassed speed, having sailed over three hundred and sixty miles in twenty-four hours.

For balance of cargo, which will be taken at very favorable rates, apply to SUTTON & CO., 84 Wall Street[6]

As to the claim of her 360-mile, 24-hour run, since no logbook from the maiden voyage has yet turned up, it is impossible to verify. If the claim is accurate she averaged fifteen knots, an excellent turn of speed, with Captain Bursley apparently driving her hard, no doubt under all the canvas his crew could set.

SNOW SQUALL's impending voyage was also advertised with pasteboard "clipper cards," colorful handouts a bit larger than a modern postcard, hundreds of them printed by Nesbitt and Company, located a block or so from the wharves. Sutton and Company.'s blue, white, and yellow card depicted SNOW SQUALL under sail with a white hull, and is one of two known contemporary images of her (though how much artistic license was involved is unknown). Her hull is at least white, with what *might* be a dark (vermilion?) stripe, but we can't say today if it's a "stock cut" from those on file at the printers', as it might have been.[7] The card also shows Sutton and Company.'s house flag, displaying a hive and swarming bees, presumably signifying industriousness. These often garish but occasionally very beautiful bits of nineteenth-century advertising ephemera, lavished around New York's South Street and Wall Street areas at a distribution cost of about a penny apiece, are now rare and highly sought after by collectors at prices ranging from a hundred dollars or so to well over a thousand.[8]

As on her maiden voyage to Honolulu, SNOW SQUALL's cargo again was extremely varied. The largest single item was 1,200 barrels of flour, followed closely by 700 bags of oats, 200 small boxes of starch, nearly 400 "hickory axles," and 100 barrels of whiskey for thirsty Californians. The cargo included brandy, nails, stoves, carts, cotton duck, quite an assortment of butter, salt pork, one lot of machinery, and various hogsheads, tierces, kegs, cases, and packages of "provisions," their nature not specified.[9] This cargo undoubtedly was assembled from a number of points of origin. The agricultural produce such as the flour, oats, butter, and pork would have been American, probably brought eastward via the Erie Canal, then down the Hudson River, while the cotton duck possibly, and the brandy almost certainly, had come originally from Liverpool or Le Havre. The important distinction between this California voyage and SNOW SQUALL's previous maiden voyage to Honolulu was that by law this was considered a "coasting" voyage between two United States ports and thus reserved to an American flag vessel. Honolulu, in the then still-independent Sandwich Islands, was technically a "foreign" voyage which a vessel flying any flag could make, and indeed the American merchant marine's share of overseas cargoes had slipped from about 90 percent at the beginning of the century to about 70 percent by 1853.[10]

But beyond Sutton and Company's labors in assembling a cargo and owner Green's arrangements for insurance, getting a crew for the roughly four-month voyage to San Francisco presented real problems for Captain Bursley. In 1853 the New York waterfront was firmly in the hands of the thugs known as "crimps"

Clipper advertising card for SNOW SQUALL's 1853 voyage to San Francisco. These colorful cards, slightly larger than a modern postcard, were passed out around New York's waterfront to drum up freight for the impending voyage.
PEABODY ESSEX MUSEUM

who ran the sailors' boardinghouses, without whose help a captain simply could not muster a crew, nor a would-be crew member connect with a ship. *In theory* a prospective crew member applied for a berth, was looked over by the captain or a mate, and joined the ship's company, if deemed competent. *In practice,* the captain had to accept whatever the boardinghouse owner or shipping master had picked up on New York's South Street waterfront. As Captain Arthur Clark noted in his memoir of the American clippers, published half a century later, getting a day's and often a night's work out of these dozen and a half roughnecks and possibly incompetents was a far cry from a Sunday school picnic.

Richard Henry Dana wrote in his classic *The Seaman's Friend,* first published in 1841 and brought out in many editions thereafter, "Usually the whole thing [i.e., shipping the crew] is left to shipping-masters, who are paid so much a head for each of the crew, and are responsible for their appearance on board at the time of sailing. When this plan is adopted neither the master nor owner, except by accident, knows anything of the crew before the vessel goes to sea."[11] What Dana failed to mention was that the would-be crew member in mid-nineteenth-century New York was indeed between a rock and a hard place. Even if he saved his pay and avoided the grog houses where the "crimps" lurked, no respectable hotel would accept him and his bag or chest, forcing him into the hands of rapacious lodging house owners who were happy to lodge him, relieve him of as much of his money as possible, and in due course dump him drunk on a vessel's deck with his two months' advance pay in their pockets.

There was a nasty racket in New York in this period. A sailor wishing to ship out had to part with five dollars, divided, it was alleged, among his landlord, an unscrupulous captain, and in some cases the shipowner. If the would-be mariner turned up to be inspected by a conniving captain he wore "some distinctive mark," perhaps a neckerchief of a certain color, indicating that he was party to the scam. By May 1857 this practice in New York had gotten so completely out of hand that the Chamber of Commerce voted to abolish the payment of sailors' advance wages to the lodging house operators to pay off their hapless tenants' debts. Waterfront paralysis set in. No crews could be obtained by any means. Within a week the Chamber was forced to "back down by the landlords, who had the sailors completely under their control."[12]

In whatever manner they were shipped, nineteenth-century seamen apparently were an improvident lot in general. Captain Samuel Samuels of the packet ship DREADNOUGHT recalled that, "the sailor's roving disposition costs him dear. I have known men to quit first-rate ships, leaving behind money due them and a good chest of clothes, for the sake of having a very short spree. And they knew, too, that after the spree they would be picked up and shipped off without a cent in their pockets. They never profit by experience."[13] On the other hand, for the unwary or simply imprudent, New York's waterfront dives and whorehouses were, as is true in "sailortowns" today, easy places to get into trouble. As one nineteenth-century "come all ye" had it:

> Last night I slept with Angeline, too drunk to turn in bed.
> My clothes was new and my money, too,
> Next morning with them she fled.

And the rueful songwriter found that he must "go to sea once more" in a "wintry wind from the west-northwest" where "Jamaica rum would freeze." The boardinghouse or saloon-keeper to whom he turned for help noted that he'd "chalked no score," (i.e., run up a tab), but offered to "give him a chance and take his advance [wages]" and ship him out. The advance wages were, of course, paid directly to the crimp.

Captain Samuels himself, in his progress aft from the fo'c's'le, had been shanghaied twice. "This was Wednesday," he wrote of one such occasion. "We could give no account of ourselves since Monday." When on one occasion early in his seagoing career, he and a friend woke up with first-class hangovers, they found themselves aboard a vessel bound for Liverpool. "Protest was useless, and we obeyed when we were ordered to man the windlass quickly

Next pages: South Street waterfront, New York. Though published in *Harper's Weekly* in 1878, some fourteen years after SNOW SQUALL's last voyage out of New York, this scene had not changed much. The major difference was that overseas cargoes were increasingly carried in foreign-flag vessels.
SOUTH STREET SEAPORT MUSEUM

under penalty of having our heads smashed."[14] According to Samuels, as the ship prepared to get underway only six out of a crew of sixteen were even able to get to their feet.

On occasion, the crimps provided men who had been drugged or who were in the fatal stages of alcohol poisoning. If one can believe Herman Melville's semi-autobiographical novel *Redburn,* published in 1849, one of the limp bodies a Liverpool crimp slung over the rail of his ship was past redemption. According to Melville, after the new and useless crew member had lain inert in his forecastle bunk for a considerable time and began to stink, one of his shipmates brought a lamp over to examine him. The flame from the lamp ignited gases from the corpse and, "to the silent horror of all, two threads of greenish fire, like a forked tongue, darted out between the lips; and in a moment the cadaverous face was crawled over by a swarm of worm-like flames."[15] The body went overboard without ceremony.

SNOW SQUALL generally carried a crew of seventeen or eighteen hands under the supervision of a chief and second mate. Those included a cook, possibly black, *possibly* Chinese, judging from some of the descriptions in crew lists such as complexion "yellow," hair "black" (though the names had been thoroughly anglicized), probably, though not definitely, a steward, a carpenter, and a boatswain.

Nineteenth-century Americans were ambivalent about seamen, essential though they were to the maritime industry. On the one hand sailors were social pariahs and respectable citizens tut-tutted over their homecoming drunken sprees among the waterfront bars. On the other hand some took an idealized view of them (in the abstract). There is a small marble statue called *Commerce* in the Heckscher Museum of Art in Huntington, New York, by New York sculptor Emma Stebbins (1815–82), commissioned in 1860, which shows a man perhaps in his early to mid twenties, clean-shaven but with mutton chop sideburns, leaning languidly, hand on hip, against a bollard. He is a handsome youth, similar to the idealized sailor holding an anchor who flanks the scythe-toting farmer on the Maine state seal (the iconography of which also includes a moose and a pine tree). Both are fashionably hirsute Greek gods in nineteenth-century seaman's shore clothes.[16] Sentimental prints for the Victorian parlor wall offered, among other subjects, *The Sailor's Return,* while printmakers such as the British Rowlandson satirized the mariner.

The reality on New York's mid-century waterfront was different. The seamen's bethels of New York and Boston, such as the Seamen's Church Institute of New York (founded in 1843 and still in operation in 2000), attempted to offer seamen clean and booze-free surroundings when in port, with liberal handouts of religious tracts which, for a guess, few of their recipients could read. But the typical crew member from New York to San Francisco in the early 1850s was either a roughneck exseaman freshly off the Liverpool packets or a totally green hand who saw a California voyage—for miserable pay—as a free passage to the gold fields.

The captain of an early 1850s clipper out of New York had several choices, none of them all that appealing. There were, if he could persuade the shipmasters to find him such, the experienced seamen. These, in an era when Americans were eschewing the sea in favor of supposed opportunities in the "Golden West," were ideally seasoned Scandinavians but more likely ex-Liverpool "packet rats," who often proved tough customers when it came to shipboard discipline, or whatever drugged or drunken refuse the crimp chose to dump aboard.

Another source of labor might be several completely inexperienced youngsters who signed on as "boys," seeking unpaid or minimally paid sea time as the first leg on their possible career towards the quarterdeck. The shipowning Tucker family of

Emma Stebbins's marble statue *Commerce,* 1860, presents an idealized view of the sailor. HECKSCHER MUSEUM OF ART, HUNTINGTON, NEW YORK; GIFT OF PHILLIP M. LYDIG III

Wiscasset, Maine, recruited these regularly, according to family historian Jane Tucker. Technically, however, the term "boy" was applied to *any* completely green hand who from lack of strength or experience could not perform the duties of an ordinary or able-bodied seaman. The "A. B.," at the top of the hierarchy before the mast, was expected to be able to perform whatever shipboard tasks were required, without exception; the boys, of course, were at the bottom of the ladder.

One such was young Charles Low, who in 1842 departed his New York dry goods store job and shipped as a boy on the ship Horatio of New York bound for China with a cargo of pig lead, lumber, and cotton goods. After Charles had secured his berth, his brother, Abiel Abbott Low, who had gotten him his unpaid job, asked him how he was "going to make a living." Charles immediately responded, "As soon as the voyage is over, I will ship again."[17] Low was a bright, ambitious youngster from a good New York family, and his talent and connections brought him rapid advancement. When the clipper Houqua (not coincidentally owned by the Lows) began her maiden voyage to China in June 1844 under veteran captain Nathaniel Palmer, who had also designed her, Charles Low was third mate. By 1847 he was master of Houqua. Captain John Whidden of Marblehead also began his career as a "boy" in the 1840s, and worked his way up to command until, in the post-Civil War maritime doldrums, he retired after a quarter century at sea.[18] A Maine captain, Charles E. Ranlett of St. George, described his own career this way:

> It was a long, hard apprenticeship, with slow promotions from the galley to the forecastle, from forecastle to the berth of second and first officer, and finally, if the boy was of the right stuff, to the quarter-deck. When that coveted place was reached, however, an honorable career was fairly in view. There would still be labor and hardship and anxiety; there would be discomfitures and reverses, but in those days, when our merchant shipping was still our pride, the master, even

of the most modest craft, felt that there was a boundless field for his ambition, and he entered upon it, rejoicing "as a strong man to run a race."[19]

These three men, just a few examples out of many possibilities, began their careers at a time when the siren song of the American West was no more than a faint murmur. By 1853 it was loud and clear, though perhaps not always on key. Simply put, twenty years earlier a youngster went to sea with relatives and friends. By the early 1850s the sea did not look as appetizing— fertile western lands or the California gold fields seemed more promising in the long run. Historian Bernard De Voto has called 1846 "The Year of Decision," the year the great westward migration really began. In the first census of 1790 the United States' center of population—the point on which population density would theoretically balance like a soup plate balancing on a knife point—was twenty-three miles east of Baltimore. By 1850 it was just southeast of Parkersburg, West Virginia, and by the outbreak of the Civil War it was near Chilicothe, in south central Ohio, many hundred miles from salt water.[20]

In any case, as SNOW SQUALL received her cargo in New York, her owner, Charles Green, was still operating two ships out of New Orleans: his first major venture, the GEORGE GREEN, which he owned with Captain St. Croix Redman of Medford, Massachusetts, and SAONE, the Maine-built "kettlebottom" which he had just purchased with Randolph Schwartz of New Orleans. Both ships were apparently freighting cotton. In the spring of 1854, as SNOW SQUALL neared the end of the English leg of her round-the-world voyage, Sarah ("Sallie") Goodwin, wife of Captain Sam Goodwin of the Maine ship ROCKAWAY, discovered that they had Captain Redman as a temporary neighbor on the New Orleans waterfront.

She wrote her mother back in Maine, "We have had one captain neighbor to us for some time, from Medford (Captain Redman of ship 'George Green'). He passes most every evening with us and is a grand talker, and as jolly as you please. We are both to start this morn, and I expect we shall go down in the same tow."[21]

Both the GREEN's and ROCKAWAY's transatlantic passages to Liverpool took about five weeks; SNOW SQUALL's from Shanghai to London took about five months. So even as SNOW SQUALL was loading in New York for her first California venture, owner Green had to attempt to keep tabs on the other two-thirds of his fleet to the extent that he could. The best shipping news was in James Gordon Bennett's *New York Herald,* whose industrious (and more than occasionally intrepid) marine reporters went out on one of the paper's "news schooners," clambered up an incoming vessel's side from a bobbing pulling boat, and copied details of the voyage from the arrival's logbook on the way in. With luck, Green and other owners might learn that day that one of their vessels had been "spoken" in latitude this and longitude that on such-and-such a date. Or a vessel (or the transatlantic steamer) might bring newspapers from a port such as Liverpool or London with the shipping news: "Arrived, vessel so-and-so of New York on such-and-such a date."

If there was no news of any sort in the paper on a particular morning, an owner, consignee, or marine insurance company could only hope for the best and fear the worst. Too often the "disasters &c." column reported that a capsized hulk, no sign of life, had been spotted—hopefully, from an owner's point of view, not on one of his vessels' regular routes nor, drifting into it, a hazard to shipping in the dark. When grim news *did* at some juncture appear, some nameless clerk at the Atlantic Mutual Insurance Company, one of New York's giants, clipped the news item, pasted it in the "Disaster Book," and jotted down the company's exposure to the loss. Several of Charles Green's vessels, ultimately including SNOW SQUALL, would achieve a dubious immortality in these "disaster books."

Meanwhile, SNOW SQUALL continued loading at the foot of Wall Street. On February 14, Captain Isaac Bursley, described as "a veteran ship-master and well liked by all," received the pleasant honor of being elected Life Member number 2,583 of the Marine Society of the City of New York. Founded in 1769, with a charter signed by England's King George III, the Society had the dual purposes of being a clearinghouse for marine intelligence (such as the locations of previously uncharted shoals) and aiding elderly or infirm members and their families. Society meetings were highly congenial social gatherings. Although the Society had honorary members from New York's maritime community, life membership (and eligibility for benefits) was reserved to those who were or had been shipmasters.

On February 22, 1853, Sutton and Company advertised for the shippers to "please hand in their bills of lading for signature at once," adding that "twenty-five tons of light freight can be taken immediately under the hatch, if sent on board this day."[22] On February 24, with the wind at sunset "fresh" from the northwest, SNOW SQUALL cleared for San Francisco and sailed the next day.[23]

Under the law, before an American vessel left for a foreign port a crew list had to be filed at the customhouse. On a vessel's return another set of papers was filed, listing deserters, deaths, additional seamen shipped, and so on. Unfortunately, customhouse records were not collected and assembled at the National Archives in Washington until the 1930s, and some material "went missing" over the years. The crew list for SNOW SQUALL's 1852 maiden voyage to Hawaii and China has not turned up. For other voyages, such as this one, with New York to San Francisco as the first leg, it is not known just how many hands were shipped, nor anything about them, because under the law and in the eyes of the clerks in the Greek temple of a customhouse down Wall Street from owner Green's office, a 16,000-mile voyage from New York to San Francisco by way of Cape Horn was technically a "coasting" passage, of no more moment than a run from New York to Boston or New Orleans. No crew list needed to be filed. Hence our knowledge of SNOW SQUALL's crews has its gaps.

What charts Captain Bursley had aboard is unknown. There were small-scale (large-area) British charts of the Atlantic available if the captain cared to pay for them out of his own pocket. There were "approaches to San Francisco" charts produced by the American government by the early 1850s. But what was available varied wildly in accuracy. A privately produced 1848 British chart,

*The East and West Coasts of South America,* though based on information from several Royal Navy captains, did not include survey data compiled by the HMS BEAGLE expedition which naturalist Charles Darwin had accompanied more than a decade earlier. God help the mariner who attempted to approach the Falkland Islands on the way towards Cape Horn using this Blachford chart!

Before leaving New York the watches were chosen. If, as seems probable from the evidence, SNOW SQUALL carried two mates, the chief mate chose first from among the bleary, shivering huddle assembled on deck, the second mate next and so on. The cook, steward, and carpenter were not expected to stand regular watches, having plenty to occupy their time, but were expected to turn to in an emergency that called for "all hands on deck." The starboard, or second mate's watch traditionally took the first four-hour evening watch (i.e., 8:00 PM to midnight) on the outward passage, the port, or chief mate's watch took that time slot homeward bound. Harking back to the days of smaller vessels, when there might be but one mate, the captain took the starboard watch. There was a nineteenth-century saying, "The master takes the ship out and the mate takes her home."[24]

Once at sea, apart from the calls to take in or set sail, which might take place many times during a day or not at all, depending on circumstances, the routine was varied only by the system of "dog watches." The origin of the term is obscure, but the practice is thoroughly therapeutic.[25] Rather than standing watch in the same time period, day after day—four hour on, four hours off— each afternoon the routine varied. After standing the noon-to-four afternoon watch, the watch on deck went below, relieved for two hours. The result is that each watch (starboard or port) takes the "graveyard watch" of midnight to 4:00 AM only every other day. It is a very welcome break in routine, minor though it may seem.

It must be emphasized that there was probably no more rigidly hierarchical society than that aboard a nineteenth-century square-rigger, whether a clipper like SNOW SQUALL or an ordinary merchantman. Every hand aboard had a set of tasks as well as a place in the shipboard social order, well-defined by custom over the years, if not centuries. The captain, of course, was at the pinnacle of the hierarchy and his power was absolute, though under the law he could be (though seldom was) fined and/or imprisoned for meting out "cruel and unusual punishment." He had complete control over the navigation and working of the vessel. The officer of the watch might, in the course of things, order minor adjustments, but if a major alteration was to take place, such as reefing a major sail, the captain supervised it. He never went aloft nor did manual labor unless he chose to.

Even his place on the quarterdeck was fixed by tradition. The weather side was his and if he came on deck from below, the officer of the deck moved to leeward. If his wife was aboard, hers was a rigidly limited social environment. She did not go forward of the quarterdeck, and apart from her husband her only company at meals would be her children, if they had accompanied her, and

*Winter at Sea—Taking in Sail Off the Coast,* by Winslow Homer. Many feet above the deck, trying to get a grip on half-frozen canvas with a life of its own was hard, dangerous work. *HARPER'S WEEKLY,* AUTHOR'S COLLECTION

the chief mate, who ate with the captain's family at the first sitting. The captain took the noon sun sight if the weather permitted. At the stroke of noon, eight bells were struck and a new ship's day at sea and logbook page began with the recording of the ship's position. It was traditional at the beginning of a voyage for the captain to call the hands aft (presumably after they had sobered up sufficiently) to give a short speech in which he told them what he would expect of them. Generally the tenor of the speech was that if they worked hard and obeyed orders the voyage would be as pleasant as wind and weather permitted. If they did *not*, the message, not always spelled out but *always* implied, was that it could be a seagoing hell.

The chief, or first mate was the ship's executive officer. The captain's orders were passed along through him, as apart from that initial speech the captain did not address the crew directly. When the call was for "all hands on deck," the captain remained aft while the chief mate took up his station on the forecastle. The second mate worked with the crew. The second, as Richard Henry Dana put it, "ought to be the best workman on board, and to be able to take upon himself the nicest and most difficult jobs, or to show the men how to do them."[26] In any case, SNOW SQUALL's watches were set, the tugboat towline cast off, and the Sandy Hook pilot dropped off of the New Jersey coast. The voyage around to California had begun. It would not be a pleasant one.

When SNOW SQUALL arrived at San Francisco on August 3, 155 days out, with one passenger from New York, the San Francisco paper, the *Alta California,* reported:

> The Snow Squall experienced very severe weather on the passage. Was 52 days off Cape Horn, 35 of which were continuing heavy [seas?] and driven as far south as latitude 60. Carried away all the iron work of the bow sprit and steering apparatus, started channels, and sustained other damage. Crossed the Equator June 23, long. 97.15 since which time have had light northerly winds and calms. On the 30th inst. was off Point

Bonita [the point on the northwest corner of the Golden Gate] a mile distant, since when they have had calm and thick fog.[27]

SNOW SQUALL's safe arrival at San Francisco was a combination of Captain Bursley's skill and a certain degree of sheer good luck. Only four years after the beginning of the Gold Rush, San Francisco Bay still lacked good navigational aids. Neither the light and fog signal at Point Bonita were yet in place, nor the fog signal, a cannon on Alcatraz Island, further in. San Francisco Bay's fogs seem to be a phenomenon unique to the Bay. They can range from a true "pea souper," top to bottom, to a band of murk, many feet thick, which hovers above the Bay obscuring landmarks higher up. (The Point Bonita Light had to be re-installed further down, *below* the fog belt line.) There had been non-compulsory pilotage in San Francisco since 1850, much of it provided by transplanted Bostonians and their schooners. These were described by an anonymous correspondent in *Hunt's Merchants' Magazine* as "than whom more enterprising, expert, and gentlemanly are not to be found

Bird's-eye view of nineteenth-century San Francisco.

On this voyage SNOW SQUALL tied up at the Vallejo Street Wharf, which is seen here in a photograph by Lawrence and Houseworth circa 1864–68. No trace of this busy waterfront remains today, long-buried under landfill.

SAN FRANCISCO MARITIME NATIONAL HISTORICAL PARK, NEGATIVE NO. A12.40, 323N

in any port in the world," and they could be picked up off the Farallon Islands, some twenty-seven miles out. It is not known if Captain Bursley engaged a pilot, but at some point he undoubtedly heard about the spectacular wreck of the mail steamer SS TENNESSEE, which had occurred in early March, just after he had left New York. TENNESSEE's captain had felt his way into the Bay in thick fog (apparently without a pilot), missed his bearings, and piled his vessel up near Sausalito, fortunately with no loss of life.

Green (or Greene) and Heath, the ship's agents in San Francisco, had their offices on the waterfront at 47 and 49 California Street, on the corner of Front Street. SNOW SQUALL lay at Vallejo Street Wharf. The street names have survived, but all traces of the 1853 waterfront have long since vanished under landfill. Indeed, by the time SNOW SQUALL reached San Francisco the tideflats were being filled and vessels could discharge beside the wharves "with convenience." Green and Heath advertised that cargo would be discharged beginning Thursday, August 4. "Consignees are requested to call on the undersigned, pay freight, and receive orders for their goods." They were sternly reminded that, "All merchandise not taken from the wharf by 6 o'clock, PM will be stored at the risk and expense of the owner."[28] If SNOW SQUALL tied up at Vallejo Street on the third and all cargo was theoretically ashore by late afternoon on the fourth, it says something about the frenetic pace of commerce in the San Francisco of the early 1850s, and a good reason for the higher rates for cargo loaded last, and on top. By August 7, John McCarty and Company was advertising whisky, sherry, butter, and sardines from SNOW SQUALL and two other vessels.[29]

Ten days after arrival in San Francisco, presumably with her Cape Horn damage patched up, SNOW SQUALL left San Francisco. Her crew list, dated August 15 (and the first of hers which has come to light), is thoroughly intriguing. Her second mate, R. D. Edmonston, was born (he claimed) in Charleston, South Carolina. Most of her crew are listed as natives of New Orleans, with fine, resounding Gallic surnames like Blatrier, Deleavon, Guillan, Letallac, and Verigeux, with an occasional Anglo such as Wilson, Cruikshank, or Taylor. But the Louisianans are in the majority of seventeen deckhands, two mates, a cook, boatswain, and a carpenter—a company of twenty-two all told. Most of the deckhands were paid thirty-five dollars per month, a fairly generous salary in the 1850s, while Joseph Vonollez, the boatswain, earned forty. At least three of the crew were illiterate, signing their mark. There is, of course, the mystery of how Captain Bursley signed on this New Orleans crew in San Francisco for the run to Shanghai. Were they "old SNOW SQUALLers," recruited by Charles Green in New York through his New Orleans connections? Were they the crew of another vessel that happened to be in San Francisco at the time? Who knows?[30]

San Francisco in 1854, looking
roughly northeast across the bay.
*HENRY BILL'S HISTORY OF THE WORLD*,
AUTHOR'S COLLECTION

100    *Snow Squall*

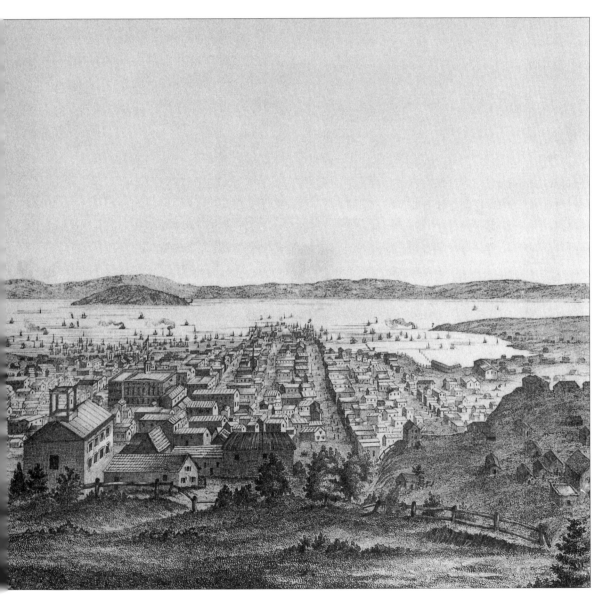

On her way to Shanghai, SNOW SQUALL made a brief stop at Honolulu. She arrived on August 28, brought "dates from New York July 19th—39 days through, which is the quickest time yet by two days," and "sailed hence for China on the morning of the 29th., with a good trade," twelve days from San Francisco.[31] Neither the Honolulu harbor masters' records nor the Hawaii newspapers give any explanation for this stopover, on which she does not appear to have discharged or loaded cargo. She arrived at Shanghai on October 2 in ballast, with Wetmore and Company as the agents.[32]

William S. Wetmore had founded the Chinese branch of the firm in Canton in 1834 and by 1853 it had offices in Macao, Lima, and Valparaiso. Wetmore retired from active participation in the firm in 1847 and settled in Newport, Rhode Island, where he built an opulent "cottage," *Château sur Mer,* where he lived until his death in 1862. He was a longtime friend of the London-based American expatriate financier, George Peabody, and named one of his sons after him. Unsurprisingly the cargo SNOW SQUALL loaded in Shanghai was consigned to George Peabody and Company in London.

However, conditions in Shanghai were far from tranquil. The Taiping Rebellion had been in progress since 1850 under the charismatic, semi-Christianized leader Hong Xiuquan. In September 1853 yet another rebel army, calling itself the "Small Swords," had seized the Old City of Shanghai and butchered government officials, although they scrupulously left the foreign settlement outside the city walls alone. Wetmore and Company's printed market newsletter, four pages on light blue paper, folded once, reported by early November that the unsettled state of the country-side, to say nothing of Shanghai, was interfering with business:

> Our accounts from the interior relative to the move-
> ments of the insurgents are conflicting, though all agree
> that their progress is still onward. Trade continues in an
> embarassed condition and in fact is only carried on by
> overcoming obstacles which a few months ago would
> have appeared insurmountable. The import market shows

no signs of improvement, and business has been confined almost exclusively to purchases of tea and silk.[33]

The westerners were in a quandary. The semi-Christian aspects of the Taipings, though not exactly orthodox, appealed to the westerners' missionary zeal, and the Small Swords occupying Shanghai, however barbarous they may have been towards Qing government functionaries, seemed fairly decent sorts. "The vigorous & intelligent manner in which Shanghai is held argues much for the peaceable character of those connected with the Revolution, and their ability to hold their conquest. Property seems to be perfectly respected, and pillage strictly forbidden," wrote Wetmore and Company to Peabody in London in November 1853.[34]

However, there is a mystery concerning SNOW SQUALL in Shanghai. The Wetmore newsletters of November 1 and 30 list her as "repairing" (though it is not stated what mishap occurred),

Shanghai in the 1850s. Watercolor by C. Middleton
PEABODY ESSEX MUSEUM, NEGATIVE NO. 8199

and she apparently did not load until December. By the end of December, with the "supply of tonnage…wholly inadequate to the wants of shippers," in part due to an increase in Chinese emigration to California, vessels in Shanghai were in "active demand."[35] Freights to New York were twenty dollars a ton for tea and thirty for silk, while those to London were seven and eight pounds (approximately thirty-five and forty dollars), a substantial premium. The repeal of the British Navigation Laws in 1850 had opened British ports to American vessels in the China trade and as SNOW SQUALL could carry 900 "cargo tons" of forty cubic feet, a voyage to London presented an agreeable opportunity for profit for her owner. By the end of December, SNOW SQUALL was loaded, consigned to George Peabody and Company in London.

Wetmore and Company sent Peabody a bill of lading for bales of raw silk costing $4,317.55. "Please receive the lot & dispose of it as advantageously as possible. We intended to have a larger shipment but the silk did not arrive in time."[36] The other British consignees were "Messrs Ben Gott, Leeds, Messrs. Gregson

St. Katharine's Docks, London, just below the Tower of London. *GENTLEMEN'S MAGAZINE*, 1826, AUTHOR'S COLLECTION

& Co., London, & Messrs. Robert Smith & Co., Manchester."[37] Captain Bursley had drawn against the freight money for repairs and "other necessary disbursements" with a ninety-day note for £2,600, drawn on Peabody and Company.[38] According to the shipping news in the English language *North China Herald*, SNOW SQUALL's cargo when she passed Wusung, downriver from Shanghai, on January 14 was 800 bales of silk and an estimated 485,000 pounds of tea.[39]

SNOW SQUALL's January departure from Shanghai was during the northeast monsoon, which blows from October to April. To set a course for the Sunda Strait in Java and thence towards the Cape of Good Hope, Captain Bursley first would have made considerable easting on the port tack to steer clear of the China coast's innumerable islands before wearing ship and turning south. A prudent captain gave the islands plenty of sea room, giving them a good berth by night and taking a position fix on them by daylight

Entrance to Bute West Dock, Cardiff, circa 1870. Due to Cardiff's extreme tidal range, the docks were "enclosed" to allow loading and discharing at all stages of tide.
COURTESY NATIONAL MUSEUMS AND GALLERIES OF WALES

as visibility was often poor in fog and drizzle. Approaching the Strait he would probably have followed the practice of other captains of anchoring at night, where possible, then proceeding cautiously towards it in daylight, taking frequent soundings.

The next leg was towards the Cape of Good Hope and around into the South Atlantic. Having weathered the Cape against the prevailing westerlies, Bursley set his course for England passing St. Helena then close to Ascension Island's volcanic peak. Coming from the southwest, SNOW SQUALL picked up the Lizard, the first landmark approaching the English Channel, in early May, then the Eddystone Light south of Plymouth, and beat up the Channel towards London, past St. Catherine's Point on the Isle of Wight, then a long eight-hour slog past Beachy Head towards Dungeness, where a tow up the Thames and a London pilot might be found. The prudent captain, such as Bursley was, stayed well offshore, ten miles or so, until closing in on Dungeness. The waters inshore, off the English Channel landmarks Portland Bill and the Start are, to put it mildly, "confused." The Race of Portland, south-southwest from the Bill, is a seething body of water, which shoals from eighteen to seven fathoms, then drops off to ten to fifteen. It is not a pleasant place, and the wind in May, as the author can attest, can be bone-chilling. It calls for a steady hand at the wheel who can steer by the sails and feel for a twitch of the rudder. It is a stretch of water through which one passes with more than a little sense of relief.

SNOW SQUALL came into Thomas Telford's 1820s masterpiece, St. Katherine's Docks, with the Tower of London just beyond on the Thames's north bank, on May 5. Her crew numbered eighteen, according to the customs Bills of Entry. The London agent was C. Gunn and her cargo to G. Peabody & Co. was 96 bales of silk, plus 704 bales of silk (probably unconsigned bales), 4,066 chests, 234 half-chests, and 2,934 packets of tea "consigned to order," plus 8 chests of "curiosities."[40] Here there is another discrepancy. According to American consular records, on arrival at London SNOW SQUALL's crew was ten American and six "foreign" rather than eighteen. Did two sailors "jump ship" between the Bills of Entry and the consular report?

After discharging in London SNOW SQUALL cleared in ballast for Newport, Wales, on May 27, proceeded to Cardiff, and left a month later on June 27 with a cargo of railroad iron.[41] As reported in the *New York Herald*, when passing the Grand Banks Captain Bursley had noted about three hundred schooners and three barks fishing.[42] She arrived in New York on August 8 with 4,057 bars consigned to Charles R. Green and apparently discharged at Wetmore's Basin in Brooklyn. In the same edition of the New York *Shipping and Commercial List* which reported SNOW SQUALL's arrival, one John Wicks of 90 Beaver Street advertised that 800 tons of Welsh rails, weighing 59 pounds per yard, were "expected to arrive soon," which may have been SNOW SQUALL's cargo.[43]

Under Captain Bursley SNOW SQUALL had made an eighteen-month circumnavigation via Hawaii, China, and Britain and in spite of one unknown misadventure crossing the Pacific, which occasioned expensive (though unspecified) repairs in Shanghai, returned safely to New York, weather and dismal crews notwithstanding. Owner Charles Green could be content for the moment.

# NOTES

[1] A. B. Becher, *Navigation of the Atlantic Ocean* (London: J. D. Potter, 1862), p. 105.

[2] Arthur H. Clark, *The Clipper Ship Era* (New York: G. P. Putnam's Sons, 1920), p. 125.

[3] Becher, p. 104.

[4] New York *Shipping & Commercial List,* February 2, 1853.

[5] Ibid., February 5, 1853.

[6] Ibid., February 12, 1853.

[7] Clipper card at Phillips Library, Peabody Essex Museum, Salem, Massachusetts.

[8] Among museum collections of these cards worth noting are those at the National Maritime Museum Library, San Francisco; the Peabody Essex Museum; and the American Antiquarian Society, Worcester, Massachusetts.

[9] *S&CL,* February 26, 1853.

[10] *Report of the Commissioner of Navigation to the Secretary of the Treasury* (Washington: Government Printing Office, 1890), pp. 134–35.

[11] Richard Henry Dana, *The Seaman's Friend* (Boston: Thomas Groom & Co., 1857), 9th ed., p. 132.

[12] J. D. Jerrold Kelley, *The Question of Ships* (New York: Charles Scribner's Sons, 1884), pp. 91–92.

[13] Samuel Samuels, *From the Forecastle to the Cabin* (Boston: Charles E. Lauriat, 1924), p. 72.

[14] Ibid., p. 46.

[15] Herman Melville, *Redburn* (London: Penguin Classics, 1986), p. 326. Improbable though this incident may seem, Bath, Maine, physician Dr. Charles Burden confirms that methane gas from decomposition could easily ignite.

[16] The pullover, tightly woven blue cotton shirt worn by Stebbins's sailor survives today in the Falkland Islands (though minus the neckerchief). An example of this virtually windproof garment can be seen at Maine Maritime Museum and the author can attest to the virtues of his twenty-year-old and much-used modern version, purchased at the Falkland Islands Company's West Store.

[17] Charles P. Low, *Some Recollections* (Boston: Geo. H. Ellis Co., 1905), p. 14.

[18] John D. Whidden, *Ocean Life in the Old Sailing-Ship Days* (Boston: Little, Brown and Company, 1908).

[19] Charles Everett Ranlett, *Master Mariner of Maine* (Searsport: Penobscot Marine Museum, 1942), p. 199.

[20] *The World Almanac* (New York: New York Daily News, 1984), p. 199.

[21] Martha Vaughan, *Sallie and Captain Sam* (Newcastle, ME: Martha Vaughan, 1992), p. 37.

[22] *New York Herald,* February 22, 1853.

[23] Ibid., February 25 and 26, 1853.

[24] Dana, p. 134.

[25] The term seems to have come into use about 1700 and *may* derive from "dog sleep," which is a "light and fitful sleep," similar to what today is called a "catnap." Or, it has been suggested, it comes from a "docked" watch.

[26] Dana, p. 149.

[27] *Alta California* (San Francisco), August 3, 1853.

[28] Ibid.

[29] Ibid., August 7, 1853.

[30] Records of the Bureau of Customs, New York, November 4, 1854. Record Group 36. National Archives, Washington, DC.

[31] *The Polynesian* (Honolulu), August 28, 1853.

[32] *North China Herald* (Shanghai), October 8, 1853.

[33] Peabody Papers, MSS 181, Box 56, Phillips Library, Peabody Essex Museum, Salem, MA.

Wetmore & Co. Shanghai Newsletter, November 1, 1853.

[34] Peabody Papers, Wetmore & Co. to Peabody, November 9, 1853.

[35] Ibid., December 28, 1853.

[36] Ibid., December 29, 1853.

[37] Ibid.

[38] Ibid.

[39] *North China Herald* (Shanghai), January 7 and 14, 1854.

[40] Customs Bills of Entry, Merseyside Maritime Museum, Liverpool. Personal communication from Michael K. Stammers, keeper, June 14, 1995.

[41] Personal communication from Basil Greenhill, National Maritime Museum, Greenwich, England, December 21, 1982.

[42] *New York Herald,* August 9, 1854.

[43] Ibid., August 9, 1854. *S&CL,* August 9, 1854.

*A Practical Discourse To Sea-Faring Men*
*That such a quantity of Lumber should be constructed and fastened together, as
to make a great floating Store-house on the water, full of conveniences for a
multitude of Seamen, <u>marine adventurers</u> and Passengers. and capable of
carrying a vast <u>Burden</u>.... This I say, is admirable.*
—Rev. Thomas Smith[1]

EANWHILE, THE CALIFORNIA MARKET appeared unpromising for a second try. Freights to San Francisco were reported as "generally depressed," and word arrived aboard the steamer via Panama cautioning against "overstocking that market with eastern goods," a caution which duly appeared in the New York shipping news.[2] Indeed, on September 26 a letter appeared in the *Shipping and Commercial List* from a San Francisco merchant who signed himself "J. W. C." (probably J. W. Coleman, a prominent businessman) gently chiding the "gentleman shippers of New York and Boston." The writer asked them if they were "still determined to believe that the same unnatural and almost fabulous state of business that existed here in '49 and '50—will always continue?" Tongue in cheek, he noted that Californians "can only consume by their utmost efforts, a few pounds of food each, per day, or wear out at the utmost rate more than one or two suits of clothes per month." He remarked, prophetically, that California's soil and climate were "well suited for agriculture."[3]

# 6

# THIRD VOYAGE:
# AUSTRALIA, JAVA, AND CHINA

One mystery surrounds SNOW SQUALL in the days after her
August 8 arrival. Whether she had been launched in August 1851
with her Muntz metal hull sheathing in place (which seems a likely
possibility) or whether she was metaled in Brooklyn in the period
while awaiting sale is unknown. In either case, the sheathing was
assumed to have a useful life of forty months and that would have
been coming to an end in December 1854 or early in 1855. The
sheathing, in overlapping sheets fourteen by forty-eight inches
(thicker at the bow, thinner towards the stern), was an alloy of 60
percent copper and 40 percent zinc, nailed to the hull over a layer
of felt. Its corrosion and wear by the abrasion of the water was
supposed to present a continuously "bright" surface to which weed
and barnacles would not cling, and meanwhile, it theoretically prevented attack on the hull by the dreaded shipworm. By the end of
forty months it would have been down to half its original thickness and ready for replacement. Did Green have SNOW SQUALL
remetaled in New York, was she remetaled during her long per-

iod of "repairing" in Shanghai, or did Green simply keep his fingers crossed?[4]

By September 20, 1854, SNOW SQUALL was lying at Pier 41 in the East River. Owner Green, working through the New York firm of Maillar and Lord, whose offices were a few doors from him on Wall Street, had decided to send SNOW SQUALL out to Australia, but there seems to have been vacillation as to which port would be her destination. On September 23 she was listed as "up" for Sydney, on the thirtieth she was advertised as sailing for Melbourne *and* Sydney in the Mutual Line, towards the end of October for Melbourne, and when she at last cleared, it was for Sydney.[5] By the end of October, SNOW SQUALL was apparently "full," though she would not leave for a few more days.

Captain Bursley seems to have left the ship and her new commander was William Gerard, of whom nothing is known beyond the fact that like Bursley he, too, was a member of the New York Marine Society, elected in January 1850. Gerard would command SNOW SQUALL for several voyages. On November 4 Captain Gerard filed his crew list at the customhouse. There were twenty-one crew members all told, all but two in their mid to late twenties. All were listed as United States citizens, though three were native Swedes. It is possible that two, natives of New Orleans, were African Americans, as their complexions are listed as "yellow" and their hair as "black." One crew member had been born in Colombia. There was also a twenty-year-old "apprentice." Five crew members deserted between the ship's clearing and sailing and had to be replaced.[6] In short, for just over three months Gerard would have to cope with whatever the boardinghouse keepers and crimps had scraped together, but he would have been delighted to have the three highly prized Scandinavians, with their reputations as excellent seamen. SNOW SQUALL finally cleared for Sydney on November 4.[7]

This Australian voyage began much like the previous one, with a run east across the Atlantic, leaving the cerulean blue Gulf Stream for the dark green mid ocean. If Captain Gerard was lucky he had a northwest, or "clearing-off," breeze to help him make his easting to where he hoped to pick up the northeast trades near the Azores in about 35 degrees north latitude. From there to just north of the Line he would have the wind off the port quarter for the month or so it took to get there, though with bad luck it could take as much as two months. The route to the southeast trades, the next "push" on the voyage, could be fickle. A vessel might pick these up just north of the equator or might spend several weeks in the calms of the doldrums. These southeast trades, fairly constant and predictable winds, began to peter out at about 20 degrees south latitude as a vessel headed south towards the band of westerlies known as the "roaring forties." On the leg toward the westerlies prudence dictated that the light canvas was sent down before entering the region of uncertain but often "boisterous" winds. On this voyage, at least, SNOW SQUALL would be sailing eastward in the South Atlantic summer.

There was honest disagreement as to just how far south a vessel should proceed before setting a course for Sydney. From their sailing directions developed while British convict ships set a course for Botany Bay from England, the Admiralty favored staying reasonably close to the Cape of Good Hope. Others, such as the U.S. Navy's Maury, suggested staying about a thousand miles south of the African continent. From the American point of view this was unexplored territory. While beginning in the late eighteenth century, American vessels such as the pioneering EMPRESS OF CHINA had rounded Good Hope en route to Canton, passing into the South China Sea through Java's Sunda Strait, by the time SNOW SQUALL set sail for Sydney American vessels had been heading for Australia for only two years or a bit less. One must assume that Captain Gerard sought the counsel of his fellow captains at the Marine Society.

Near the end of February, at the height of the Australian summer, Captain Gerard picked up the lightship on Sow and Pigs Shoal, then the lighthouse on South Head, before heading past the bold headlands through the mile-wide harbor entrance to the anchorage in Watson's Bay outside of Port Jackson, as Sydney's harbor is known. It is nearly landlocked. The 1855 edition of Horsburgh's *India Directory*, a standard nineteenth-century reference work, called it "one of the best and safest harbours in the world."[8] Sydney, in 33 degrees south latitude, has a climate much like Southern California's. The deeply indented harbor has a total coastline of just over one hundred fifty miles but is actually only fifteen miles wide, east to west.

SNOW SQUALL's arrival may have been witnessed by the "cavalcades of welcome" which often thronged the promontory, eight miles from town by the Old South Head Road, to look at the incoming vessels as they dropped anchor in Watson's Bay for inspection and to drop off mail and newspapers. The handsome white lighthouse on South Head, known as Macquarie Tower, was designed by convict Francis Greenway, who received a pardon from Governor Macquarie at its dedication in 1817.

It might have been a few more days, depending on the wind and the availability of space on Sydney's waterfront, before she proceeded up the harbor. SNOW SQUALL at last arrived in Sydney on February 21, 1855, with a general cargo and six passengers: William Gordon with a party of three, and "Messrs Congreaves, Mattison, and O. R. Willer." The *Sydney Morning Herald* commented that she was "a splendid American clipper ship, but has made a long passage of 105 days from New York, having had headwinds nearly all the voyage."[9] The Australia route described above seems to have been the usual one but SNOW SQUALL simply had bad luck.

Her cargo list included grocery items such as 200 cases of fruits, nearly 200 barrels of apples, over 300 packages of "groceries," and barrels of salt pork. There were eleven cases of "cards," whether business or playing not specified, but if the latter, the players could smoke the tobacco consigned to Hussey, Bond & Hale, Wilkinson Brothers & Co., or "to order," i.e., F. W. Clarke & Co., the ship's Sydney agents. There were cases, packages, bales, and bundles of laths, chairs, candles, brooms, window sashes, doors, boots, and a fair quantity of "slops," this latter presumably clothing to be sold to gold hunters at outrageous prices. There was also a considerable amount of "machinery," some of it consigned to Ebsworth & Co., the rest "to order." As she had on previous voyages, SNOW SQUALL carried several thousand feet of lumber.

Although the wide variety of cargo items bespoke a rapidly growing seaport, it must be remembered that Sydney was hardly a frontier shanty town. By the time of the California "forty-niners" and the shacks and tents of infant San Francisco, Sydney was over sixty years old. The discovery of gold in New South Wales in 1851 had, moreover, triggered another "gold rush" similar to California's, though much of the gold field action later shifted to the state of Victoria. An 1855 view of Sydney Cove from Fort Macquarie shows a modest town, not quite yet a city, with at least one three-story building. Another view, looking down over the harbor past Garden Island, shows a fair amount of shipping in Sydney Cove with the Botanic Gardens, certainly a sign of some sophistication, off to the right. (It should be noted, however, that in the 1850s a botanic garden was a source of scientific study of exotic and medicinally useful plants, not yet considered a public "pleasuring place.")

The most intriguing item in the cargo list is "1 package" consigned to "C. [G?] Train and Co." George Francis Train, scion of the American shipping firm of Enoch Train, had been sent out to Melbourne, Australia, in 1853, where he established a shipping firm which, it is said, earned $95,000 in its first year. Train also had the wit to introduce coaches built in Concord, New Hampshire, to the Melbourne–Sydney run. These, with their superior suspension, eased the bone-jarring journey and were an immediate success. Train, however, left Australia in 1855 to begin an eccentric career of American railroad building, pamphleteering in support of the Irish Fenians, and an unsuccessful bid for the presidency.[10]

As is well known, from the eighteenth century on, in addition to what adventurers ventured into the Australian frontier to try their hands at farming and other pursuits, Britain had adopted a policy of shipping convicted criminals to its faraway colony, some of them guilty of offenses, such as petty larceny or prostitution, which might not even bring a jail term today. But the rush to the Australian gold fields, whether it was by hopefuls from the British Isles or by disillusioned Californians (some of them Australians who had joined the American gold rush), produced a change in British colonial policy towards Australia. "It would appear a solecism," wrote a British official to the governor of New South Wales in late 1852, "to convey offenders at public expense, with the intention of at no distant time setting them free, to the immediate vicinity of those very gold fields which thousands of honest labourers are trying in vain to reach."[11] Britain ended the policy of shipping felons to eastern Australia in 1853 and to western Australia in 1858.

But the area surrounding the gold fields had a severe shortage of farm labor. Imported foodstuffs, many of them American, were in high demand, as an unnamed American consul reported, "at least until the Australians pay more attention to agricultural pursuits, which will hardly be the case so long as they can find gold nuggits [sic] weighing $98\frac{1}{2}$ lbs. each."[12] The best quality American flour ("and none else need be exported," wrote the consul) fetched from $15.60 to $16.80 a barrel at a time when gold was worth $19.20 an ounce.[13]

In Australia captains encountered the same problem that caused them difficulties in San Francisco: crew desertion. As Captain Clark would complain in his *The Clipper Ship Era*, a goodly portion of the crew was "suddenly possessed with the desire to get to the…mines."[14] Desertion was endemic and American consuls reported sourly to Washington that with the resulting labor shortage in Australia the colonial authorities were not noticeably helpful in recovering deserters. Captain Gerard discharged two men in Sydney and apparently lost two more by desertion. The anti-government rioters protesting stiff licensing fees in December 1854 at the Ballarat gold fields, 70 miles west of Melbourne, apparently included not a few Americans.

The five new hands shipped were all listed as "American citizens,"[15] *but,* as the consul in Sydney reported a few years later, "The law requiring two-thirds American seamen is constantly and systematically broken by [seamen's] protections [i.e., certificates of citizenship] being openly bought and sold to persons who are neither native-born nor naturalized citizens of the United States, by owners, masters, agents, and seamen conjointly." He also complained that scheming sailors took advantage of the law "to extract money from American shipowners, under the pretense of cruel treatment."[16]

His crew brought back up to strength, Captain Gerard cleared from Sydney for Batavia (modern Jakarta) on March 27. Aboard as passengers were Mr. and Mrs. Crawford with one child and two servants, and a Mr. Neuyts, plus cargo from three Sydney firms. Buyers and Learmouth shipped thirteen cases of cigars, Lender and Company a case of percussion caps and five cases of "fancy ware," and J. Crawford shipped the ingredients for club soda: a soda water machine, three cases of vitriol (sulfuric acid), and two hundred dozen soda water bottles.[17] These last, most likely, would have been of the type known as "torpedo bottles," thick glassware with an elliptical bottom, hence the name. Once filled and corked they could not stand upright like a modern bottle but had to be laid on their sides, thus keeping the cork wet and preventing the soda water's bubbles from escaping.[18] SNOW SQUALL arrived at Batavia on June 9, with that good news reaching the United States by the end of August.[19]

SNOW SQUALL sailed for Java just before the changing of the monsoon. Between Australia and Java, the southwest monsoon did not really set in until early May. In the meantime, winds could be quite baffling. In late April 1865, it took the ship MEMNON of Boston six days to get north through Sunda Strait. As the captain fretted, a passenger, Harvard-trained naturalist Albert Bickmore, had plenty of leisure to observe the Java coast. He noted the poisonous snakes swimming in the sea, the bits of volcanic pumice floating by, and the thunderstorms that rolled down from the mountains. By early afternoon, he wrote, "Lightnings would be seen darting their forked tongues around the mountain

*The Strait of Sunda, Compiled from the Most Recent Surveys.* The detail shows Batavia (Jakarta) and the long mole.
JAMES IMRAY & SON, LONDON, 1868.
AUTHOR'S COLLECTION

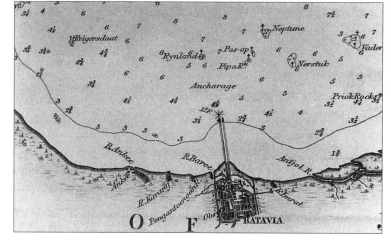

*The Strait of Sunda* detail, showing Sunda Strait. Anjer is near the bottom. Once a popular stop for fresh provisions and water, it was devastated by a tidal wave following the eruption of Krakatoa in 1883.
JAMES IMRAY & SON, LONDON, 1868.
AUTHOR'S COLLECTION

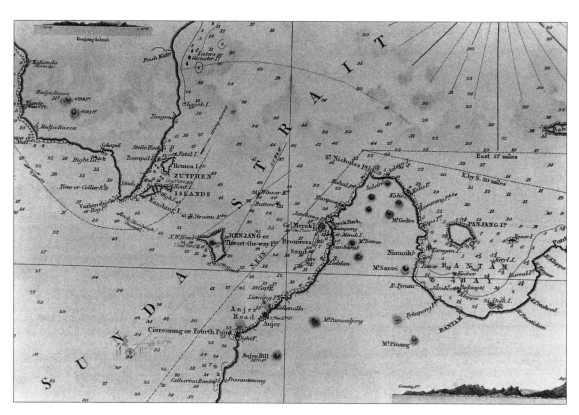

crest: and then, as if the winds had broken from the grasp of their king, thick cloud masses would suddenly roll down the mountainsides, lightnings dart hither and thither, and again and again the thunders would crash and roar enough to shake the very firmament."[20] For the mariner on shipboard, it was thoroughly miserable. "The planks burn under his feet; in vain he spreads the awning to shelter himself from the broiling sun," wrote the Dutchman Jansen.[21] Bickmore recalled that those six days slatting about, with the temperature between 88 degrees and 90 degrees F, "were the most tedious and oppressive I ever experienced."[22]

Meanwhile, if a vessel was becalmed, there was the omnipresent danger from pirates in the waters from Java to Malaysia. A merchantman rolling helplessly was an all too tempting and potentially lucrative prey. Captain John Whidden recalled the preparations of his ship, DANUBE, which was armed with four deck guns (two smoothbore, two rifled), muskets, boarding pikes, sabres, cutlasses, "and a magazine with plenty of ammunition." Not without reason, the pirates in this area were regarded as "cruel and bloodthirsty [a] set of scoundrels as ever scuttled ship or cut a throat." If a suspected pirate drew uncomfortably near, with one of its crew suspected of climbing aloft to prepare to drop a nauseating stink bomb, someone got a gun or rifle ready "to drop him before he got there." This accomplished, "in ninety-nine cases out of a hundred they would haul off, and nothing further would be heard from them."[23]

This was no idle precaution as these bombs, essentially clay grenades, were filled with sulfur and brimstone, often with a goodly addition of human or animal excrement. Tossed into an open hatch and exploding belowdecks, they produced highly poisonous hydrogen sulfide gas. One must wonder, though, reading Whidden, how many perfectly innocent native craft were fired upon on general principle. On the other hand, a prudent captain traversing constricted areas in these waters today stations crew with automatic weapons on the bridge wings—just in case.

Off to starboard on the eastern shore of the strait lay Cierco-rang, or Fourth Point, and two miles east northeast beyond it Anjer Road and the village of Anjer. Here an incoming or home-ward bound vessel might obtain fresh provisions such as pigs, poultry, vegetables, and water, brought by boats from shore, de-spite the fact that the anchorage is quite open. Behind Anjer 5,000- foot Mount Karang raised its "crest of green foliage," before a Batavia-bound vessel such as SNOW SQUALL rounded Java's westernmost extremity of St. Nicholas Point and stood to the eastward, past Bantam Bay towards Batavia, some forty miles away. A prudent captain anchored at night in these shoal waters.

The Dutch had arrived at Bantam in 1596 to trade in pep-per, then the only export commodity, though nutmeg became a major one as well. Bantam soon proved a thoroughly disease-ridden spot, and in 1619 the Dutch set up permanent operations at Batavia, though it was held by the British from 1811 to 1816. By the 1850s the original settlement walls had been torn down and Batavia sprawled to the south—and higher, healthier ground. The port itself boasted imposing neoclassical government build-ings, arranged along a system of canals: in other words, a micro-cosm of Holland in the East Indies.

In the harbor shoal mud flats extended quite a way from shore towards the anchorage. The ingenious Dutch had built a "canal" northward through and past the flats. "Its sides are well walled in, and extend out some distance toward the shipping, on account of the shallowness of the water along the shore. At the end of one of these moles, or walls, stands a small white light-house, indicating the way of approaching the city, which cannot be fully seen from the anchorage," wrote Bickmore.[24]

After an incoming vessel had been boarded by an officer from the guard ship, a list of crew and passengers handed over, and the ship's company given a clean bill of health, it was neces-sary to row ashore, up the canal, and go to the appropriate office before permission to trade with private merchants could be obtained from the local official, the Shabundar. This seems to have been not always immediately forthcoming. In the case of Bickmore's Memnon, it apparently took some haggling.

Sometime in June 1855, Snow Squall left Batavia for points west. She is listed in New York and Portland papers as in Batavia on June 9, variously reported as bound for Colombo, Ceylon,[25] and for China.[26] Her cargo of cigars and soda water ingredients entered Batavian social life, and they conjure up a portrait of the end of the day. The Dutch houses, reported Bickmore, had broad verandas "where the inmates sit in the cool evening and receive the calls of their friends." The expatriate Dutchman regarded "a cigar, or pipe, and a small glass of gin" (possibly laced with soda) as "indispensable things to perfect happiness."[27] Snow Squall brought the cigar and the fizz.

News of her subsequent whereabouts reached owner Green in New York in late October when he learned that she was "in port" in Hong Kong on August 10.[28] Minus two crew members discharged in Hong Kong, she arrived in Shanghai on August 17 with a cargo of "sundries."[29] There is no mention of the usual exports from Java such as coffee and pepper.

At Shanghai in February, government forces had succeeded in recapturing the old walled city from the rebels. By the time of Snow Squall's arrival most of the damage had been repaired and for the moment, at least, things were back to normal. There had been one important exception, however: during the "Small Swords" occupation of Shanghai, with the customhouse in hostile hands, government collections—and foreign trade—came to a complete halt for a spell.

In theory Shanghai could have functioned as a free port, with no tariffs whatsoever, but apparently rivalry among the foreigners at Shanghai prevented this from happening. The British, for example, were dismayed when a Prussian ship left Shanghai without paying duties, arguing that absent a customhouse at which duties could be collected, no duties need be paid, and worried that other foreign vessels not paying duty might be able to undercut the market.

The solution, which would set an important precedent for the future China trade, was devised by British consul Rutherford Alcock. Thenceforth foreigners collected their own duties, took a percentage for their expenses, and in due course turned over the money to the government. This was eventually formalized as the Customs Inspectorate, run by westerners rather than Chinese, a system which lasted for many years. There was also the question of western neutrality during the conflict. In theory, during the rebellion both the British and Americans were neutral, though in practice they tended to hinder the government forces. The French, under direct attack during the rebel siege, were definitely and self-servingly pro-government.[30]

*Chart of the Coast of China from Canton to Nanking, by I. Purdy.* The water-stained chart from which this detail is taken was used by Captain Philip Dumaresq on his shanghai voyages of 1858, 1859, and 1860. R. H. LAURIE, LONDON, 1851. AUTHOR'S COLLECTION

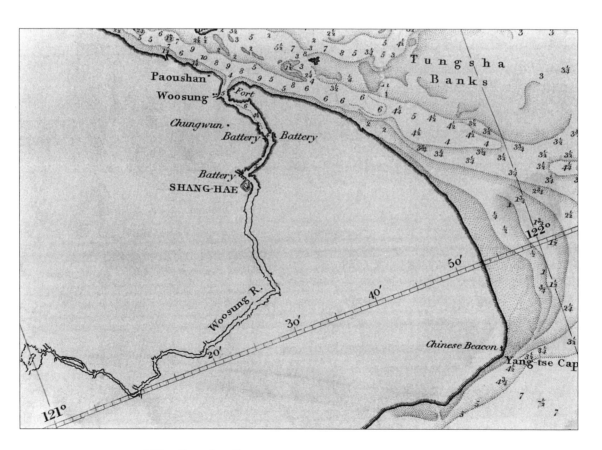

On August 7 the American consul at Shanghai reported that the business season was "just opening" and estimated that exports would be about double those of a year before. Imports, however, were small because it would take some time to dispose of the "enormous quantities" of goods which had piled up while the city was in rebel hands. Shanghai, he predicted, had a great future. "The great valley of the Yang-tse-Kiang is the commercial field and this port is the entrepôt." He foresaw that the Chinese would find that Shanghai, being nearer the tea and silk districts than Canton, could offer better prices and that eventually they would "abandon their old and long route."[31]

On this visit, once again SNOW SQUALL's Shanghai consignee was Wetmore and Company, but there is a somewhat nagging mystery. In the weekly English-language *North China Herald* for

Buildings of Russell & Company, Shanghai.
PEABODY ESSEX MUSEUM

the month of September, under the heading "destination," SNOW SQUALL is listed as "for sale." Had Charles Green given Captain Gerard orders to find a buyer, if possible? Apparently no buyer was found, as on September 29 she is listed as "up for N.Y." with "early" dispatch.[32] She cleared on October 6 with "teas &c." dispatched by Wetmore,[33] dropped downriver to Wusung, and finally left on the thirteenth in company with the ships R. B. FORBES and HORATIO. She passed Java Head on November 6 and arrived in New York on January 21, 1856, with teas and silks consigned to Green.[34] There were 14 packages of silk and nearly 8,000 chests of tea for Brown Brothers, a thousand or so chests for S. W. Goodridge, nearly 1,600 chests for A. Robertson, Jr., and 16 packages of silk for Duncan, Sherman and Company. The rest of the cargo of tea, silk, and unspecified merchandise was "to order" and was probably sold at auction.[35]

Shortly before SNOW SQUALL reached New York, in heavy weather on December 4 an Irish seaman, "Nicholas Powers of Waterford fell from the mizzen topgallant yard overboard and was lost."[36] Apparently he had come aboard in Australia or the Orient. Handling canvas aloft was hazardous at any time, but in the North Atlantic winter the half-frozen sailcloth was a formidable opponent for the shivering crew perched precariously on the foot rope below the yard. Powers's fall could have come from any one of a number of causes: the surging topgallant could have knocked him overboard; it was getting toward the end of a long voyage and a frayed becket might have given way. Whatever the cause of the fall, even if the sailor survived it, in "heavy weather" there was no hope of recovering him even if his heavy winter clothing had not pulled him down within minutes. A seaman's life under sail in the nineteenth century was a dangerous one with an accident rate four times greater than coal mining. Roughly half the deaths at sea were caused by falling or being washed overboard as happened to the unfortunate Powers.[37]

In early to mid February 1856 SNOW SQUALL went into the "balance dock" on the East River below Pine Street for caulking, coppering, and a general overhaul. The New York Balance Dock was exactly what its name implies—a vessel went into the dock and was "balanced" on her keel with her sides supported by long shores to the sides of the dock. SNOW SQUALL came off the dock shortly before February 18, once again prepared for sea.[38]

## NOTES

[1] Rev. Thomas Smith, *A Practical Discourse to Sea-Faring Men* (Boston: John Boyles, 1771).

[2] New York *Shipping and Commercial List*, September 2 and 9, 1854.

[3] Ibid., September 26, 1854.

[4] Francis B. Dixon, *The Law of Shipping and Merchants' and Shipmasters' Guide* (New York: Henry Spear, 1859), Section 617, p. 523: "A deduction of one-fortieth from the expense of repairing or replacing the metal sheathing, or any part thereof, after first deducting the value of the old metal and nails, shall be made for every month since the vessel was last sheathed, until the expiration of forty months, after which time the cost of re-metaling or repairing the same, shall be wholly borne by the assured." Unfortunately, the annual *American Lloyd's Register*, which listed the date of each vessel's remetaling, did not begin publication until 1858 and such routine maintenance was not noted in the New York newspapers.

[5] *S&CL,* September 23–November 4, *passim.*

[6] Records of the Bureau of Customs, Record Group 36, New York, November 4, 1854. National Archives, Washington, DC.

[7] *S&CL,* November 8, 1854.

[8] James Horsburgh, *The India Directory* (London: William H. Allen, 7th ed., 1855), vol. II, p. 854.

[9] *Sydney Morning Herald,* February 22, 1855.

[10] Train's pamphleteering is described in general terms in his entry in the *Dictionary of American Biography,* Dumas Malone, editor (New York: Charles Scribner's Sons, 1936), vol. IX, pp. 626–27.

[11] Quoted in Manning Clark, *A Short History of Australia* (New York: NAL Penguin, 1987), pp. 123–24.

[12] *Report of the Commercial Relations of the United States with All Foreign Nations* (Washington: A. O. P. Nicholson, 1856), p. 80.

[13] Ibid.

[14] Clark, *The Clipper Ship Era,* p. 122.

[15] The crew list filed in New York in November 1854 was amended on arrival in January 1856 to reflect desertions, discharges, and new hands during the voyage. Record Group 36, National Archives.

[16] *Report of the Commercial Relations of the United States with All Foreign Nations for the Year Ending September 30, 1857* (Washington: William A. Harris, 1858), pp. 18–19.

[17] *Sydney Morning Herald,* March 28, 1855.

[18] When the top layer of over a century's worth of rubbish was being removed from SNOW SQUALL in 1986 a number of these "torpedo bottles" were found along with more modern debris. These were later identified by the Jones Museum of Glass in Sebago, Maine, as being of the mid-nineteenth century type, though having no verifiable direct connection

with SNOW SQUALL's career. When opened and ready for table use, the bottle was placed upright in a holder, sometimes of very elaborate design, rather like placing an egg in an egg cup.

[19] *Portland Eastern Argus,* "Shipping News," August 20, 1855.

[20] Albert S. Bickmore, *Travels in the East Indian Archipelago* (New York: D. Appleton and Company, 1869), pp. 16–17.

[21] Matthew Fontaine Maury, *The Physical Geography of the Sea* (New York: Harper & Brothers, 1855), p. 107.

[22] Bickmore, *Travels,* p. 16.

[23] John D. Whidden, *Ocean Life in the Old Sailing Ship Days* (Boston: Little, Brown and Company, 1908), pp. 217–18.

[24] Bickmore, *Travels,* p. 27.

[25] *Portland Eastern Argus,* August 18 and 20, 1855.

[26] *S&CL,* August 22, 1855.

[27] Bickmore, *Travels,* p. 32.

[28] *S&CL,* October 27, 1855.

[29] *North China Herald* (Shanghai), August 25, 1855.

[30] For a more detailed analysis of the customs problem and the creation of the Inspectorate, see Linda Cooke Johnson, *Shanghai from Market Town to Treaty Port 1074–1858* (Stanford: Stanford University Press, 1993), pp. 290–91 and chapter 11.

[31] *Hunt's Merchants' Magazine and Commercial Review,* vol. 34 (January–June, 1856), pp. 393–94.

[32] *North China Herald* (Shanghai), September 29, 1855.

[33] Ibid., October 13, 1855.

[34] *New York Herald,* January 22, 1856.

[35] *S&CL,* January 23, 1856.

[36] *New York Daily Tribune,* January 22, 1856.

[37] Eric W. Sager, *Seafaring Labour: The Merchant Marine of Canada 1820–1914* (Kingston: McGill-Queen's University Press, 1989), pp. 224–25.

[38] *New York Daily Tribune,* February 18, 1856.

*The anchor is weighed and the sails they are set.*
*Away to Rio!*
*The girls we are leaving we'll never forget,*
*For we're bound to the Rio Grande.*
—CAPSTAN CHANTEY[1]

*When this voyage is beaten by any sailing vessel,*
*we shall be ready to give her credit for it.*
—*NEW YORK HERALD*, MAY 13, 1856

IN EARLY 1856, with the New York coffee market active and California freights stagnant at just over thirty cents a cubic foot, down from ninety to ninety-five cents three years earlier,[2] owner Green decided to send SNOW SQUALL on a quick voyage to Rio de Janeiro, even though other clippers, such as the famous FLYING CLOUD, were then loading San Francisco cargoes. Details of this voyage, as gleaned from the shipping news in New York's *Herald* and *Daily Tribune* are sketchy. Again under Captain Gerard, SNOW SQUALL cleared for the "East Indies" on February 20 and sailed the next day on the high tide just after ten in the morning, with a west-southwest wind.[3] She arrived back in New York on May 12, thirty-four days from Rio de Janiero (hardly the "East Indies!"), but a round trip which was worthy of some mention in the *Herald*:

> A few days since we mentioned the fact of her arrival at Rio from New York in the unprecedented space of 28 days. She has occupied but 79 days in accomplishing her voyage out and back. When this voyage is beaten by any sailing vessel, we shall be ready to give her credit for it.[4]

# 7

# TRIUMPH AND DISASTER:
# THE VOYAGES OF 1856–58

Her incoming cargo was not reported in the shipping news, but it was most likely coffee. In this period Brazil was far and away the world's largest coffee producer—over 300 million pounds a year, almost three times the production of second-place Java. Indeed Brazil produced over half the annual supply of the beans. The people of the United States and Canada were serious coffee drinkers, between them consuming over 200 million pounds each year, while the traditionally tea-drinking British made do with about 40 million. Flour was the major American export to Brazil with just over 300,000 barrels in 1854.[5] However, Baltimore's high-quality "Howard Street" flour, which supposedly kept better in hot climates, seems to have been preferred over the New York product in general, so it is even possible that SNOW SQUALL sailed south in ballast, as did other vessels.

By June, though California freights remained stubbornly stuck at about the thirty cents level,[6] Green arranged to send SNOW SQUALL around to San Francisco in W. C. Annan and Company's Eagle Line. By the end of the month she was loading at Pier Ten and an advertisement in the *Shipping and Commercial List* restated this list of the virtues of the "splendid extreme clipper ship SNOW SQUALL, Loyd, Commander," printed on Annan's handout advertising cards: "This beautiful little clipper has proved her superior sailing qualities by beating the entire clipper fleet on her last voyage from China, and her speed and early day of departure offer superior inducements to those wishing to lay down their goods in San Francisco in time for the Fall trade."[7] The rather pedestrian artwork on the card, printed in a dull shade of green, now in the collections of New York's South Street Seaport Museum, shows a man trudging along, braced against the wind of what is apparently a "Snow Squall."

But here a mystery concerning this voyage crops up. Who was her master on it? The evidence is contradictory. In the advertisement quoted above her master is given as Loyd, and in the listings of vessels up for San Francisco, Loyd's name also appears.[8] But when she cleared for San Francisco her captain is given as "Gerrand" (possibly a typographical error).[9] To further complicate matters, just over two months after leaving New York SNOW SQUALL was partially dismasted and a "protest" (i.e., a sworn statement) filed at the American consulate in Montevideo was signed by Thomas Loyd. To *further* complicate things, when the ship finally arrived at San Francisco, the captain is Gerard, but Lloyd (or Loyd) took her on to Manila and New York. It is this kind of thing which leaves even Clio, the Muse of History, scratching her head, and wondering just a bit about nineteenth-century orthography!

The known facts of this voyage are mainly drawn from Loyd's Montevideo protest,[10] which, since no SNOW SQUALL logbooks from any voyage appear to have survived, gives us at least a glimpse into the events of 1856. A marine protest is, in the words of an 1859 work, *The Law of Shipping*, "a declaration or narrative, by the master, of the storms or bad weather, which the vessel may have encountered, the accidents which may have occurred, and the conduct which in cases of emergency he had thought proper to pursue."[11] It may be as simple as filling in the blanks on a "boiler plate" printed form at a consulate or customhouse, the master

blandly attesting that his vessel had had "a boisterous and tempestuous passage," which is certainly preventive action in case there were claims
of cargo damage on arrival, but it is not at all in-
formative as to details. Or, as in this case, an "extended protest," where a clerk takes down a
captain's testimony, can be a lively relation of
harrowing events, useful later on in settling just
who, the owner or the consignees, is responsible
for losses on the voyage. As will become apparent in discussing the problems which arose from
SNOW SQUALL's final voyage, the sequence of
events and actions taken can be crucial under
"The Law of Admiralty," a most ancient and arcane body of precedent which goes back to medieval times and beyond. Indeed, when St. Paul
was shipwrecked, precedents for dealing with
the aftermath were already in place.

Clipper card for SNOW SQUALL's
1856 voyage to San Francisco in
W. C. Annan's Clipper Line.
SOUTH STREET SEAPORT MUSEUM

At five o' clock in the afternoon of July 6,
1856, carrying a cargo of "Sundry Merchandise,"
the "extended protest" reads, on leaving New York Captain Loyd
"discharged the Pilot and Tow Boat, made all Sail, and proceeded
to Sea, with the wind from the Southward." SNOW SQUALL was
not heavily laden—drawing eleven feet, she was six feet lighter
than her normal draft of seventeen. According to the Sandy Hook
Pilots' records, her pilotage (based on loaded draft) was $19.91.[12]
This was, incidentally, a not inconsiderable sum, better than half a
month's wages for a skilled shipwright.

By eight in the evening the highlands of Navesink, New Jersey, bore west by north, from which bearing Loyd "took his departure," the moment from which a voyage officially began. After
that a vessel's deck log, the inviolable record kept by the chief
mate, ran from noon to noon.[13] The winds and weather continued
"moderate" until August 19, when approaching the latitude of
Uruguay (though well offshore), SNOW SQUALL encountered hard

gales from the westward. At four in the afternoon the crew double reefed the topsails and furled the mainsail and spanker, then later in the day when the weather abated, "made sail accordingly," possibly following the old adage:

> Rain before wind: tops'l sheets and halyards mind.
> Wind before rain: hoist your topsails up again.

Five days later disaster struck. It was blowing hard in squalls. Just before midnight a heavy squall from the southwest took the ship aback, carrying away the fore topgallant mast and fore topmast studdingsail and yard. Loyd took in sail and double reefed the topsail, and next morning reefed the main.

It is worth noting that in his account of the incident, while reporting the loss of the topgallant and a studdingsail, Captain Loyd makes no mention of either a skysail or a royal, which would have been set above the topgallant. When SNOW SQUALL set out on her delivery voyage to New York in 1851, she reportedly had standing skysail poles and yards, which seem to have gone missing by 1856. It may be that early in her career one of her captains had decided that skysails were just a bit more canvas aloft than the ship could handle comfortably. In the case of the clipper RAINBOW, whose lofty sail plan was controversial right from the beginning, she was dismasted on her maiden voyage to China in 1845, and her captain shortened her rig when she was repaired at Hong Kong. As to SNOW SQUALL's absent royals, it is possible that preparing for the approach to Cape Horn Captain Loyd had sent the royals down. Yet he was flying studdingsails, about which there was some occasional controversy. (Some captains, in fact, would argue that royals, as well, were more trouble than they were worth, putting too much strain on the masts.) The Boston *Commercial Bulletin* was one of the skeptics, claiming that "short passages are made with strong, fair winds, when studdingsails cannot be carried." It suggested that shipowners direct their captains to keep a record of episodes with and without studdingsails and royals, noting the speed of a vessel before they were set and while they were set. Such an experiment, the *Bulletin* editorialized, would "enable them to judge whether these light sails are worth the expense bestowed upon them, or not."[14]

Loyd pressed on towards Cape Horn. On August 31 he observed that "the Ship made more water than usual." On September 2 there were "hard gales" which split the fore topsail. (Apparently Snow Squall still carried single topsails, rather than the double or split topsails which had come in during the early 1850s). By September 5 Snow Squall was in 43° 41' south latitude, just north of the entrance to the River Plate. At midnight it had been clear weather with a light breeze, with no inkling of trouble ahead, when just after two in the morning the ship was struck by a "sudden squall," which, from its violence might have been what is known in those latitudes as a *pampero*. If a pampero strikes during daylight hours, it can be a fine, sunny day offshore, when suddenly the horizon to the southwest looks as if some great hand had scribbled over it with grease pencil. The sun continues to shine, but the dark smudge spreads. Mariners experienced in these waters shorten sail to the bare minimum and batten down everything possible. When the storm hits it is of fairly short duration, say an hour or so, but severe. The wind screams through the rigging. The air is full of spray. Visibility is down to zero in sheets of rain, and the temperature drops like a rock, for it is a mass of cold, dense air falling that produces a pampero. It is like being in a car wash in a wind tunnel during a New England October.

That is in daylight. At two in the morning aboard Snow Squall perhaps the only warning Captain Loyd and his crew may have had was when the stars to westward began to dim and then vanish. When the storm hit, the only light on deck was the dim yellow glow of the oil lamp illuminating the compass in the binnacle. Fortunately, on a square-rigger like Snow Squall, the position of every line, run through its fairlead and coiled and draped over its belaying pin, followed a time-honored pattern, vessel to vessel, for there is no blindness darker than a storm at sea on a moonless night, and when the sea attacks, memory and touch are the tools of salvation. One is not afraid because there is no time for it. The drill, in SNOW SQUALL's case performed ceaselessly in daylight and darkness during the two months since leaving New York, took over. Even the greenest hand, unless a total incompetent, knew by this time the location of each pinrail and pin and when necessary could count—by feel if necessary—one, two, three, "Got it."

Within minutes or less SNOW SQUALL lost her main topmast, main topgallant mast, main topsail yard, the main top, and the main trestle trees. In other words, everything above the mainmast itself lay in a wet, writhing tangle on deck or overboard, battering the hull with every surge of the sea. The futtock shrouds below the main top were in ruins, as were the mizzen topgallant mast, with its backstays, the fore topmast studdingsail boom, the main topgallant studdingsail, the fore and main braces, the fore and mizzen topsail braces, and various other gear. "The wreck swinging about, tore the mainsail to pieces, split [the] mizzen topsail, and in consequence of the high sea running," Loyd ordered the overboard wreckage cut away, "fearing they would pierce the ship's bottom."

With the crew slipping, stumbling, and cursing, it apparently took nearly twenty-four hours to restore some kind of order to a chaos. It is one thing to climb aloft, even by feel, because, like the pinrail, there is a known progression to it. But when the familiar is strewn or dangling about in illogical, shin-barking, pitch-dark disarray, about all one can do is to hack it into manageable fragments.

The following day, at two in the morning, Loyd "close reefed fore Topsail and handed it, & commenced clearing the Wreck." The wind finally moderated by six in the evening, and early the next day Loyd "wore Ship, and shaped a course for the port of Montevideo, to repair damages." After splitting several more sails and discovering that "the fore topgallant yard [was] badly sprung," on September 14 SNOW SQUALL's weary captain and crew let go the anchor "one league" from the Punta Brava lighthouse. If the weather was clear, first to appear as they came in would have been the nearly 500-foot-high hill, from which the Montevideo got its name, then the spires of the cathedral. The next day Loyd took a pilot to go in (though judging from consular reports the local pilots were of uneven competence in the shoal and treacherous estuary of the River Plate), anchored "in conformity with harbour regulations," then called for a survey to assess the damage.

Montevideo in the 1850s was a city of about 16,000 inhabitants. Uruguay had just gone through a wrenching nine-year civil war during which many of the cattle whose hides were its major export had been slaughtered. Most American vessels, after discharging their cargoes of agricultural products and lumber, generally headed across the estuary to Buenos Aires for a return cargo of Argentine hides for New England's burgeoning shoe industry.

On the first of October, in the quiet of the American consulate, as the clerk's pen scratched against the pages, Loyd set out and swore to the terrifying events of three weeks before and "did declare to protest against the High Winds, Squally Seas & Currents" which had reduced SNOW SQUALL's rig to a tangle of trash, declaring that his ship had been "tight, staunch & strong" and that "his Officers, Crew, and himself used their best Exertions, for the

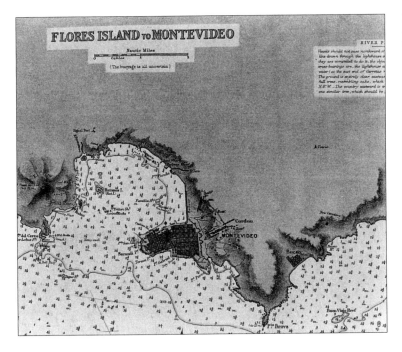

Detail from *River Plate*. Though the estuary of the River Plate is broad, it is very shallow, and undoubtedly Captain Loyd had a leadsman taking soundings constantly.
JAMES IMRAY AND SON, LONDON, 1883. AUTHOR'S COLLECTION

*Triumph and Disaster* 135

Preservation of said Ship." The document, "being distinctly read out to them," was witnessed by first mate Richard Wilkinson and seamen William Stein and Alberto Rodrigez. Here there was no ambiguity about Loyd's connection with SNOW SQUALL. He signed the protest in a fine, swashing Victorian hand, "Thos Loyd Master."

With repairs underway, Loyd anticipated a reasonably expeditious resumption of the interrupted voyage. However, just short of two months later, SNOW SQUALL was nearly ready for sea when she "was run into by the Spanish brig CORA, which carried away jibboom, fore topgallant mast, and mainmast head."[15] Repairs to this further indignity took another three weeks.

After SNOW SQUALL finally left Montevideo, she was twenty-two days from Montevideo to Cape Horn, off the Cape three days in "moderate weather," crossed the equator in the Pacific on January 7 in 106 degrees west longitude (rather close to the South American coast), picked up the northeast trades in 30 degrees north latitude, then dawdled for a week, making only about forty miles a day. By the end of January she was off the Golden Gate for two days in "light winds," but arrived on January 31, 1857, with Gerard apparently again in command, 208 days out of New York. On the passage from Montevideo one of the crew, William Brown, "fell from the anchor and was drowned." Not exactly a record run, 208 days from New York, but certainly a memorable one.[16] It is likely that SNOW SQUALL was towed to her berth on the North Beach waterfront. San Francisco's Merchant Transportation Company offered towage "to and from sea" for a vessel of her tonnage for the sum of $150. Towage merely "from wharf to stream" was only $40.[17]

Her cargo intended for the "fall season" was long overdue, and there was some confusion as to who would handle it. San Francisco's *Alta California* ran two advertisements the day after SNOW SQUALL's arrival. W. C. Annan of Battery Street, in whose Eagle Line she had run from New York, announced that she was ready to discharge at Battery Wharf and notified consignees "to call on the undersigned, pay freight and general average deposit, and receive orders for their goods," adding that, "All goods remaining on the wharf after 4 PM will be stored at the risk and expense of the owners thereof." The second advertisement was for R. S. Haven, who announced that consignees should call at *his* Battery Street office. Haven claimed that "the undersigned is alone authorized to receive the same and the goods will not be relinquished until these requisitions are complied with."[18] He was the younger brother of a well-known San Francisco insurance adjuster, Joshua P. Haven. The acerbic Caspar T. Hopkins, in his memoirs of this period, published in a number of issues of the *California Historical Society Quarterly*, had little good to say about the Haven brothers. The elder he called "uneven, unsystematic, and unbalanced," while the younger was "a good adjuster when sober," which, Hopkins added gratuitously, "was seldom the case."[19] Just how the dispute between Haven and Annan was resolved is unknown, but in early February, when SNOW SQUALL was about to sail for Manila on the next leg of her voyage, Haven was handling the arrangements.

Left to right: Vallejo Street, Broadway, and Pacific Street wharves, 1863.
SAN FRANCISCO MARITIME NATIONAL HISTORICAL PARK, NEGATIVE NO. A12.15237

However the squabble between agents was settled, by February 5 SNOW SQUALL's cargo began to appear on the San Francisco market. Geo. Howes and Company on Sansome Street was advertising four hundred reams of printing paper of "Superior quality and manufacture of Messrs. H. V. Butler & Co.,"[20] while James Patrick offered a thousand kegs of Old Colony nails of "assorted sizes."[21] In a few more days Washburn's "Grocery and Provision Auction House" at the intersection of California and Front Streets, offered "for the account of whom it may concern," dried peaches from SNOW SQUALL's cargo, while Smiley Brothers, another firm of auctioneers at the corner of Sansome and Sacramento, were about to sell "on behalf of underwriters, damaged on voyage," quite an assortment of men's clothing, including coats, pants, and vests. McRuer and Merrill offered, "for the account of the underwriters," fifteen bales of brown sheetings.[22]

Park and White, opposite the post office, offered three hundred cases of Hostetter's Bitters, "ex Snow Squall." This Pittsburgh patent medicine was popular in the mining camps. Heavily laced with alcohol and quinine, its label, emblazoned with St. George and the dragon, claimed that, "One wine-glass taken three times a day, before meals, will be a swift and certain cure for Dyspepsia, Liver Complaint, and every species of Indigestion." If a miner had a touch of the malarial shakes, the quinine soothed the spasms, and presumably the three wineglasses the psyche. Hostetter's remained a popular nostrum well into the twentieth century.

SNOW SQUALL had taken a fairly severe pounding on this voyage, between her dismasting and her collision in Montevideo, and Captain Loyd had noticed that she was making more water than usual, so presumably with a nudge from the surveyors, on February 10, "a fine day," she came up San Francisco Bay under tow to the floating drydock at Mare Island Naval Shipyard.[23] At 10:30 the next morning SNOW SQUALL went "on the dock." She was found to be "open on the starboard and a little copper off the keel and stern," but further examination the next day revealed that she was "generally open," requiring that all of her sheathing be stripped, and that she be caulked and "coppered all over." The next three days saw atrocious weather and little shipyard work took place. On February 16, a cloudy day but at least no longer raining, the yard hands were at work indoors and outdoors and SNOW SQUALL was refloated.

Even before SNOW SQUALL went into drydock, R. S. Haven advertised her imminent departure for Manila. This "A-1 first-class clipper ship" was scheduled to leave on the 14th (though she did not actually clear until February 19 or sail until the 20th). Meanwhile, freight and cabin passage could be arranged either through Captain Loyd on board or through Haven. SNOW SQUALL would have passed south of Hawaii, gone just north of the Marianas, then proceeded south along the west coast of Luzon to reach Manila at the end of the northeast monsoon, a voyage of over 4,000 miles.

After loading at Manila SNOW SQUALL sailed for Sunda Strait on April 10 and arrived in New York via the Cape of Good Hope on August 4 with a thoroughly unglamorous but extremely useful cargo, reported in the *New York Herald* as, "hemp to C. R. Green."[24] It had been another frustrating voyage. She had light winds

The floating dry dock at Mare Island Naval Shipyard, Vallejo. After the partial dismasting and collision in Montevideo in 1856, SNOW SQUALL arrived in San Francisco in late January 1857, 208 days from New York. From February 11 to 16 she was repaired and remetaled in the dry dock. Mare Island had opened in 1854 and in 1855 received the dry dock, which had been built in New York and brought around Cape Horn in several sections. The vessel shown in this circa 1870 photograph is probably the USS PORTSMOUTH. The navy yard closed in the late 1990s.
MARE ISLAND NAVAL SHIPYARD

through the Indian Ocean, then hit heavy weather approaching the Cape, which took a full two weeks to round. She passed the island of St. Helena in the South Atlantic on July 3.[25]

That summer of 1857, as it would turn out, was an enormously trying one for New York's business community, particularly those with large outstanding loans. Green, who later claimed that he had never, ever, borrowed money, apparently weathered the Panic of 1857 successfully, though obviously he had to keep his fleet of vessels gainfully employed if possible. Whether Green had sniffed the financial wind, liked not what he smelled, and prepared for the blow, or whether he was just being a thrifty and prudent Yankee as usual is unknown. There had been portents. The end of the Crimean War and the resumption of grain shipments from Russia had lessened European demand for American wheat. Interest rates in London had risen and investors sold off American railroad stock, with the result that stock pledged as collateral on western real estate loans lost value. In August the New York branch of the Ohio Life Insurance and Trust Company (in spite of its name actually a banking firm), battered by embezzlement and non-producing loans, suspended payments. The fragile financial house of cards collapsed, and many firms, including the publishing house of Harper & Brothers, went under, at least temporarily. The Richmond, Virginia, *Examiner*, quoted in the *New York Herald* of August 30, reported that, "The whole west is gridironed over with railroads owned by bubble companies.... The banks explode but asseverate with great emphasis that they are solvent though obliged to 'suspend for a short time.'"[26] It was a short-lived but severe financial disaster.

Charles Green responded by sending SNOW SQUALL to Rio via Richmond, Virginia, probably with a cargo of flour from the Richmond mills. She cleared New York for Richmond on September 3,[27] and the Richmond customhouse for Rio on September 22. She had a crew of nineteen, ten of whom apparently deserted in Rio. They were replaced in December by thirteen hands shipped in Rio: a third mate, no wages given, two ordinary seamen at sixteen dollars per month, and ten seamen at eighteen dollars.[28] SNOW SQUALL arrived in New Orleans on January 29, 1858, towed up from the Passes by the tug PHOENIX, with eight hundred bags of coffee, consigned to "master," for Captain Loyd or Green's agents to dispose of as best they could.[29] On February 23 SNOW SQUALL again left for Rio with a cargo of beef, flour, pork, and lard, commodities which undoubtedly had come down the Mississippi to the entrepôt above the delta.[30] She left Rio on April 25 and returned to New Orleans on May 26, towed up by CONQUERER to the quarantine station, carrying a cargo of 8,950 sacks of coffee to Schwartz and Company. But the market was "dull"; the New Orleans *Bee* had "heard of no transactions today worth reporting."[31] This was to be SNOW SQUALL's last voyage between Rio and New Orleans. Shortly before SNOW SQUALL arrived another of Charles Green's ships cleared for Liverpool with a cargo of cotton, wheat, lard, and lumber. She was the 1,292-ton DICTATOR, built in Robbinston, Maine, in 1855. Green had purchased her in November 1855, from William G. Train of Boston, adding a fourth vessel to his fleet.

It is worth noting that in his annual message to the Louisiana legislature early in 1858, Governor Robert Charles Wickliffe sounded a note which presaged troubles to come. "The doctrine of State rights," he said, "the cornerstone of our system of government, the great bulwark against centralization...appears to be making progress." He went on, "The cardinal principle of our system is, that we are not one nation, with a supreme government at Washington, but an aggregation of thirty-one sovereign nations, with certain specified powers."[32] The good news, as least as it concerned shipowner Green, was that operations against the rebels in China had begun early in the year. In August the short-lived transatlantic telegraph cable carried its "first news dispatch direct from Europe," announcing the end of the war in China. The cable broke down shortly thereafter and so, though no one knew it, did the fragile Chinese truce. Green ordered Captain Loyd to take SNOW SQUALL to Boston to load for a voyage to Shanghai.

## NOTES

[1] The origins of this famous chantey may go back to before the Mexican War. It may be a product of the gold rush. The late Stan Hugill claimed that "Rio" referred to Brazil's Rio Grande do Sul, rather than Rio de Janeiro, but Maine Maritime Museum's former curator, Robert Webb, no mean chanteyman himself, is positive that *Away to Rio* would have been sung on the voyages described here.

[2] *Annual Report of the Chamber of Commerce of the State of New York for the Year 1856* (New York: Wheeler and Williams, 1859), p. 207.

[3] *New York Herald,* February 22, 1856.

[4] Ibid., May 13, 1856.

[5] *Report of the Commercial Relations of the United States with All Foreign Nations* (Washington: A.O.P. Nicholson, 1856), pp. 652–53.

[6] *Annual Report,* p. 207.

[7] New York *Shipping and Commercial List,* June 28, 1856.

[8] Ibid., June 21, 1856.

[9] *New York Herald,* July 3, 1856.

[10] Protest: Ship SNOW SQUALL of New York. Consulate of the United States, Montevideo, October 1, 1856. Records of the Department of State, Consular Records. Record Group 84. National Archives, Washington, DC.

[11] Francis B. Dixon, *The Law of Shipping and Merchants' and Shipmasters' Guide* (New York: Henry Spear, 1859), p. 174.

[12] Records and Logbooks of the Sandy Hook Pilots, July 1856. Stephen B. Luce Library, SUNY Maritime College, Bronx, NY.

[13] On one Maine ship, SHENANDOAH, family tradition has it that the mate was logged in by the captain, one James "Shotgun" Murphy, as being drunk on his watch. Mate Alvord simply noted for the rest of the voyage that "the Captain was sober again today."

[14] Quoted in *The Mercantile Marine Magazine,* May 1861, p. 156.

[15] *Alta California* (San Francisco), January 31, 1857.

[16] Ibid.

[17] Ibid., February 4, 1857.

[18] Ibid., February 1, 1857.

[19] "The California Recollections of Caspar T. Hopkins." Photocopies from the *California Historical Society Quarterly*, pp. 257, 352. n.d.

[20] *Alta California* (San Francisco), February 5, 1857.

[21] Ibid.

[22] Ibid., February 7, 11, and 12, 1857.

[23] Mare Island Naval Shipyard logbook, quoted in letter to the author from Mrs. Sue Lemmon, shipyard historian, May 26, 1992.

[24] *New York Herald,* August 5, 1857. "Manila hemp," the product of the *Musa textilis* plant, has been called "the most valuable of all fibres for cordage." *Encyclopaedia Britannica,* 11th ed. (New York: The Encyclopaedia Britannica Company,

1911), vol. XIII, p. 580.

[25] *New York Herald,* August 5, 1857.

[26] Ibid., August 30, 1857.

[27] Ibid., September 4, 1857.

[28] Records of the Bureau of Customs. Record Group 36.

National Archives.

[29] *New Orleans Bee,* January 30, 1858.

[30] Ibid., February 23, 1858.

[31] Ibid., May 27, 1858.

[32] Ibid., January 21, 1858.

S NOW SQUALL left New Orleans July 5, 1858, and dropped
down below the Southwest Pass the next day, loaded with a
general cargo, much of it agricultural produce. She arrived
in Boston a short two weeks later, tying up at Battery Wharf on
the northeast corner of the waterfront.[3] Drays, or heavy wagons,
hauled bales of cotton along Atlantic Avenue to Beebe and Company, Farwell and Company, and Seaver and Company, while a
thousand pigs of lead went to Farwell. Leather dealers J. A. and
Minot Tirrell received large consignments of hides.[4] Meanwhile,
Charles Green's three other vessels were active in what the Boston
*Shipping List and Prices Current* called "The European Fleet." The
GEORGE GREEN under Captain Fairbanks left Mobile on April 8 and
was at Kronstadt (near St. Petersburg, Russia) by July 3 in company with the HARRY BLUFF. The BLUFF's captain (and part-owner),
St. Croix Redman, had left Mobile on February 22 and was now
loading for Boston. Meanwhile, DICTATOR, under Captain Zerega,
had left New Orleans on May 27 and was in Liverpool by June 29.[5]

144

# 8

## TO SHANGHAI, AGAIN AND AGAIN: 1858–61

After discharging, SNOW SQUALL went into James and John Dillon's Fort Hill Dry Dock at the foot of Broad Street where she was surveyed and remetaled.[6] This was her first survey by the newly formed American Lloyd's. It may be that the gimlet-eyed Boston surveyor disapproved of the sheathing job done at the Mare Island drydock in California only the year before, because sheathing was supposed to last forty months before needing replacement when down to roughly half its original thickness through wear and corrosion. Sheathing was depreciated at the rate of one-fortieth of its value per month for marine insurance purposes.[7] In any case by August 11 SNOW SQUALL was at Long Wharf under Captain Loyd, loading for Shanghai.[8]

Her cargo once again was quite varied. There was a considerable quantity of lumber and coal, topped off with nearly two thousand packages of "domestics," i.e., cotton cloth from the mills of Lawrence or Lowell. There were four boxes of sewing machines, fifty casks of medicine, fifty-one boxes of scales, and small

Aboard SNOW SQUALL as a "boy" in 1858 was sixteen-year-old Edmund Rice. Rice kept a fairly detailed diary on the voyage. When the Civil War broke out he volunteered and was commissioned a captain in the Fourteenth Massachusetts Infantry, later transferring to the Nineteenth Massachusetts. For heroism at Gettysburg during Pickett's Charge Rice was awarded the Medal of Honor. He stayed with the army, retiring as a brigadier general in 1903.

COURTESY OF STEVEN J. NITCH

shipments of glassware, tobacco, and twine. There was even one piano, possibly one of the famed Boston Chickerings.[9] She carried a crew of twenty-one, most of them in their twenties, though one Alexander Brown, born at Gay Head on Martha's Vineyard, was a venerable thirty-nine. Where the crew hailed from when they shipped in Boston was not recorded, but their birthplaces ranged from Eastport, Bangor, and Camden, Maine, to New York and Boston, with two listed as "no proof." Wages, where they appear on the crew list at all, averaged ten dollars a month. The chief mate, Charles van Dolan, made twenty-seven dollars, and a Henry Nash, probably the second mate, twenty-five. Only six of the crew shipped in Boston were still aboard when SNOW SQUALL returned to the United States ten months later.[10] Of more than passing interest are two young crew members, fourteen-year-old Theodore Catlin of Deerfield, Massachusetts, and sixteen-year-old Edmund Rice of Cambridge. Both apparently shipped as "boys." Edmund was five foot eight with a "dark" complexion, brown hair, and hazel eyes. A photograph taken in 1861 of Edmund in his new army uniform, admittedly a rather solemn occasion, shows him gazing steadfastly at some point well over the photographer's head, not at the camera.

Young Catlin and Rice were both of very good families. Catlin's was an old Deerfield name going back to the seventeenth century. His father, John, had run a baggage wagon line to Boston, gone into business briefly in Georgia, and returned to Deerfield in 1841, two years before Theodore was born. Edmund Rice was born in Brighton and grew up in Cambridge, where his father was in the real estate business, described in the 1850 census as "land dealer," doing a fair amount of development in Malden. It has not been possible to determine how these two youngsters were recruited for SNOW SQUALL. Through Charles Green's Boston connections? Through Captain Thomas Loyd, or A. A. Frazar and Company, who handled SNOW SQUALL's Boston affairs? The trail is cold. In any case it appears that after just shy of three years as a student at Norwich University, a military school in Vermont, Edmund had decided to take a break and go to sea. If practice on other vessels is any indication, it is likely that the callow youths were not berthed with the roughnecks of the rest of the crew. Aboard the Bath ship W. F. BABCOCK in 1883, the boys were apparently housed in a separate room in the forward deckhouse, next to the galley, according to a sea journal kept by Maria Murphy, wife of the famous captain, James F. "Shotgun" Murphy. And when a giant wave stove in the deckhouse, one of the BABCOCK's boys moved into the mate's quarters.[11]

On August 21, two days before SNOW SQUALL was to depart, Arthur W. Austin, Collector of the District of Boston and Charlestown, issued Edmund Rice a Seaman's Protection Certificate. This was simply a document stating that Edmund had produced evidence that he was an American citizen, in some ways a holdover reaction to the British impressment tactics which helped bring on the War of 1812. And on this voyage young Edmund kept a diary. It is one of the few firsthand pieces of evidence relating to SNOW SQUALL's voyages—fascinating in what it relates, maddening in what it does not, but on the whole a far better literary production than the journal kept by the author when *he* went to sea at about Edmund's age![12]

Rice began his sea journal with, "The Snow Squall left the end of Long Wharf Boston at 12 o'clock on morning August the 23 & commenced to work as soon as we left the wharf." He noted that "the pilot was giving orders and we were hoisting sails, the wind at our stern. Both owner and pilot left us out the lower port." This last remark confirms observations made on SNOW SQUALL during archaeology in the Falklands, namely that there was a port (or ports) in the 'tween-decks suitable for loading long lengths of lumber or railroad rails. It would have been a low duck and a scramble for Charles Green and the Boston pilot to get into the pilot schooner's yawl boat, but apparently they made it without incident.

That evening the watches were set. Rice was in the port or "larboard" watch under the first mate. He makes no mention of dog watches, the two-hour watches from four to six and six to eight in the afternoon that broke up the daily routine. "We have 4 hours on & 4 hours off night and day. We sweep the decks in the afternoon & wash them in the morning at four o' clock." Five days out, trouble erupted. One crew member refused to obey the second mate, who grabbed him by the throat, whereupon the crewman drew his knife and threatened to stab the mate. At this point Captain Loyd came up, ordering the mate to "put some irons on him & lash him to the mast," though he was released at nightfall.

Unless there was a need to work the ship, Sundays were traditionally the crew's "washing day & mending day," as Rice put it. SNOW SQUALL had picked up the Gulf Stream, the weather was getting noticeably warmer, and on his first Sunday afternoon Rice spotted a flying fish. SNOW SQUALL apparently was no "hell ship," at least as far as the boys were concerned. "The Captain is like a father to us. The carpenter is one of our best friends. So is the steward and the cook. They give us what remains after the officers have eaten." That Sunday the steward brought the boys half of a plum pudding and Rice noted that, "We fare great and better than the sailors." He also recorded happily that he had not yet been seasick. The next day Rice was sent aloft to furl the mizzen royal which, he commented was "the highest sail on the mast." In other words, as in 1856–57, there were no skysails set.

By September 12, just shy of three weeks out, SNOW SQUALL was at 17 degrees north latitude, 42 degrees west longitude, approaching the equator in rainy weather, making around ten knots, with a restive crew. Rice commented gloomily that "there have been signs of mutiny this week," though apparently trouble never erupted as he never mentioned the subject again. The next night and day it rained hard; hard enough for SNOW SQUALL's crew to scoop up water from the deck and fill the empty water casks. However, Rice groused, the water "does not taste very good after the men have walked through it barefooted & shoes on."

The incident raises an interesting question. Many vessels of SNOW SQUALL's period had a cylindrical iron water tank abaft the mainmast, resting on the keelson and extending to the weather deck from which it could be pumped. Indeed a July 1870 contract between New York's Comstock and Company and SNOW SQUALL's owner, Charles Green, to run his ship the GEORGE GREEN to San Francisco specifically stated that "it is understood and agreed that the ship's having a water tank no other water is to be carried below decks."[13] As this stipulation is contained in a printed charter form on which other blanks might be filled in as needed, the tanks must have been fairly common, as, for example, in the 540-ton "clipper barque" MERMAID, launched at Boston in 1851, the same year as SNOW SQUALL. She had a 2,000-gallon tank.[14] They filled SNOW SQUALL's water casks on September 13, but by October 24 the crew had been put on a water allowance of a gallon a day. Was Captain Loyd simply prudently hedging his bets or were the casks the only, possibly leaky, water storage on board?

The diet at sea of course revolved around salt beef or salt pork, but on September 18 SNOW SQUALL's crew managed to catch an albacore after unsuccessful attempts at other fish. "We had it Sunday afternoon," wrote Rice, "and it tasted like veal." SNOW SQUALL crossed the equator approaching Cape St. Roque, at the eastern tip of Brazil, on September 25, and that evening "Father Neptune" came aboard to initiate the green hands as "shellbacks" by "shaving" those who had never crossed the Line—though light-hearted, a rite of total humiliation. Rice was the second in line. "The lather was not put on very thin; it was made of tar and grease. The brush a large paint brush, the razor a piece of board." Once having become a "shellback," should Rice ever ship out again he could, in his turn, help initiate hapless neophytes.

Cape St. Roque was the turning point for South Atlantic voyages. SNOW SQUALL ran close enough inshore near Pernambuco so that Rice could "see the land very plain," and a local log boat passed nearby, though he could not quite make out any buildings. At that point vessels bound for Valparaiso or San Francisco around Cape Horn set a course to pass inside the Falkland Islands, while China or Australia-bound vessels set a course to pass south of the Cape of Good Hope to pick up the prevailing westerlies. SNOW SQUALL approached the Cape, borne along by the prevailing westerlies. Rice does not record how close SNOW SQUALL passed to the Cape. Generally speaking vessels bound into the South China Sea began to ease northward in about 40 degrees north latitude, hoping to pick up the southeast trades in about 20 degrees south latitude, more or less.

Nine days after crossing the Line SNOW SQUALL came up on and "spoke" an English ship, ELECTRIC SPARK, bound from London for Bombay, then passed her handily. "The Englishmen did not like to see us pass them very well," recorded Rice smugly. By Sunday October 9 they were running under double-reefed topsails and a week later, approaching the Cape of Good Hope, it was "blowing a gale all the time" and getting colder. In another week they were in "about 43° [south] latitude, 38° [east] longitude," "spring off the Cape & we have many a cold night." Rice apparently had no sea boots and his friend the cook lent him a pair, though Rice declined the offer of some thick socks, saying that he had sufficient. There was wind, snow, and hail, and the sails were frozen stiff while SNOW SQUALL bowled eastward, occasionally logging sixteen knots.

After rounding the Cape they headed northeast and the weather became warmer. Rice had by now taken up the steward's duties. And then, on November 12, Rice's friend, the cook, George Harper, died. "No one was near him when he died. As soon as it was found out he was sewn up in his blankets and hove overboard. No one thought anything of it when they hove him over. The men simply took off their hats. The Captain didn't even come on deck." Harper, according to the crew list, was thirty-two, from Greensborough [North Carolina?], described as having a "dark" complexion and "woolly" hair. Many African Americans shipped out as cooks or stewards on American vessels in this period. Does the incident show a certain indifference on the part of Harper's crewmates and Captain Loyd? It's hard to say. Certainly, as witness Harper's offer to lend young Edmund Rice his boots, a friendship had grown between the cook and the youngster, but Rice's only expression of grief is his comment on Captain Loyd's refusal even to say or read a few words over his body or witness the burial at sea.

Since Captain Loyd seems to have chosen the so-called "Eastern Passages" rather than the more usual route through Java's Sunda Strait, by November 28 they were "in sight of the Spice Islands." Timor lay off the starboard bow. There were flying fish and killer whales. The crew caught a shark and had some of it for breakfast on, as it turned out, Rice's seventeenth birthday, but he confessed that he "did not like it much." He preferred the porpoise they harpooned the same day and pronounced it "very good." By December 3 something was very much amiss aboard SNOW SQUALL, and Rice reported that he predicted that they might put into the first available port since "the Captain, Mate, steward, two men, and a boy are sick & the cook dead." Two days later, Alexander Brown, the steward from Gay Head on Martha's Vineyard, died on Rice's sea chest. "As soon as he died the men were ordered to sew him up and throw him overboard, but the men would not do it until he was cold. The Captain is worse and another one of the men are sick." On December 13 the chief mate, Charles van Dolan, died. According to the crew list, he was twenty-seven.[15] On December 11 Rice had recorded, rather gloomily, that with the sickness aboard, "no one knows where we are." The approaches to the China coast are not, from all available evidence, a place in which to be lost, with many charted (and at that period some uncharted) snags. When they buried the mate on the afternoon of December 13, shoved overboard from the plank from which two others had slid, there was talk that "there was bad luck in it."

By December 19 the second mate and the carpenter were running the ship. Rice accused them in his diary (though certainly not in public) of carrying too much sail. "I think we will lose our masts before we get to Shanghai." There had been alarums and excursions. On the day the mate died SNOW SQUALL sighted "a lot of boats in the water," coming from a nearby island. Ill though he was, Captain Loyd ordered his crew not to let them come on board, but "they collected together and tried to board us," as Rice recorded. SNOW SQUALL fired a cannon and the ball went "between two of the boats." If a newspaper story which appeared some forty years later is correct, it would appear that due to his military training at Norwich, such as it may have been, Rice had been given command of one of SNOW SQUALL's small swivel guns. He is supposed to have fired a round of "lead pipe and nails." The pirates (if such they were) hung around until it was obvious that all of SNOW SQUALL's guns were loaded, then retreated to shore. Rice recorded that, adding to the tensions, "an earthquake shook the ship for two or three minutes," noting dryly that it had been "an eventful day to me."

Christmas Day was not a pleasant one, with much work taking in sail. Instead of the traditional plum pudding, gingerbread was served, but Rice does not mention who had taken over the late cook's duties. At least SNOW SQUALL was now in green, not blue, water and Rice thought they were approaching land. The two days after Christmas brought heavy gales. By December 28 SNOW SQUALL was "beating up and down the coast," Captain Loyd now had hoisted the signal for a pilot, and by the end of the day the ship lay at anchor. There was no further evidence of sickness.

On December 30 the pilot, who Rice thought was English, arrived in a small junk and SNOW SQUALL began to work upriver past Wusung to Shanghai, a process which took several days of heaving up the anchor, making sail, then anchoring again, which Rice described as "harde work." During the arduous process, twenty-year-old John McFarlane (or McFarland) of Boston, perhaps the "hard case" who had given trouble early in the voyage, attacked the first mate. He was later brought to trial before the American consul, fined ten dollars (a month's wages) for "Court expenses," and "sentenced to be put in irons aboard of Ship at the discretion of [the] Master."[16] He jumped ship on August 23, forfeiting whatever more pay he had coming to him eventually, probably considered by Captain Loyd and his mates "good riddance."

At last on January 3 SNOW SQUALL lay at anchor off the foreign concessions, her cargo consigned to Ullett and Company.[17] Rice was delighted to receive mail from home. His parents had written him from Cambridge on September 20, in care of the American consul W. L. G. Smith, with family news and enclosed a passport, so that if Edmund wanted to return home "any other way" he could do it, providing Captain Loyd consented. He was to sign a draft on his father for his passage money, which Edmund's father was sure would be agreeable to Loyd. But the senior Rice cautioned his son, "Dount [sic] you try to come home any other way except by the vessel unless the Capt. is willing." Edmund was to pass on his father's respects to Captain Loyd and to "Mr. Nash," who was probably by now the chief mate.[18] In any case, he elected to stay with his ship, and on Sunday, January 9, he got shore leave, "the first time on land for 4 months & 18 days." He is remarkably laconic regarding this first excursion in an exotic Chinese port except to note that he went "inside of the wall & to the Temple of Tosh, there [sic] God that they worship."

While in Shanghai Captain Loyd became involved in a dispute with Russell and Company, another consignee, over the payment of freight he had brought out. The "point at issue" before Consul Smith was whether the freight should be paid in Chinese currency (taels) or in "Mexican dollars." Apparently Loyd lost his case and payment was to be in dollars, with the captain assessed for "court expenses" of $10.90.[19]

As SNOW SQUALL discharged and began taking on return cargo, Rice jotted down a few incidents of note. By January 16 two British men-of-war had come into port. Given the timing they were possibly from the expedition up the Yangtze to see what river ports might be opened up under the recently signed Treaty of Tientsin, in which the Imperial Government made further concessions to Britain. On Washington's Birthday "the American ships displayed their bunting and fired salutes sunrise, noon, and sunset."

SNOW SQUALL had suffered desertions: three on January 24, two more on February 20 that Rice recorded, and apparently eight more, with one crew member, Jeremiah Bumpus discharged at Shanghai with "no wages due to him."[20] In the end Captain Loyd would ship fifteen new hands in Shanghai and sailed with "one Frederick George, a destitute American Seaman sent home by the Consul."[21] According to the *North China Herald*, SNOW SQUALL left Shanghai on March 21 with "tea and sundries" dispatched by Ullett and Company, while on her arrival at New York the *Herald* gave a departure date of March 22, most likely taken from the "official" beginning of the voyage in the deck log once SNOW SQUALL had dropped the pilot and the traditional entry made, "So begins this voyage."[22] She went down past Wusung with 597,810 pounds of green tea and "sundries."[23] On Sunday, March 20, while apparently preparing for departure or dropping down towards Wusung, as Rice recorded, "we ran over a Chinese fishing boat. We were going about ten knots an hour. I suppose all hands were drowned."

*Shanghai* by Sun Qua.
PEABODY ESSEX MUSEUM AND
VOSE GALLERIES, BOSTON

There was some excitement aboard SNOW SQUALL on the homeward passage. On April 3 Rice reported, "I think we are racing with a ship, 'Romance of the Seas.' She started a day before we did. We caught up with her in the 6th day out. I have seen her two or three times since." On April 5 ROMANCE was several miles astern of SNOW SQUALL when both ships anchored for the night, forty miles north of the Gaspar Strait, and by April 7 "nearly out of sight astern." On April 9 SNOW SQUALL anchored off Anjer, on the east side of the Straits of Sunda, to "take in some provisions & fruit & a couple of monkeys."

Apparently, in the urge to beat ROMANCE, nearly a hundred feet longer than SNOW SQUALL and theoretically, therefore, a faster ship, Captain Loyd clapped on every scrap of sail he could, occasionally with disastrous results. On April 13 SNOW SQUALL lost "two booms, one yard, and a sail," two days later the mainsail and main topmast staysail went, and on the twenty-fourth two more studdingsail booms.[24] But SNOW SQUALL boiled on, and by

May 5 the Cape of Good Hope lay off the weather bow. It was the kind of race that would be repeated nearly a decade later in 1866 when the British tea clippers ARIEL and TAEPING raced up the English Channel to the London docks after their record ninety-nine-day runs from Fuzhou, a race which climaxed John Masefield's thrilling novel *The Bird of Dawning*. The SNOW SQUALL versus ROMANCE race was not to be a record-setter. They had left Shanghai when the monsoon was petering out. ROMANCE had passed Good Hope two days before but SNOW SQUALL was two days in the lead when she crossed the Line during the night of May 28. SNOW SQUALL arrived at Sandy Hook on June 22, ninety-two days out, and ROMANCE the next day. The *New York Herald* didn't call it a race but merely commented that SNOW SQUALL brought "teas &c to Charles R. Green." The New York *Shipping and Commercial List* noted 814 half chests of tea to Westray, Gibbes and Hardcastle, 3,001 "packages [of tea?] to Brown Brothers & Co., 6,587 do ["ditto"], and "fire crackers and other merchandise."[25]

Edmund Rice did not follow the sea. When the Civil War broke out he volunteered and was commissioned a captain in the Fourteenth Massachusetts Infantry in April 1861, later transferring to the Nineteenth Massachusetts. Wounded at the Battle of Antietam, he rejoined his regiment. At the Battle of Gettysburg, the Nineteenth Massachusetts Volunteers rushed in to reinforce the line which Pickett's charge had broken and "for twelve minutes received the enemy's fire at a distance of less than fifteen paces." With Rice the Union officer "nearest fighting the enemy in the [Union's] whole line, he fought until he fell," until reinforcements held Pickett in check with "the single thin line of his regiment." For this he was awarded the Medal of Honor. Rice stayed with the army, finally retiring as a brigadier general in 1903. He died in 1906.[26] Edmund Rice's shipmate, Theodore Catlin, apparently stayed with the sea, but with tragic consequences. Inscribed on a stone in the Catlin family plot in Deerfield is, "Also remembrance of Theodore Fay, son of John and Josephine Catlin lost at sea, Mar. 10, 1860, AE 16." There are no further details available.[27]

On July 11 SNOW SQUALL cleared New York for Shanghai, again under Captain Loyd, drawing sixteen feet. Her outward fee from the Sandy Hook Pilots was thirty-six dollars. She may have been delayed in getting clear of New York. Though high water on the eleventh was just after six in the morning, the next day's *Herald* reported three ships in the bay, "bound out," in hazy weather with a light southerly wind.[28] SNOW SQUALL arrived at Shanghai on November 5, consigned to Ullett and Company, cleared for Amoy on November 30, and departed on December 5 laden with "sundries etc." She arrived back at New York on March 21, 1860, with a thousand "half chests" of tea to Westray, Gibbes, and Hardcastle, nearly three thousand "packages" to Brown Brothers, and more "packages" and silk "to order," i.e., Green's account.[29] She carried two passengers, a Mrs. F. Van Fleet, age forty, and her ten-year-old son.[30] There is no mention in the *New York Herald*'s generally detailed shipping news of a stop at Amoy. Instead she is supposed to have actually left Shanghai on December 19, passed Anjer Point on January 2, the Cape of Good Hope on February 5, and crossed the equator on February 27 (in light winds "since leaving the Cape"). In other words a respectable, though not remarkable, passage of ninety-two days, apparently without incident.

At this point it may be useful to take a look at SNOW SQUALL's owner's overall operations on the eve of the American Civil War. SNOW SQUALL was but one part of Charles R. Green's fleet, the only one, as far as can be determined, which returned regularly to her home port of New York. Green owned three other vessels: the GEORGE GREEN, the HARRY BLUFF, and DICTATOR; the GREEN and the BLUFF were owned in partnership with Medford, Massachusetts, Captain St. Croix Redman, who was captain of the latter. From what can be determined in the shipping news columns of the New York *Shipping and Commercial List* for 1860, the GREEN often ran between New Orleans and Havre with one voyage from New Orleans to Genoa, while the BLUFF ran to Havre from Mobile and Key West. DICTATOR apparently operated in the Pacific under a Captain Zerega: San Francisco to Hong Kong, then on to Batavia where she loaded for Amsterdam. Meanwhile Green had insured the GREEN and the BLUFF with the Mercantile Marine Insurance Company of Boston, each for a year: the GREEN for $6,250 at an annual premium of $501 and the BLUFF for $10,000 at an annual premium of $751.[31]

This "snapshot" of Green's peacetime operations is undoubtedly far from complete, as some arrivals and departures at ports where his vessels called may simply not have been reported in the shipping news columns, and it is possible, indeed likely, that he carried insurance policies with more than one company. Since none of Green's business papers from this period have come to light, it is impossible to know the details of how he conducted his operations. It seems likely, given the start of his career in New Orleans, that he retained connections there, but he would have had to have connections in other ports as well: if the GEORGE GREEN, for example, ran regularly to Havre, who brokered the cotton cargoes, arranged for the remittance of freight money, and so on? And all of this complicated business took place before the transatlantic (or even transcontinental) telegraph was in operation. Finally, although Green's apparently was a successful shipping business, according to his credit reports cited earlier, the American shipping industry had undergone a long, slow decline from its peak about 1825. In 1825, 95.2 percent of American imports and 89.2 percent of exports were in American flag vessels. By 1860 those numbers had slipped to 63.0 and 69.7 percent respectively.[32] The causes were many and varied, and the brief but severe Panic of 1857 had certainly hastened the decline, but the bottom line was that a shipper or agent in New York was less concerned about which flag a vessel about to load at South Street flew than with which vessel offered the more attractive freight rate. Only the coasting trade between American ports was reserved—by law—to American flag vessels (as it still is today), yet the coasting trade was a relatively small part of Charles Green's overall business.

When SNOW SQUALL arrived back in New York in March

1860, the waterfront was in the doldrums. The *Herald* reported gloomily that "such a universal dul[l]ness had not been known for thirty years and there were hundreds of ship carpenters in New York and Brooklyn who did not know which way to turn to make a living. Nor are the prospects for a turn for the better at present very encouraging."[33] The late March news from Shanghai, which reached New York towards the end of June, was also not reassuring. It was unknown if they were connected with the Taiping rebels but "numerous bands of marauders" threatened several Chinese cities, "particularly Hangchow, a great commercial centre, through which pass the bulk of the Tea and Silk crops to arrive at this place."[34]

Undeterred, Green sent SNOW SQUALL out to Shanghai once again as the California trade was "dull." Under Captain Loyd she cleared on June 16 "for Shanghai and a market" and arrived on November 10, consigned again to Ullett and Company.[35] On November 30 she cleared for Amoy and departed on December 5 with a cargo of "sundries etc."[36] This would be her last departure from Shanghai. She arrived at Amoy on December 12. Aboard was a cargo which included 1,700 bales of cotton, a large quantity of woolens, and twenty cases of "merchandise," apparently articles which were unsalable at Shanghai, with a total value of $29,115.50. She left Amoy for New York January 5 or 11, 1861, with 14,655 packages of tea, the produce of Fujian Province, value $146,500, and arrived at New York on April 4 with her tea consigned to Olyphant and Company and W. C. Pickersgill and Company. She had made, the *New York Herald* reported, the "shortest passage from China of the season," eighty-two days from Amoy and seventy from Java Head. SNOW SQUALL had "outstripped all her competitors in the China fleet this season." The *Herald* also reported in the same issue that South Carolina had cut off supplies to Fort Sumter in Charleston Harbor and that "The Secession Army [was] Ready for War."[37]

However, once again the shipping news pointed up the element of chance. Under Captain Loyd SNOW SQUALL had indeed outstripped the competition, but it was a combination of seamanship and luck. On January 29, in 11° 41' south latitude, 100° east longitude (roughly five hundred miles southwest of Java), SNOW SQUALL "spoke" (i.e., passed within hail of) the clipper SANCHO PANZA of Boston. The PANZA had left Fuzhou, about 125 miles north of Amoy, on New Year's Day but four days later encountered a twelve-hour typhoon during which, as Captain Loyd proceeded on, she "was hove down for 4 hours, losing an entire suit of sails, bulwarks etc. and had 7 feet of water in the hold when she righted."[38] The unlucky PANZA limped into New York nine days after SNOW SQUALL's stunning arrival, having been battered by another gale in the Atlantic four days earlier. She had shipped a sea which stove in her forward deck house and filled the cabin.[39]

---

NOTES

[1] *Hunt's Merchants' Magazine,* vol. 34, 1856.

[2] *Report on the Commercial Relations of the United States with All Foreign Nations* (Washington: A. O. P. Nicholson, 1856), p. 514.

[3] *Boston Daily Advertiser,* July 30, 1858. Boston *Shipping List and Prices Current,* July 31, 1858.

[4] Boston *Shipping List,* July 31, 1858.

[5] Ibid., July 28, 1858.

[6] Ibid., August 7, 1858. *American Lloyd's Register of American and Foreign Shipping* (New York: 1859).

[7] Francis B. Dixon, *The Law of Shipping and Merchants' and Shipmasters' Guide* (New York: Henry Spear, 1859), p. 524.

[8] Boston *Shipping List,* August 11, 1858. There is a discrepancy in the spelling of the captain's name. It appears in the *Shipping List* as "Lloyd," but elsewhere, as in consular documents, as "Loyd," with a single "l."

[9] Ibid., August 28, 1858. Though the list of Boston exports to China for the period August 10 through 27 does not mention SNOW SQUALL specifically, she was the only vessel to clear from Boston for China during that period.

[10] Crew List, Boston, August 23, 1858, Records of the Bureau of Customs, Record Group 36. National Archives, Washington DC.

[11] Sewall Family Papers, Maine Maritime Museum, Bath, MS-22, Box 529, Folder 1, entry for March 27, 1883. I am indebted to Professor John Battick for this reference.

[12] Edmund Rice Diary, August 23, 1858–June 23, 1859. Steven J. Nitch Collection ©1997 by Steven J. Nitch.

[13] Cornelius Comstock Papers,

vol. C-92, Baker Library, Harvard Business School.

[14] *Boston Atlas,* April 9, 1851.

[15] Crew List, August 23, 1858, Record Group. 36, National Archives.

[16] Judicial Report of Cases Heard and Determined at Shanghai, U.S. Consulate, April 12, 1859. *National Archives Microfilm Publication M 112, Roll 4.* General Records of the Department of State, Record Group 59. National Archives.

[17] *North China Herald* (Shanghai), January 8, 1859.

[18] Moses and Eliza Rice to Edmund Rice, September 20, 1858. Steven J. Nitch Collection.

[19] Judicial Report.

[20] Certificate of Discharge, Shanghai, March 9, 1859. Records of the Department of State, Consular Records, Record Group 84. National Archives.

[21] Amended Crew List, New York, June 22, 1859. Records of the Bureau of Customs. Record Group 36. National Archives.

[22] *New York Herald,* June 23, 1859.

[23] *North China Herald* (Shanghai), March 26, 1859.

[24] Quarterly Consular Report from Amoy, *Microfilm Publication M 100,* General Records of the Department of State, Record Group 59. National Archives. The departure date is also given as January 11 in the *New York Herald* of April 5, 1861, which reported her arrival. There may again be the discrepancy between "clearance" and actual departure. See also the New York *Shipping and Commercial List* for April 6, 1861.

[25] To repeat, there was considerable debate in the maritime community as to whether or not these sails were worth their trouble.

[26] *New York Herald,* June 23, 1859. *S&CL,* June 25, 1859.

[27] William Arba Ellis, *Norwich University 1819–1911: Her History, Her Graduates, Her Roll of Honor* (Montpelier: The Capitol City Press, 1911), vol. 2, pages unnumbered.

[28] Letter to author from David R. Proper, The Memorial Libraries, Deerfield MA, December 21, 1993.

[29] Records and Logbooks of the Sandy Hook Pilots, Stephen B. Luce Library, SUNY Maritime College, Bronx NY. *New York Herald,* July 12 and 13, 1859.

[30] *S&CL,* March 24, 1860.

[31] Passenger list microfilm, New York Public Library, transcribed by Norman Brouwer.

[32] *Risk Book,* Mercantile Marine Insurance Company of Boston. Baker Library, Harvard Business School.

[33] *Report of the Commissioner of Navigation* (Washington: Government Printing Office, 1890), pp. 134–35.

[34] *New York Herald,* March 21, 1860.

[35] *S&CL,* May 26, 1860.

[36] Ibid., June 16, 1860.

[37] *North China Herald* (Shanghai), December 1 and 8, 1860.

[37] *New York Herald,* April 5, 1861. *S&CL,* April 6, 1861.

[38] *New York Herald,* April 5, 1861.

[39] Ibid., April 14, 1861.

*Vessels trading to ports beyond the Cape of Good Hope, or Cape Horn must have two suits of courses, top-sails, jibs, spankers, and fore topmast staysails and be metal sheathed within one foot of load line.*

—AMERICAN LLOYD'S REGISTER, 1861[1]

THE AMERICAN CIVIL WAR had begun. The question which immediately began to trouble American shipowners, SNOW SQUALL's Charles R. Green undoubtedly among them, was whether the Confederacy would issue "letters of marque" under which, as had happened during the War of 1812, armed, privately owned vessels, operating under the authority of a belligerent, could capture vessels of that belligerent's enemy. A letter in the *Times* of London, quoted in the *New York Herald,* opined that if the British government "conceded the Confederacy the right to be treated as a belligerent," then southern privateers might bring their prizes into neutral ports and have them condemned by Confederate prize courts.[2] It was a deeply troubling situation which induced panic in some quarters. By August at least five American vessels had been sold in Liverpool, and a report from Rio said that there were over a hundred American vessels lying there "which had their sails unbent and would possibly remain so for some time" for fear of rebel privateers.[3] In Java an American vessel reportedly was "unable to find employment here owing to her

# TWICE TO MELBOURNE AND BEYOND, AND TWO BAD SCARES: 1861–63

flag—the insurance offices declining at the moment to accept risks on property in American bottoms."[4]

It has to be emphasized that it is not a matter of how accurate some of this information was; the United States had never before had to deal with a major civil insurrection and there was obviously an active rumor mill in action, but this is what shipowners read in their morning paper, however they chose to deal with it. Green chose to wait and see. As it turned out, once the Union blockade was in place Confederate privateers lacked ports into which they could bring prizes for condemnation by a prize court. The Confederate navy's raiders, such as the CSS ALABAMA and CSS FLORIDA commanded by officers of the Confederate navy, burned or "bonded" their captures. The Confederacy would ultimately wound Charles Green financially with the burning of one of his vessels. Meanwhile Virginian Matthew Fontaine Maury, whose wind and current charts and sailing directions had revolutionized the merchant marine's choice of sailing routes, had cast his lot with the Confederacy. As a tribute to his sterling hydrographic achievements, in happier times he had been elected a member of the venerable and prestigious Marine Society of Salem, Massachusetts. When news of Maury's defection reached Salem, the outraged Yankee mariners ordered that his portrait be turned with its face to the wall.

On April 21 the HARRY BLUFF, one of the two ships Green owned with St. Croix Redman, arrived at New York in ballast under Captain Redman from Havre via Mobile, apparently having gotten out in the nick of time, and again arrived back from Havre in ballast in early October.[5] The BLUFF's outward cargoes were almost certainly cotton. The Confederacy had decreed an embargo on cotton exports and while Britain, for the time being, enjoyed a substantial stockpile, there was a severe shortage in France. Meanwhile, by presidential proclamation, the United States began seizing Southern-owned or partially Southern-owned vessels at New York and Baltimore. On September 21 New York customs surveyor Andrews seized the Massachusetts-built bark LAMPLIGHTER, which was one-eighth owned in Charleston and one-sixteenth in Savannah. "After the shares which are forfeited to the federal government have been disposed of the vessel will be allowed to proceed on her voyage," reported the *Herald*.[6] A little over a year later, in October 1862, LAMPLIGHTER was captured and burned by the Confederate raider ALABAMA.

By mid October seamen were a scarce item at New York, "the government having induced a great number to ship in the Navy."[7] In early November came the news that Captain Charles Wilkes of the United States Navy had forcibly removed Confederate Commissioners Mason and Slidell, bound for England, from the British Royal Mail steamer TRENT off Cuba. The Confederates were held at Fort Warren, an island in Boston Harbor, in fairly comfortable quarters (allowed to keep their considerable hoard of Cuban "segars" and to receive dainties from shore). Wilkes received a hero's welcome when he arrived at New York, but he had stopped and boarded a vessel flying a neutral flag and Britain felt the insult deeply. British forces in the Canadian Maritimes near the Maine border were beefed up while diplomatic negotiations proceeded, and there was a distinct possibility of an Anglo-American war. At the end of 1861 the United States backed down; in early 1862 the commissioners at last left for England aboard a British warship and the tumult subsided, though to this day it raises interesting questions of international law and the rights of neutrals in wartime.

Meanwhile Charles Green had business to attend to. In August freights to San Francisco had been "very dull," reported at twenty-five to twenty-seven cents a cubic foot though it was "understood" that lower rates had been accepted. By mid September things had not much improved to San Francisco but freights to Australia kept edging upward. By the third week in September freights to Melbourne were thirty pence a foot ($0.525) and by early October they had risen to thirty-two and a half pence a foot ($0.568).[8] (Freights to Australia were quoted at New York in sterling rather than dollars since they would be collected at Sydney or Melbourne.) The San Francisco market remained persistently "dull," as SNOW SQUALL lay across the East River at Wetmore's Basin in Brooklyn, but when Melbourne freights rose gratifyingly Charles Green made up his mind. On October 5, though SNOW SQUALL still lay at Wetmore's, she was listed as preparing to sail for Melbourne. By October 19 she was loading at East River Pier 10. Maillar, Lord, and Quereau's Kangaroo Line, whose Wall Street office at number 108 was fairly near Green's, were the New York agents. SNOW SQUALL was advertised as "the extreme out and out clipper," having "elegant state-room accommodations." Lord and Company would handle things in Melbourne.[9]

From the report of James F. Maguire, United States consul in Melbourne, American carriages continued to be in demand and "agricultural implements and harvest tools of American make are also much used."[10] At New York SNOW SQUALL loaded fifty-two "packages" of carriages and a miscellaneous cargo of hardware. Axes were a large item as were shovels and spades, sluice forks, picks, handles, and brooms. There were several large consignments of "oil," "coal oil," and "kerosene oil." Foodstuffs included canned oysters and lobster, hops, and yeast powder. Down below, as "stiffening," were a hundred tons of pig iron.[11] There were five passengers in the "elegant accommodations": Mr. and Mrs. Norton, and Messrs. John Flynn, M. Symonds and V. B. Nolton.[12] SNOW SQUALL had a new captain, twenty-nine-year-old James Sullivan Dillingham, Jr., a native of West Harwich, Massachusetts, newly listed on the American Shipmasters Association's *Register of Approved Shipmasters.*[13] He had commanded the ships NABOB and KIT CARSON and most recently had served as one of the "Acting Masters" of USS RHODE ISLAND, sometimes known as "Little Rhody," under Lieutenant Stephen D. Trenchard. Apparently life in the navy did not suit Dillingham, for he obtained his discharge shortly before assuming command of SNOW SQUALL. One suspects that life aboard a navy supply ship was just a little bit too dull for a man who had been around Cape Horn!

Captain James Sullivan Dillingham, Jr., took command of SNOW SQUALL in 1861 after a short stretch in the U.S. Navy. Here, in a family portrait, he stands on the left. The seated gentleman is James S. Dillingham, Sr.

At the same time that SNOW SQUALL was loading for Melbourne, another of Green's ships was about to head that way. The HARRY BLUFF, glowingly advertised as "the A-1 extreme clipper ship" (which was stretching things more than a bit), was loading at Pier 13 with "fine accommodations for first and second cabin passengers all on deck. The accommodations for second cabin passengers are unsurpassed for comfort, light, and ventilation." The BLUFF was to run in R. W. Cameron's Pioneer Line, carrying the U.S. mails.[14]

Dillingham shipped a crew of nineteen in New York. Twenty-eight-year-old Richard Sears, a native of Massachusetts, was chief mate, with twenty-two-year-old N. B. Washburn, another Massachusetts Yankee, as second. Two of the crew were apparently African Americans, described as "complexion black, hair woolly." These were Peter Musell, born in Canada, and Shepperd Patterson, a Pennsylvanian. The average age of the crew was just under twenty- five. The oldest man aboard was thirty-seven-year-old John McIntire. Wages are listed only for crew members: three at twelve dollars a month and one at ten. Significantly, all four deserted, three at Melbourne and one a few months later at Penang.[15] Apparently it was a reasonably uneventful passage, as Captain Dillingham does not seem to have filed an extended protest with Consul Maguire at Melbourne following his arrival on February 19, 1862,[16] just the standard piece of printed "boiler plate" in which a captain attested to "boisterous and tempestuous weather on the voyage."[17] The desertion problem at Melbourne was a trying one for both captain and consul. Maguire complained that captains too often paid a seaman all or part of his wages and winked at his desertion, not giving him a proper discharge, then swore before the consul that he had used "all lawful means to prevent such an occurrence." Had the seaman been properly discharged, the captain, by law, was supposed to deposit three months' extra wages with the consul to provide for his expenses until he re-shipped. Under Melbourne port regulations, without a proper discharge he could not legally ship out and eventually "becomes a heavy charge upon the government," the lack of a discharge "being no obstacle to his obtaining relief from the consul."[18] Obviously Maguire was becoming more than a little annoyed. In any case, Dillingham shipped three replacements for his deserters, two at about seventeen dollars a month and the third, an "ordinary seaman," at about thirteen,[19] and cleared for Anjer Point in ballast on March 16.[20]

SNOW SQUALL arrived at Singapore on April 21, consigned to Hutchinson and Company. Apparently Ordinary Seaman James Neill, shipped at Melbourne, was lost overboard on April 2. Having shipped two new hands at twelve dollars a month, SNOW SQUALL left for New York via Penang on either May 6 or 8. She lost one seaman to desertion in Penang and discharged the carpenter.[21] There was one anxious period off the Cape of Good Hope on July 17 when SNOW SQUALL "experienced an exceedingly violent gale from the westward, with a very high irregular sea, causing the ship to labor heavily." She was off the Cape for nine days in company with "more than twenty ships." After passing the Cape she experienced "alternate light westerly winds, calms, and gales," passed Saint Helena on July 31, crossed the equator on August 14 in 44° 30' west longitude, and before arriving at New York was "three days to the northward of the Capes of Delaware." Captain Dillingham had been completely out of touch with the progress of the Civil War since reading a New York newspaper of April 1 in Singapore or Penang, so it was with gratitude that on August 30 he spoke the schooner N. B. BORDEN bound from Bristol, Rhode Island, for Cuba. Captain Collins kindly gave him recent papers which brought him up to date. Later that day he also spoke the bark BRUNSWICK, headed for New Orleans, which had fallen to Union forces on April 25, and then arrived at New York on September 5, a hundred days out of Penang with "tin, rubber, pepper, &c." consigned to owner Green.[22] SNOW SQUALL anchored out "in the stream" for several days, then by September 9 was unloading at East River Pier 11.[23]

By September 13 it was announced that SNOW SQUALL's next voyage would be out to Melbourne for R. W. Cameron and Company. As on the previous voyage, the cargo was extremely varied and almost entirely hardware items with a bit of tobacco, mackerel, and pork thrown in. Once again there were over six hundred cases of kerosene, coal oil, and naptha, an indication that SNOW SQUALL was a repeat early carrier in what came to be known as the "case oil" trade. There were eight carriages and twenty-seven "boxes of carriages," twenty boxes of rolling pins, hatchets, axe handles, axles, and brooms, and nearly fifteen thousand "pieces [of] lumber."[24] It may be that to load this lumber through the rectangular cargo port in the 'tween-decks near the foremast SNOW SQUALL shifted over to Ford's Basin by November 19.[25]

Captain Dillingham brought his twenty-one-year-old wife with him. Annie Maria Shillaber Dillingham was five feet, four inches tall, described in the crew list as having a light complexion and dark hair. Also aboard was an Ellen Boyd, but whether she was a friend of Mrs. Dillingham's or had been shipped as a stewardess is unknown. There were twenty names on the crew list (including Mrs. Dillingham), and Richard Sears again shipped as chief mate.[26] SNOW SQUALL began her voyage shortly after 9:00 AM when the steam tug DAY SPRING brought Captain Dillingham and the Sandy Hook pilot out.[27] The crew hove the anchor up with "strong breezes from the North West and fine weather." At 10:00 AM the tug cast off and the crew set topsails and the foresail. An hour later the pilot left in the pilot schooner's pulling boat and SNOW SQUALL set "all plain sail." At noon the twin red sandstone towers of the lights on New Jersey's Navesink Highlands bore "W.N.W. ½ W distant Eighteen miles," and Dillingham began his log, with winds and courses noted on a slate from noon to noon and scrupulously copied into the logbook each day by Chief Mate Sears, with whatever additions and corrections Captain Dillingham chose to make.

Although December 6 and 7 were squally, with SNOW SQUALL for a time running under "close reefed topsails" alone, by the end of the seventh conditions had moderated and it was possible to set the royals. Nothing more "of moment" occurred on the voyage (though "pumps were carefully attended to") until on February 16 SNOW SQUALL "passed Port Phillip's Head at the entrance to Hobsons Bay" on the final leg towards Melbourne, which lies at the north end of Hobsons Bay. The weather was threatening, with a strong breeze, when SNOW SQUALL anchored about 8:30 PM with fifty-five fathoms of chain, furled the sails, and set the watch. By midnight it was "thick and rainy" with a strong breeze. "So ends... this passage of 76 days from New York."[28] It is approximately thirty miles from Port Phillip's Head to Hobsons Bay. In the nineteenth century the bay itself, roughly three and a half miles wide and two miles deep, was only partially useful as an anchorage, "nearly all the eastern half of the bay being occupied by a shallow bank." However there was "good anchorage in 3 to 5 fathoms, over stiff mud and clay."[29] When news of SNOW SQUALL's arrival reached the United States, the Portland, Maine, *Daily Press* called it "an extraordinary passage."[30]

Approach to Melbourne Harbour on Australia's south coast. SNOW SQUALL made two voyages to Melbourne, arriving in February 1862 and 1863. On the second voyage she lost both anchors. New anchors and chain had to be brought out from shore.
AUSTRALIAN NATIONAL MARITIME MUSEUM, SYDNEY

The next morning Captain Dillingham and the pilot went ashore. Dillingham came back aboard at five in "strong breezes and thick rainy weather" and at eight they let go the starboard anchor with fifty fathoms of chain and increased the scope to seventy-five fathoms on the port. The following day began with "fresh gales and thick foggy rainy weather" with a "heavy short sea heaving into the bay." Although Dillingham does not give the direction from which the gales were blowing, Port Phillip Bay is fairly shallow (in many places less than sixty feet deep), and a gale from the south across that thirty-mile shallow fetch would have produced the conditions he describes, with SNOW SQUALL's bow pitching upwards repeatedly and bringing the anchor chain up short. At four in the morning "paid out all of the port chain and 35 fathoms on the starboard. The ship pitching hard and surging very heavy on her chains."

At two in the afternoon the port anchor chain parted and they "paid out all our starboard one and brought her up again," setting a signal for a pilot (an ensign at the fore topgallant masthead) and one for a steamer (a "rendezvous" flag at the peak of the mizzen).[31] At three the pilot arrived and at four a steamer brought an anchor and forty-five fathoms of chain, giving SNOW SQUALL's crew the end and carrying out the anchor. By that time the weather was beginning to moderate somewhat though the weather was still "thick and rainy." At eight the next morning SNOW SQUALL's crew began the slow process of "heaving ahead" and had the port anchor up by noon and the starboard anchor up by three. The steam tug HERCULES took SNOW SQUALL in tow and brought her further in to anchor again, with "moderate breezes from the west and fine weather" at last. SNOW SQUALL began lightering cargo ashore on Friday, February 20, though the weather was again "unsettled." A week later Captain Dillingham, Chief Mate Sears, and the carpenter, Edward Seaburg, appeared before U.S. Consul Blanchard to make a marine protest relating the events.

Dillingham had problems with desertions in Melbourne. In a deposition before Consul Blanchard he swore that between March 7 and 9 eight seamen had jumped ship before SNOW

Queen's Wharf at Melbourne's
West End.
AUSTRALIAN NATIONAL MARITIME
MUSEUM, SYDNEY

SQUALL departed for Penang via Anjer in ballast.[32] There is, however, a slight discrepancy. Dillingham's deposition is dated March
21. However the Melbourne *Argus* reported that she "entered out"
on March 13 and finally cleared on March 16.[33] She arrived at
Singapore, consigned to Hutchinson again, on April 28 and the
Singapore newspaper reported that her actual departure date was
March 24. It may well be that, after clearing and the necessary
paperwork taken care of, Captain Dillingham simply had to wait
for favorable winds before actually setting sail. She is listed as
"repairing" at Singapore in early to mid May and left for Penang
on the nineteenth,[34] arriving at Penang on May 29 and sailing for
New York on June 11.[35]

SNOW SQUALL arrived at New York on September 14 and
apparently anchored below the city before proceeding to East
River Pier 46 the next day. The shipping news in the *New York
Herald* of September 16 was matter of fact: "Arrived ship Snow
Squall, Dillingham, Penang 94 days, with mdse. to Chas R. Green.

June 20 lat 5 29N. lon 93 25E. spoke ship Living Age of Bucksport, from Akyab for Falmouth. 40 days out."[36] But the story on page three of the *Herald*—and on the front page of the *Times*—was a rouser. The *Times* headlined it, just below a story on the siege of Charleston:

ANOTHER PIRATE AFLOAT
A Bark-rigged cruiser in the South Pacific—
Her Attempts to Capture the Clipper Ship
Snow Squall—Interesting Narrative of
Capt. Dillingham—Description of the Rover—
A suspicious Steamer Seen.

The *Times* had the story *slightly* wrong. SNOW SQUALL's encounter with CSS TUSCALOOSA took place in the Atlantic, not the Pacific, just off the west coast of South Africa, but Dillingham's was a good yarn, just the same. On July 28, "lat. 33° 05 south, lon. 15° 45' east Cape of Good Hope, bearing southeast by south, one half

Singapore, circa 1850. SNOW SQUALL called at Singapore in 1863. On arrival at New York she discharged 1,503 slabs of tin, which was a major Singapore export. It was shipped loose in slabs, about forty slabs to a ton. A nineteenth-century manual on stowage advised that a "careful tally" should be kept when loading tin.
MAINE MARITIME MUSEUM

east, distant 160 miles; 3¼ o'clock PM, made a sail ahead, with which we came up very rapidly." The stories in the *Herald* and the *Times* were apparently transcribed directly from SNOW SQUALL's logbook and differ in a few non-fatal details but Dillingham's account, as printed in the *Times*, continued:

> Soon made her out to be a bark standing the same course as ourselves, under whole topsails, we having royal and topsail stunsails set. Set our ensign, which was answered by the American ensign. We ran under her lee to speak to her. As we approached her we observed no name on her stern, which aroused our suspicions. We were soon hailed, "Where from and bound?"; which having answered, we asked "What ship?" and received for reply, "Heave to, and I'll send a boat alongside of you." To which we promptly replied, "Aye, aye." At this moment her three starboard ports were opened and as many guns run out, and upon us, we being about a ship's length from her.
>
> Of course, we were now fully aware of the character of the stranger, and having a smart ship under foot, were fully resolved to surrender only when the last hope of escape was gone. Requesting my wife to return to the cabin, I ordered the helm hove up and all possible sail made. The stranger, now observing our movements, fired a blank shot at us, which, having no effect, was soon followed by a solid shot, which fell short about thirty feet; at the same time the Confederate flag took the place of the Stars and Stripes. We now shot ahead of her, when she made sail as fast as possible, and gave chase after us. It soon became but too apparent that she was too light for us, being in good ballast trim, while we were very deep—the wind in the meantime becoming light and unsteady, with every prospect of a calm.
>
> We therefore, on consultation, deemed it advisable to lighten the ship as the only possible chance of escape

and immediately stove several casks of water, and hove overboard a considerable quantity of heavy provisions, and then reluctantly sacrificed a small portion of the cargo. At about 6 o'clock the chase swung broadside to and fired a shot at us, but without effect, and then continued the chase. Soon after this, finding we were distancing him, we desisted from lightening the ship, all hands uniting in thanks to God for His gracious deliverance.

There is a Winslow Homer wood engraving which appeared in *Harper's Weekly*. It depicts an American captain and his wife, spyglass in hand, observing the rapid approach of the dreaded Confederate raider ALABAMA. It is a moment of high drama, for it is obvious that the American vessel is doomed, a scenario which was played out all too often with the hapless captain later watching from the deck of the ALABAMA as flames licked up at the sails and rigging of his recent command and possibly lost investment. Approaching the equator on September 1 Dillingham sighted a steamer, which headed towards SNOW SQUALL "evidently desiring to communicate with us. Not fancying his movements, we hauled by the wind under all sail." Dillingham changed course after dark, just in case, and reached New York safely.

There is another version of SNOW SQUALL's narrow escape, the deck log of the Confederate raider TUSCALOOSA. Captured off Brazil by the CSS ALABAMA and fitted out, renamed, and armed as a "tender," the 348-ton bark CONRAD, built in Philadelphia in 1857, was described by one of ALABAMA's officers as "a beautiful specimen of an American clipper," and as "new, well-found, and fast."[37] However, the CONRAD was carrying cotton when captured and typically vessels built for that trade were a good deal bluffer and "boxier" than SNOW SQUALL. The TUSCALOOSA's log differs, from SNOW SQUALL's, on several interesting points. Dillingham wrote of the wind becoming "light and unsteady." The Confederate log speaks of a "stronger breeze & squally weather with drizzling rain with heavy sea." After the TUSCALOOSA had fired the solid shot that fell short, "we loaded a second time on account of the strong breeze and *her being the clipper ship the Snow Squall* [emphasis added] she left us very rapidly after loading we trained on her again and fired but it also fell short." The TUSCALOOSA continued the chase until six in the evening with all sail set, and an hour and a half later was sailing close-reefed.[38] Obviously weather conditions so close onshore can change rapidly, but whether Captain Dillingham was justifying his actions in jettisoning cargo and stores, or Captain Low of the TUSCALOOSA was figuratively throwing up his hands is impossible to say. In any case SNOW SQUALL discharged a cargo at New York of tin, pearl sago, sago flour, pepper, chairs, gum benzoine, tapioca, cubebs (a spice similar to pepper), nutmeg, and other items.[39] American clipper historians Octavius Howe and Frederick Matthews claim that Captain Dillingham was handsomely rewarded by the New York insurance underwriters for having saved SNOW SQUALL and her cargo, but it has not been possible to verify this.

## NOTES

[1] *American Lloyd's Register of American and Foreign Shipping* (New York: E&G Blunt, 1861), p. xxiii.

[2] *New York Herald,* June 6, 1861.

[3] Ibid., September 8, 1861.

[4] Ibid., September 12, 1861.

[5] Ibid., April 22, 1861; October 10, 1861.

[6] Ibid., September 22, 1861.

[7] Ibid., October 19, 1861.

[8] New York *Shipping and Commercial List,* August 3, 1861—October 2, 1861. The exchange rate, as published in I. R. Butts's *The Merchants' & Shipmasters' Manual* (New York: I. R. Butts, 1860), p. 118, was that fourpence sterling equaled seven cents U.S. or a rate of 1d=1.75¢. £= $4.84. As the Civil War dragged on, the American paper currency (the "greenback") lost much of its value. By 1864, when it became necessary to forward SNOW SQUALL's cargo, payment had to be made in gold, not paper.

[9] *S&CL,* October 5, 19, and 23, 1861.

[10] *Commercial Relations of the United States with All Foreign Nations for the Year Ending Sept. 30, 1861* (Washington: Government Printing Office, 1862), p. 91.

[11] *Melbourne Argus,* February 20, 1862.

[12] Ibid.

[13] Typescript copy of 1864 *Register of Approved Shipmasters and Officers of Merchant Vessels Holding Commissions from the American Shipmasters Association.* Dillingham was #397. Phillips Memorial Library, Penobscot Marine Museum, Searsport, ME.

[14] *New York Herald,* November 8, 1861.

[15] Records of the Bureau of Customs, New York, July 11, 1861, Record Group 36. Records of the Foreign Service Posts of the United States, "Arrivals and Departures," Consulate General, Melbourne, 1862, No. 13, February 19, 1862. Record Group 84. National Archives, Washington, DC.

[16] *Melbourne Argus,* February 20 and 21, 1862.

[17] "Arrivals and Departures," February 19, 1862. Record Group 84. National Archives.

[18] *Commercial Relations,* p. 91.

[19] "Arrivals and Departures," Record Group 84. National Archives.

[20] *Melbourne Argus,* March 18, 1862.

[21] *Singapore Straits Times,* April 26, 1862. Departure from *Straits Times,* n.d. Loss of Neill from crew list.

[22] *New York Herald,* September 6, 1862.

[23] *S&CL,* September 6 and 10, 1862.

[24] *Melbourne Argus,* February 18, 1863.

[25] *S&CL,* November 19-29, 1862.

[26] Records of the Bureau of Customs, Record Group 36. National Archives. The date of the original crew list is uncertain, but it was returned to the Custom House at New York on SNOW SQUALL's return in September 1863. (Date illegible.)

[27] "Arrivals and Departures," Record Group 84. National Archives. Dillingham's protest filed at Melbourne February 19, 1863.

[28] Ibid.

[29] Alexander George Finlay, F. R. G. S., *A Directory for the Navigation of the South Pacific Ocean* (London: Richard Holmes Laurie, 1884), p. 1044.

[30] *Portland Daily Press,* April 27, 1863.

[31] James Horsburgh, *The India Directory* (London: William H. Allen, 1855), 7th edition, p. 120.

[32] "Arrivals and Departures," Record Group 84. National Archives. Dillingham's sworn statement of deserters.

[33] *Melbourne Argus,* March 14 and 17, 1863.

[34] *Singapore Straits Times,* May 2, 5, 16, and 19, 1863.

[35] *Portland Daily Press,* July 30, August 21, 1863. *New York Herald,* September 15, 1863.

[36] *New York Herald,* September 16, 1863.

[37] *The Logs of the CSS ALABAMA and the CSS TUSCALOOSA Kept by Lieutenant John Low, CSN.* W. Stanley Hoole, ed., (University of Alabama, Confederate Publishing Company, 1972), p. ix.

[38] Ibid., pp. 46–47.

[39] *S&CL,* September 19, 1863.

*Before her anchors could be made ready, she was carried forcibly upon the rocks at the entrance of the Strait of leMaire, where she remained fast.... A fresh breeze sprung up when the ship was floated off and was worked clear.*

—CAPTAIN JAMES S. DILLINGHAM, JR.[1]

SNOW SQUALL had arrived in New York in September 1863 and was "seen" by an American Lloyd's surveyor in November. Though her metal sheathing, put on in December 1860, was perilously close to the end of what the underwriters termed its useful life for insurance purposes, it was not replaced, perhaps because of wartime shortages. The surveyor classed her A-2—meaning that shippers should perhaps think hard about using her for highly perishable cargo. When Lloyd's began classing American vessels in 1858, SNOW SQUALL received A-1½ rating because she was built of a variety of woods. At twelve and a half years, SNOW SQUALL was not a "young" vessel by any means, but over the years Charles Green had apparently maintained her well, putting in twenty new hanging knees and a "new lower rig" as needed.

SNOW SQUALL had had a close call with TUSCALOOSA and Green had lost his DICTATOR to the Confederate raider GEORGIA in late April, but rather than joining other shipowners in panicking, as he prepared to send SNOW SQUALL to sea once more he was dickering with the shipbuilding Sewalls of Bath, Maine, for a new

# 10

# THE FATAL VOYAGE: 1864

ship to replace DICTATOR. Apparently Captain Simonson, of the New York firm of Cornelius Comstock, one of Green's Wall Street neighbors, had been in Bath on his behalf to look at a new ship under construction, though a definite deal had yet to be struck.

San Francisco freights had been holding fairly steady at thirty-five to forty cents per cubic foot and by November 14 SNOW SQUALL was at Pier 46 on the East River, "up" for San Francisco in Comstock's Clipper Line.[2] The same issue of New York's *Shipping and Commercial List* that reported this ran a brief story on a serious problem. Notwithstanding other American shipowners reflagging their vessels, and in some cases laying them up because of Confederate raiders, there was a shortage of seamen for American vessels. The U.S. Navy had been draining off the available supply since the war started, and the *List* predicted that the shortage would "cause serious embarrassment to the maritime commerce of the Country."[3] About a week later it reported that only about a quarter of the vessels in New York seeking overseas cargoes "are covered by the American flag, whose shelter commerce once so eagerly sought."[4] Not in the case of Charles R. Green, who bucked the tide, though SNOW SQUALL's imminent departure for San Francisco was in the "coasting" trade reserved (still) to American-flag vessels. Long-ago decisions now enshrined as accomplished deeds were made on evidences and nuances of evidence which have mostly since disappeared. Green took gambles and seems to have won a good many of them, but all a historian can do is to guess what hunches such a dimly visible protagonist played.

As mentioned, SNOW SQUALL was to run in Cornelius Comstock's "Clipper Line for San Francisco." Although details are sketchy, Comstock, with offices at 96 Wall Street, a few minutes' walk from Charles Green's, was established as a "shipping and commission merchant" by 1859. By the late fall of 1863, as SNOW SQUALL prepared to receive cargo, Comstock's San Francisco contact was one Albert Dibblee, a transplanted Hudson Valley New Yorker, with whom Comstock would maintain relations long after SNOW SQUALL. Shipowner Green contracted with Comstock to advertise for and handle incoming freight. Comstock took a small percentage ($2\frac{1}{2}$ percent) off the top and guaranteed Green a certain amount, with anything over the guarantee going to Comstock in lieu of New York freight commissions.

Green, for his part, agreed to give SNOW SQUALL a fresh coat of black paint outside and white in the 'tween-decks, and in the case of Green's ship the HARRY BLUFF, had to make sure there was a "full set of patent ventilators." The ship "shall be kept tight, staunch, well fitted, and provided with every requisite, and with men and provisions necessary for such a voyage." Meanwhile Comstock had local printer George Nesbitt run off a batch of colorful "clipper cards" advertising the voyage, which one George Clark passed out around the South Street waterfront at a dollar per hundred.[5] It is not known if Comstock had a muslin advertising banner lettered for SNOW SQUALL, though it was often done.

Item number one on the cargo list was just over eighty tons of steamer lump coal, consigned to Dibblee and Hyde as Comstock's San Francisco agents, for which the freight was nearly

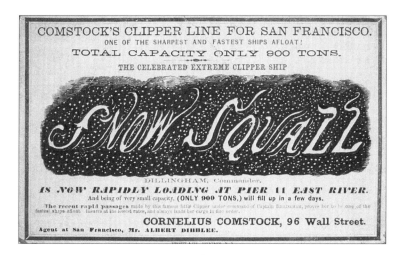

Clipper card for SNOW SQUALL's 1864 voyage to San Francisco in Comstock's Clipper Line. Printed by South Street-area printer George Nesbitt, one George Clark passed them out around the waterfront for a fee of a dollar per hundred.
PORTLAND HARBOR MUSEUM

seventeen hundred dollars. On December 12, E. Franklin Glaser signed the receipt on Green's behalf, noting that "quantity unknown."[6] This coal, and its condition and quantity once it reached San Francisco, would cause a great deal of contention later on. As with SNOW SQUALL's other previous San Francisco cargoes a great variety of goods came aboard: two hundred cases of alcohol, fifty cases of canned lobster (a popular "convenience food" in nineteenth-century California), tobacco, whisky, and what was simply described as "liquor." Sixteen carboys of acid were stowed on deck. The last cargo item to come aboard was a considerable quantity of explosives from the Hazard Powder Company of Delaware for a freight charge of $993.40 (apparently Hazard had been recently and *very* quietly bought up by its Delaware neighbor, E. I. du Pont). By New York Harbor regulations this had to be loaded well out in the harbor at Bedloe's Island, and Captain Dillingham billed Comstock fifteen dollars for "moving ship to take powder."[7] It must be remembered that the freight money was to be collected in San Francisco, so both Green and Comstock had made fairly substantial outlays in New York and would not see a return on their investments for a number of months.

On this voyage SNOW SQUALL carried a crew of nineteen: a first mate at fifty dollars a month, a second mate at thirty-five, a carpenter, steward, and cook at thirty each and seven hands (pre-

*The Fatal Voyage*     *181*

sumably skilled able-bodied seamen) at twenty-five dollars, four at
twenty, one at eighteen, and two "boys," who made a piddling ten
dollars a month each. Captain Dillingham was paid $125 per
month.[8] A figure of "primage" at 5 percent appears in Comstock's
tally of freight loaded but it is unclear if this went to Dillingham
as a bonus as had been the custom in the past (referred to tongue-
in-cheek as a captain's "hat money"), or if it was reserved as
rebates for shippers who did all of their business with a single carrier like Comstock. One of the boys was sixteen-year-old Hubert
Taylor, whose father ran a successful ironworks in Brooklyn. Like
the clipper's teenaged diarist, Edmund Rice, on the 1858 voyage,
arrangements had obviously been made to get the youngster
signed on, either through Cornelius Comstock or, as seems more
likely, through the senior Taylor's Wall Street connections.

Young Hubert, who kept a fascinating, though somewhat
sketchy, journal on the voyage, saw shipping on SNOW SQUALL as a
means of getting to San Francisco to join a chum who was travelling out there by steamer. He was an enterprising youth who had
organized a teenage militia in Brooklyn and had been offered, and
turned down, an appointment to West Point, as he had his heart
set on joining SNOW SQUALL, though he immediately regretted it.
A portrait of Hubert, painted when he was twenty (which includes
what *might* be SNOW SQUALL in the background) shows a slight,
serious young man with reddish-brown hair, by then sporting a
wispy goatee.

Hubert began his pocket diary on New Year's Day, the day
before SNOW SQUALL was to sail. He spent New Year's working
hard and turned in late, longing "to be ashore to enjoy myself
with the rest of the folks" and accounting himself "very lonesome"
as he gazed mournfully across to the lights on the dim Brooklyn
shore.[9] He does not record where he berthed aboard the ship but
it seems unlikely that his doting father would have permitted
him to be thrown in with the rest of the crew, who had been
scraped up somehow from the New York waterfront, and there
is some (though admittedly skimpy) evidence that he was at least

At the age of sixteen, Brooklyn native Hubert Taylor signed on for the voyage for ten dollars a month as a means of getting to San Francisco. This portrait by Junius Brutus Stearns, a friend of the Taylor family, was painted when Hubert was twenty. The ship in the background is presumably SNOW SQUALL.
COURTESY OF JEREMY TAYLOR

minimally kept an eye on. In any case, SNOW SQUALL sailed on January 2. Hubert recorded that it was "very cold. Snow & Ice on deck. I could hardly stand up, fingers and feet nearly frozen." He had his last sight of land (probably New Jersey's Navesink Highlands) early on that short January afternoon and wished himself "home, beside a warm fire."

At least, unaccustomed as he was to rough shipboard victuals, the steward and cook took pity on him and slipped him some leftovers from the cabin table. Apparently cargo stowage had not been to Captain Dillingham's liking, as day after weary day all hands were employed "shifting cargo." Not quite two weeks out of New York, on a night watch pumping ship, Hubert got into an altercation with fellow crew member "Irish Jim," and recorded triumphantly that he'd won the tussle by nailing Jim "right under the eyes." On January 16 there was a bit of excitement when SNOW SQUALL was "chased by two vessels supposed to be privateers," one of which, wrote Hubert, was a steamer. "We about ship and soon got out of her reach," rejoicing that SNOW SQUALL was a "fast Sailing Vessel." Captain Dillingham may be excused for having been prudent to the point of mild paranoia, because the preferred route towards Cape Horn was just off the easternmost point of Brazil, Cape St. Roque, and Confederate commerce raiders, such as CSS FLORIDA, were known to be lurking there, but one must also understand that a sixteen-year-old green hand's remarks may overstate the facts.

The diary then has a long gap, broken only by the sighting of an unidentified sail on February 2. But on February 24 they sighted land, and about four that afternoon SNOW SQUALL "struck ashore on Tiera del fuego [sic] in trying to go through Strait of le Maire." Patagonia is, in general, a thoroughly inhospitable coast with a few anchorages suitable for brief layovers, and then, as now, with no port where repairs could be had. The native Fuegians, whose campfires, seen from afar, had given the large island its English name of "Land of Fire," were unpredictable aborigines and well-meaning British attempts to "civilize" them had failed utterly. They simply did not wish to be "civilized" and on occasion had massacred those who had attempted it, including those who had kidnapped Fuegians in order to "educate" them and return them to raise their compatriots to a presumably higher level of culture. Tierra del Fuego was, in short, a miserable and dangerous place in which to meet disaster.

Le Maire Strait is about twelve miles wide. It is a spectacular landscape with snow- and ice-covered mountains rising almost vertically on the mainland to about six thousand feet above the sea, a South Atlantic Ice Age geography even in mid summer. It offered a shortcut that shaved a day, more or less, off the passage to the Pacific around Cape Horn. Earlier captains had avoided the whole encounter by running outside of the Falkland Islands, some three hundred miles to the eastward, but by mid century it was pretty

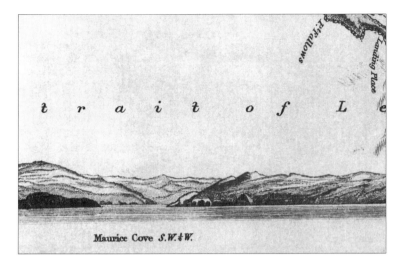

Maurice Cove S.W.¼W.

Strait of le Maire, shown in an Admiralty Hydrographic Office chart dated 1841: *The South-Eastern part of Tierra Del Fuego (with Staten Island, Cape Horn, and Diego Ramirez Islands),* surveyed by Captain Robert FitzRoy, R.N., and the officers of HMS BEAGLE.
STEPHEN PHILLIPS MEMORIAL LIBRARY, PENOBSCOT MARINE MUSEUM

Strait of le Maire.
PHOTO BY C. W. ELIOT PAINE, COURTESY OF DR. JOHN CONSTABLE

well agreed that this was an unnecessarily chicken-hearted approach. Dillingham had made at least one run to San Francisco, in 1857 in the clipper KIT CARSON, so he was familiar with his options. He did have the two volumes of Horsburgh's *Sailing Directions* (one of the "standard" guides) aboard,[10] and Horsburgh's description of le Maire was brief and rather laconic. Other guides to South Atlantic navigation spoke repeatedly of le Maire's sometimes nasty tide rips, cautioning captains to choose their slant of wind and time of tide with care before attemping the inside passage and suggesting that it had best be done by daylight.

As Captain Dillingham described the events of February 25 (his date and Hubert Taylor's differ), SNOW SQUALL "was standing along the *Land* [emphasis is Dillingham's], weather moderate, rain falling, and wind light from the southward and eastward." At 1:30 PM, with the ship about nine miles offshore, the wind came around to the northeast. "At Four PM while still standing along shore the *wind suddenly died away* and the *current* rapidly *swept the ship in towards shore*, so that in a few moments, and *before her anchors could be made ready,* she was *carried forcibly upon the rocks* at the entrance of the *Strait of Le Maire,* where she remained fast."[11] Dillingham ordered the boats put overboard (which Taylor interpreted as preparing to abandon ship) and ran out a line with an anchor to try to heave the vessel off, but by the time these were adjusted, "a fresh breeze sprung up when the *ship floated off and was worked clear.*" He had to order the 270-foot cable (worth eighty dollars) cut away.[12] A survey revealed that the rudder was badly damaged and that there were several feet of water in the hold. Dillingham decided to run northeast to Port Stanley at the eastern end of East Falkland Island, the only port of refuge where SNOW SQUALL might be repaired.

It was not a decision he took lightly. Repairs there were notoriously expensive, as he had discovered in January 1860 when he brought his leaking KIT CARSON into Stanley for "extra pumps," but he had no other option. There simply were no ports of refuge on the mainland within practical reach. Curiously, his narrative of events makes mention of an attempt to "weather Cape Horn," though "ultimately" he set a course for Stanley, where SNOW SQUALL arrived on March 2. Dillingham's course towards the Falklands presumed a landfall at tiny, bluff Beauchêne Island at the southwestern end of the archipelago. Fortunately the weather seems to have held reasonably fair. Although the fact was not published until about forty years later, after heavy weather off Cape Horn a strong current sets in which sets vessels much more to the northeast than they reckoned. The south shore of East Falkland, particularly around Bull Point, is littered with the bones of vessels whose captains were further inshore than they thought. As one walks about Bull Point today, burrowing "Jackass" (Magellanic) penguins peer shyly out from beneath what were once deck beams, and a line of salvaged nineteenth-century ships' timbers marches northward, supporting sheep fence.

There are, however, some misconceptions about the Falklands and their sometimes turbulent weather. Though it has been known to spit a few flakes of snow or sleet even in the South Atlantic summer, the squalls are generally of short duration, and in general the climate is moderate, though windy. The final misconception is that the Falklands are very nearly part of Antarctica! In point of fact, at not quite 52 degrees south latitude, Stanley is roughly as far south of the equator as Liverpool is north.

The Falkland Islands, shown on a John Tallis map circa 1851. Stanley's harbor is at the extreme right. It is quite apparent that the delineator of the penguins at lower left had never seen one.
AUTHOR'S COLLECTION

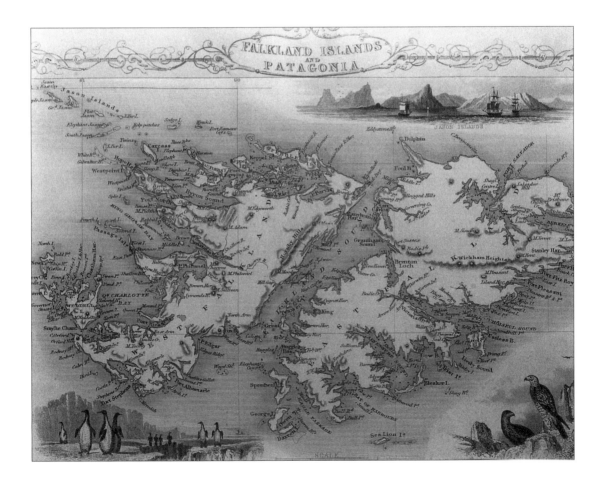

To reach Stanley's nearly landlocked harbor SNOW SQUALL had to sail eastward along the coast of East Falkland, with the low, rolling pastures of Lafonia (named for an early settler) to port. There, in a treeless landscape, cloud shadows raced along the grass covered hills. To the north, in the distance, rose East Falkland's highest mountain, 2,300-foot-high Mount Usborne. Low, sandy Cape Pembroke marked the turning point to head westward into Stanley's outer harbor of Port William, and Hubert Taylor noted that headwinds from the west delayed them for a day. Once into Port William, the narrow entrance to Port Stanley lay to the south. Dillingham picked up a local pilot and headed in. Only one fathom of water lay on the western entrance at York Point but deep water, four to five fathoms, was close by Navy Point to starboard.

Stanley Harbor, looking west.
ORIGINAL DRAWING BY CAPTAIN
G. H. ELLIOTT, ROYAL MARINES.
*ILLUSTRATED LONDON NEWS*, 1867,
AUTHOR'S COLLECTION

The small settlement of Stanley, population just under four hundred, lay to port on the south side of the harbor, a cluster of houses clinging to the steep slope, but unprepossessing as it might

be, it was Dillingham's only hope of repairing Snow Squall. He anchored near shore, and Taylor recorded that his captain "hired Pumpers to pump ship during the night" to relieve the ship's exhausted crew.[13] The Stanley harbor master's *Shipping Register* for 1864 lists Snow Squall as the fourteenth vessel to enter that year. Among the *Register*'s entries are, "Whither bound: San Francisco; Cargo: General; No. of days out: 59; Number of crew: 14" (they apparently did not count the officers and "idlers" such as the cook), and under Remarks, "Been ashore in the Strait of Le Maire, Ship leaky and Rudder damaged, Went ashore 26th February, 1864," and in another handwriting, "& Ultimately condemned."[14]

On March 7 Dillingham wrote Mr. Pine, the Falklands' colonial secretary, announcing that "after much delay and trouble from the weather &c," he was at last ready to begin discharging his cargo of explosives and asked Pine to have government carts ready to take the powder to the magazine.[15] He attempted, initially, "to stop the leak…without discharging,"[16] and hired "diving apparatus" from Stanley's J. M. Dean and Son for fifteen pounds "for use in sending Diver under the bottom of the 'Snow Squall' to ascertain damages and stop leak. (Cargo on board)."[17]

Stanley was an excellent port of refuge, but as the many nineteenth-century hulks which line its shoreline attest, an expensive and difficult place to get repairs. There was, for example, no drydock nor a slipway where a vessel of Snow Squall's size could be hauled out. In June 1860, the American commercial agent in Stanley, William H. Smyley, appointed ten years earlier, reported sourly about Stanley, "I generally send American destitute seamen to Montevideo, to the United States consul there. The passage rate from this to that port is high, and the accomodations [*sic*] execrable; but, were I to quarrel with the Falkland [Islands] Company, they would not take the men at any price." Warming to his attack Smyley continued, "There is little to entice our ships here, and few ever call unless they are in distress and cannot avoid it. Ships' bills on the United States will scarcely be taken, and even mine on the government often refused at any price."[18]

In truth Smyley was hardly the ideal ally for an American captain in trouble. He had owned and captained sealers out of Newport, Rhode Island, for years (and sent useful navigational notes back to Matthew Fontaine Maury for his *Sailing Directions*), but the British authorities, while acknowledging that he had on many occasions bravely rescued distressed mariners, took a very dim view of some of his other activities, which they regarded as downright illegal. In 1854 he had brought the USS GERMANTOWN to Stanley in a bit of "gunboat diplomacy" when the crews of two American sealers were arrested for alleged livestock poaching. The British claimed that he was not above donning a Royal Navy uniform, warning off American sealers and then, of course, harvesting seals himself—in short, a thoroughly freebooting nineteenth-century frontier adventurer who eventually accused Dillingham of having bungled things.

Meanwhile, Dillingham made a determined effort to save his ship. On April 24 he hired what proved to be the leaky hulk of the British MARGARET at two pounds per day (roughly ten 1864 dollars) to receive his cargo, and another hulk into which to dump the troublesome coal before "heaving down" SNOW SQUALL to try to find and stop the leak. In the first set of accounts for expenses in Stanley there was one item of six pounds, thirteen shillings for "Ten Gallons of Rum for the Laborers." In the accounts the item is explained as, "Grog (rum) appears to be an institution peculiar to the Falkland Islands; in the present instance laborers refused to work without it."[19]

In a letter written after his return to New York Captain Dillingham described some of his troubles in Stanley:

> Finding that I must discharge, I immediately secured a
> hulk, the only place of storage obtainable, to receive my
> cargo. The "Snow Squall," still leaking badly, was hauled
> alongside the hulk, and proceeded to discharge with
> her own crew, aided by an equal or greater number of
> men hired ashore. The hoisting of cargo was done by

hand. Packages were slung, hoisted, and swung over the rail, and then the hulk's tackles were hooked onto the goods lowered into the hold of the hulk, where they were stored, about as in loading a vessel for sea. The discharging was done as rapidly as circumstances would permit, taking as good care of everything as we could. It occupied in the neighborhood of three weeks....

As to damage from the cargo from breakage, I know that some did occur, notwithstanding the care exercised. I myself saw some damage by breakage of packages &c arising from accident or carelessness of the men...but cannot state the goods or [identifying] marks. Every precaution possible was also used to prevent pilfering and stealing, watch being kept...while the work was going on, but it was impossible to see all the men at all times, and there must necessarily [have been] opportunities occurring for stealing....[20]

Dillingham then prepared to "heave down" SNOW SQUALL to try to find the leaks. In the heaving down maneuver a vessel is lightened as much as possible, then brought over on her side as far as possible, exposing her bottom. It is simple in theory and fairly tricky in practice, involving, in SNOW SQUALL's case, a good deal of improvised pulling and hauling. Dillingham ran up a considerable bill for lumber, cordage, work on the pumps, and so on. When we examined the existing portion of the hull in the 1980s there was evidence of metal sheathing having been removed, probably in an attempt to find the leak itself. Perhaps over-optimistically, Dillingham had had new sheets of metal punched for re-installation.

One intriguing piece of evidence has surfaced to explain a possibility for the failure to locate the leak. In 1861–62 another Maine-built vessel, the ship SCREAMER, voyaged from Saigon, where she had gone aground briefly, to Mauritius to load lumber for London. Early in the voyage she began to leak seriously, and at a stopover in Cape Town a diver failed to locate the leak and additional crew was hired to pump. On arrival in London, after what must have been a harrowing voyage, SCREAMER went into drydock and when the water went out she poured out water like a shower-bath. On examination, once the sheathing was taken off, a large section of her planking had been seriously eaten away by marine worms. Examination of SNOW SQUALL after her 1987 recovery revealed worm damage and it is possible that SNOW SQUALL's leak, exacerbated by her grounding, was invisible under the metaling, which could not be completely removed in the Falklands.

Meanwhile Captain Dillingham had trouble with his crew. On March 16 the "Carpenter, Cook & a sailor" were sent to Stanley's jail "for mutiny." The carpenter was sentenced to six weeks, the other two to a month. Hubert Taylor was appointed acting steward.[21] Unfortunately details of this insubordination were lost when the Stanley Town Hall burned about fifty years ago; they might have made for interesting reading.

Dillingham had engaged the Falkland Islands Company, and day after day SNOW SQUALL's bill with the F. I. C. continued to mount up. The F. I. C. had received its royal charter from Queen Victoria in 1852 and by 1864 was the owner of considerable acreage in the Falklands in addition to what it had purchased from Samuel Lafone of Lafonia. Though early projections of profits to be made in the Falklands had proved to be overly optimistic, by 1864 the F. I. C.'s sheep ranching operations were *just* beginning to show black ink. In part, the F. I. C.'s difficulties had stemmed from its early refusal to bring J. M. Dean (who provided a diver to look for SNOW SQUALL's leak), into the business, and over the years the Dean family proved to be extremely tough business rivals. In a small, sparsely settled colony many thousands of miles from the Mother Country, such rivalry could be fierce. The F. I. C. was agriculture-oriented. Dean "could do any work connected with shipping or sealing from practical experience, coopering his own [seal] oil and knowing how to dry wrecked goods to make the most of them."[22] In addition, he offered credit at his store, undercutting the F. I. C.'s terms. In short, Stanley had a nasty business war. Over the years, when a vessel such as Snow Squall was condemned (or wrecked) the Deans, and later others, moved in swiftly while the apparently timid F. I. C. managers awaited instructions from the home office. In Snow Squall's case they acted resolutely.

In addition to all of the hardware items (and all of it, including lumber, had to be imported to the treeless Falklands or salvaged from other vessels), there were wages to be paid to local workers, the hire of vessels to transport cargo items, the rent on storage hulks, and the feeding of Snow Squall's crew. Under the law a shipmaster might abandon his vessel when the cost of repairs exceeded half of the value of the vessel *after* repair, and Dillingham had yet to find the leaks.

After several surveys Snow Squall was condemned on April 23 and her crew paid off, though Chief Mate Sears was then hired to supervise the pumping of the leaky Margaret, and to keep an eye on the cargo. On the twenty-sixth Dillingham wrote Falklands governor James George MacKenzie, "I beg permission from your Exelency [*sic*] to bring my ship in near the shore so that she will ground at about half tide that I may avoid the expense of pumping. I design to place an anchor off shore to prevent her beating higher up until I have entirely dismantled her, when I propose to pump her out and place her as high as she will come upon the beach. Your Exelency [*sic*] would confer a great favour upon me by allowing me, for the present, to place her near the F. I. Company jetty as I desire in that vicinity to arrange the Spars, Rigging &c &c for sale by auction."[23] Governor MacKenzie gave his permission, providing the Falkland Islands Company had no objections. Dillingham forwarded a letter of assent from their manager, James Lane, so Snow Squall was moved to what proved to be her final resting place. Dillingham had expressed his belief that once moved to her final berth Snow Squall could still be used as a storage hulk (a common practice in the treeless Falklands)—in other words, an instant warehouse—but she settled with a heavy list to port and apparently was never resettled on an even keel. She became a source of salvaged lumber, judging from several photographs taken in the 1880s showing piles of it on her deck next to a temporary "gin pole" derrick to move it around.

Dillingham had run up a very substantial bill with the Falkland Islands Company. The F. I. C. quite commonly allowed a stranded captain leeway to do this then offered to settle the account at a bargain for them. In May the F. I. C. purchased the hull of SNOW SQUALL for £435 (just over $2,000).[24] At about the same time, almost everything from SNOW SQUALL that could be removed was auctioned off, item by item. They went at very low prices as it was definitely a buyer's, not a seller's, market. The lower main rigging was knocked down for fourteen pounds while the topmast and royal backstays went for just over thirty-four. Everything, including the ornate cabin paneling, with its "pilasters of burnish gilt," and furniture went. The paneling brought eight pounds, the cabin furniture three. The grinning dragon figurehead, for which there did not appear to be a ready market, stayed in place. Individual lots of "rope," generally speaking, went for more than the ship's wheel, four to seven pounds per lot as against a mere three for the wheel. (This last item, had the practices of some other American vessels in the China trade been followed, might have been a quite handsome production with brass inlay, purchased in China. If so, it would point up the "fire sale" nature of the auction.) One capstan brought just over three pounds while another went for just one pound, fourteen shillings. All in all the sale of "the ship and her effects" raised £1,174.5.10 ($6,536.10), "provisions and spare materials" £373.13.6 ($2,107.68) and "damaged cargo" £142.6.8 ($792.22) for a total of £1,695.6.0 ($10,610.20). During her sojourn in Stanley, SNOW SQUALL had run up a bill with the Falkland Islands Company of £2,924.11.9 ($16,722.90). Dillingham paid off the remainder with a ninety-day draft on Brown, Shipley, and Company of London for £1,229.5.9.[25] (All dollar figures are in 1864 dollars.)

Meanwhile, there had been the "tidying up." Captain Dillingham voyaged to Montevideo in May aboard the schooner ONEMEA (and offered to convey government dispatches should the governor wish). From "Monte" he went to Buenos Aires where he engaged the 600-ton bark ORSINI of Freeport, Maine, captained by Hiram Smith, for ten thousand dollars in gold (no Civil War greenbacks), to take the cargo on to San Francisco. The ORSINI arrived in Stanley on July 17, nine days out of Buenos Aires, with a crew of fourteen and "one passenger" (Dillingham?).[26] It took about two weeks to stow the cargo aboard the ORSINI, which sailed for San Francisco on August 16. But there had been a hitch which infuriated Commercial Agent Smyley no end. By law Captain Smith had been supposed to take on some of SNOW SQUALL's crew (as many as two men for each hundred of the ORSINI's register tons), thus getting them off Smyley's hands, and he did not. Smyley now had two crews to get home somehow: SNOW SQUALL's and those of the ship FRANK PIERCE, who had been rescued after their ship capsized off Cape Horn. All were now "on the hands of the Consulate." On August 18 the irate Smyley wrote Secretary of State Seward:

> Some days previous to his [i.e., Captain Smith's] sailing I requested him to take ten of the men who were on the Consulate which he agreed to do. I had the men in readiness and only waited for him to say at what time he wished me to send them on board, when to my surprise he got his vessel under weigh [sic] and left the port without the men. I am well aware that he did it intentionally, he not wishing to take them, for certain reasons....[27]

The "reasons" were quite likely that Captain Smith was well aware of the "attempted mutiny" and decided he could do without potentially rebellious SNOW SQUALLers. In any case, continuing his dispatch to Seward in this thoroughly testy vein (one can almost visualize his wattles quivering and his pen scratching irritably), he was "sorry to inform [Seward] that Captain Dillingham has conducted his business so badly that it will be ruinous to his employers and the underwriters," adding that he would now have to charter a vessel to take the "stranded crews" to Montevideo and suggested that it should be "charged to Capt. Smith."[28]

Smyley wrote his dispatch to Washington on August 18. SNOW SQUALL's Dillingham seems to have been fully aware that Smyley was criticizing him behind his back. On August 9 he wrote Governor MacKenzie, "As certain parties are calling in question either directly or indirectly my proceedings since I have become a resident of this colony, I beg to ask, as a great favor, should your Exelecy [sic] not deem it incompatible with your position," to "certify as to the manner in which I have conducted my business during my stay at this port." Dillingham went on to explain that "more than three months after the event, a man comes to this colony after an absence of quite six months and objects that the ship which I condemned here from utter inability to repair her should have been repaired and that instead of employing a hulk in which to stow the cargo I should have employed certain warehouses on shore...." Dillingham complained (without mentioning Smyley by name) that as the criticism was coming "from a man who from his position will by strangers be suffered to judge unfortunately," MacKenzie should check with Stanley's harbor master to get the facts. He assured the governor that he would keep any reply "confidential" while he was in the Falklands and that it would only be used in Dillingham's "native land," i.e., once he got back to the United States.[29]

Whether delighted to have a chance to take a poke at troublesome Smyley or out of sympathy for Dillingham or both, on August 12 MacKenzie responded with a warm letter in which he gave Dillingham credit for a "conscientious desire to do your duty, and with a bona fide intention of benefiting all parties concerned."[30]

One SNOW SQUALL crew member seems to have arranged his own escape. Young Hubert Taylor joined the ship WOOSUNG of Liverpool, which sailed on May 6 for San Francisco after watering in Stanley. He celebrated his seventeenth birthday on the voyage and arrived in San Francisco on July 17, happily clutching his souvenir from the Falklands—a penguin skin. Captain Coleman of WOOSUNG reported "the ship Snow Squall, from New York for this

Captain Dillingham had gotten SNOW SQUALL away from the CSS TUSCALOOSA in 1863. Unfortunately, as he was trying to get home in 1864 his luck ran out. The Baltimore bark MONDAMIN, on which he was a passenger, was captured by the CSS FLORIDA a few days out of Rio de Janiero. Dillingham lost all his charts, instruments, and books and eventually reached Massachusetts "all used up."
U.S. NAVAL HISTORICAL CENTER

port, as having been condemned at the Falkland Islands."[31] ORSINI arrived at San Francisco on November 4.[32]

In whatever manner Smyley repatriated the rest of SNOW SQUALL's company, about September 8 Captain Dillingham took passage on the mail schooner FOAM (formerly the yacht on which yachtsman and author Lord Dufferin had cruised to Iceland) for Montevideo and from there took a steamer for Rio de Janeiro. At Rio he took passage on the Baltimore bark MONDAMIN on what he hoped was the last leg of his return to the United States. Unfortunately, a few days out of Rio, on September 26, "after a chase of six hours, the barque was captured by the Confederate steamer [CSS] Florida, taken possession of by a prize crew, and, the following morning, the crew and passengers were put on board CSS Florida, and the barque was burned by the prize crew," as Dillingham deposed at Boston in March 1875. MONDAMIN's captain, forty-year-old Abraham Phinney, like Dillingham a Cape Codder, had already lost one vessel to FLORIDA, the brig CLARENCE in May, 1863; now FLORIDA, under Captain C. M. Morris, had pounced on him again. As both captains deposed in their claims under the "Commissioners of Alabama Claims" arbitration after the Civil War, the Confederates seized their personal effects as well as Phinney's bark. Phinney testified that he lost his "nautical instruments, books and charts, clothing, and other effects" to the value of $202.00, and that he had thirty dollars in expenses getting home.

Dillingham apparently had the wit to make out a detailed inventory of what was seized, which he got Morris to sign. It is a bit difficult to determine Dillingham's total personal loss as some valuations are expressed in "gold" and some in "currency," but it was substantial. Dillingham's claim was denied under the arbitration but it is, in effect, a catalog of what a prudent Yankee captain would have aboard for a voyage around Cape Horn into the Pacific.

2 chronometers

2 Vols. Horsburgh's Sailing
   Directions [for the Pacific]

2 Pacific Ocean Sailing
   Directions

2 Nautical Almanacks [*sic*]

1 China Pilot

1 Pacific Ocean Directory
   (Kuholt)

1 Summers New Method

1 Ward's Star Tables

1 Blunt's Coast Pilot

1 Brownlow's Planisphere

1 Straits Sunda Chart
   (Particular)

1 Gaspar Straits Chart ditto

2 Tunis Straits Charts ditto

1 Gulf Siam ditto

2 China Sea No. 1 and No. 2
   ditto [likely Imray British
   "bluebacks"]

1 ditto Java to Malacca
   (Particular)

3 Eastern Passage, No. 1, 2

1 Large Chart of Australia

1 ditto of California

1 ditto of Indian Ocean
   (Irving)

1 West Coast of S. America

1 North Atlantic

1 South Atlantic

1 Coast of N. America to
   Capes of Delaware

1 ditto to Cape Henry

1 South Pacific

and then:

1 Spy Glass, worth $30 gold

1 Pr. Opera Glasses, $25 gold

1 Sextant, Spencer, Browning
   & Co., $160 (currency)

1 Brass framed Octant, ditto,
   $65 currency

Dillingham had, in effect, lost his carefully assembled tools of his trade as a bluewater captain. Apparently he and Captain Phinney were transferred from FLORIDA to a "Spanish schooner" which landed them at San Juan, Puerto Rico, from which they took passage on the schooner CASTOR for Baltimore.[33] MONDA-

MIN's owner, Thomas Whitridge of Baltimore, eventually received $9,149.38 in compensation but Dillingham lost out for some reason.[34] What Phinney received is unknown. It was FLORIDA's last capture. On October 7 she herself was captured by the USS WACHUSETT in the neutral harbor of Bahia, Brazil, an extremely dubious action under international law, against which the Brazilian government protested vigorously.

Dillingham reached New York on November 20, "entirely used up by his exertions at Stanley, his Capture by the 'Florida' etc., etc.," and went home to Chelsea, Massachusetts, "to be cared for there," as his employer, Charles Green, wrote Dibblee and Hyde in San Francisco.[35] In the same letter Green urged Dibblee and Hyde to suggest to the San Francisco insurance adjuster, Thomas N. Cazneau, that "if he thinks proper to put in some compensation for Captain Dillingham, who has saved the underwriters on Cargo a much heavier loss, by his good management at the Faulklands [sic] (one of the worst places a cargo *could* get into) & his favorable charter of the 'Orsini'—I think it will be approved by all."[36] So much for Commercial Agent Smyley's dyspeptic remarks! Dibblee and Hyde disagreed, however, with Green's proposal, suggesting that the underwriters—should they choose to do so—*might* suggest that course of action, though they sounded a bit dubious.

Shortly after Dillingham's return home he received an irate letter from Cornelius Comstock on the subject of SNOW SQUALL's cargo of coal. Writing from Chelsea the day after Christmas he replied to Comstock's letter, which must have arrived Christmas Eve. "Yours of the 23rd came to hand on Saturday evening but too late to be answered but I hasten to attend to it this morning." Obviously gritting his teeth, Dillingham wrote Comstock that "as to the Coal in the 'Snow Squall' in relation to which you address me, I beg to say that the coal received all the damage it was possible for salt water to do to it from Feb 27th the date of the ships grounding to April 12th the day of its being discharged, for we were not enabled to keep the watch [water?] constantly out of the holds as we were generally obliged to *'suck the pumps'* and then attend to other duties about the ship while the water accumulated. By adopting this course only were we enabled to reach port with the ship." Comstock apparently had complained not only about the coal's condition but that far fewer than the eighty-odd tons supposedly loaded in New York (the coal was receipted for with the notation "quantity unknown.") had reached San Francisco. Sighing, Dillingham continued, "I do not know how to account for it falling short so much [nearly one-fifth] for I went into the hold of both the 'Snow Squall' and hulk myself to see that it had been thoroughly cleaned up and found this had been done. Of course it was quite impossible for us to prevent some considerable quantities from falling between the vessels while swinging it from one to the other [in batches of about a hundred pounds] as the weather was usually very rough.... I had no idea that anything like this amount had been lost."[37] It should be remembered that all of this unloading and loading of packages and coal was carried out during the South Atlantic wintertime, when the weather, though not as bitterly cold or snowy as a New England winter can be, often hovers just about at the freezing mark with blustery winds. Hence the demand from Falklanders hired to handle cargo for an occasional tot of rum.

The ORSINI had arrived at San Francisco on November 4 and now the intricacies of settling SNOW SQUALL's affairs began. It must be remembered that freight was collected on arrival and that up to this point neither owner Green nor New York agent Comstock had derived any income whatsoever from the voyage. For unknown reasons the ORSINI was consigned to the well-known San Francisco firm of W. T. Coleman, rather than Dibblee and Hyde, the original consignees, but on learning of this arrangement Green wrote both them and Coleman at the end of August (the exact date is unclear), via the Panama steamers, transferring all transactions to Dibblee and Hyde.[38] Affairs were now in the hands of insurance adjuster Cazneau, whose office in the Exchange Building on Battery Street opposite the customhouse apparently was marked by a huge wooden anchor, "as big as the bower of a man-o'-war," of which, unfortunately, no photograph seems to exist. Cazneau was an insurance broker, "adjuster of marine losses and averages," notary public, and offered "consultations upon all Insurance and Maratime [sic] Subjects."[39]

In a period of colorful characters in San Francisco, Thomas N. Cazneau was definitely one of the more colorful. He was born in Boston March 14, 1812, the younger son of a sea captain. The Cazneaus were an old seafaring family which came to Boston from France in 1687; other Cazneaus (though not his father, William) were members of the prestigious Boston Marine Society. By 1842 Thomas was in New York and active in insurance and in the New York Fusiliers, where he and his company had a piece of music, *Cazneau's Quick Step*, dedicated to them. About 1850 he arrived in the mining town of Columbia, California, where he ran a popular "resort," with a barroom, restaurant, and theater, which later burned. In 1859 he moved to San Francisco, where he joined the Haven Brothers' marine insurance adjusting firm. After the departure of the alcoholic R. S. Haven (who had handled SNOW SQUALL's somewhat confused affairs in 1857), Cazneau took over the business, which he ran until his death in 1873. He was described as a "small man, with hatchet features, black hair and beard (dyed till his death), a limber tongue, and charming manners," active in Democratic politics and again in the militia, though one cynic described it as "invincible in peace, invisible in war." Cazneau was also active in the Sausalito Land and Ferry Company, which developed Sausalito, where there is today a Cazneau Avenue. This, then, was the man selected to try to untangle SNOW SQUALL's affairs.[40]

The other player in the 1864 SNOW SQUALL drama was Albert Dibblee of the firm of Dibblee and Hyde. He was a transplanted New Yorker born at Clermont on the Hudson, not quite a hundred miles north of New York City, on February 9, 1821. The first Dibblees had settled in Connecticut in the seventeenth century. During the American Revolution two of the three Dibblee

San Francisco merchant Albert Dibblee, the agent for SNOW SQUALL's cargo, which finally arrived aboard the Maine bark ORSINI. Dibblee was an extremely hard worker, sometime member of San Francisco's "Committee of Vigilance," and active behind the scenes in city politics.
COURTESY OF PROFESSOR ARTHUR MEJIA

brothers were Tories and fled to Nova Scotia while Albert's grand-father joined the Continental Army in New York. Albert's father, a circuit court judge, moved to New York City when Albert was seven. A judge's salary was barely enough to support six children, much less to educate them properly, so at age sixteen Albert be-gan a career in banking. In 1849, remembering the family motto, "Cautiously but Fearlessly," he gambled on California and bought a varied selection of goods, hired a clerk to go to San Francisco with him, and embarked on the ship MARTHA in November 1849 with office fixtures, two portable houses, and a 36-foot sailboat, arriving after a passage of 197 days.

He became a success, due to an enormous appetite for work and meticulous attention to detail. Like other San Francisco entre-preneurs of his period he was plagued by fires, bank failures, and in his case the death of one partner and an apparent betrayal by another. He lived over his business, eating in local restaurants, and sometimes staying up until dawn to take care of business corre-spondence. He was what would be called today a "workaholic," but it paid off. Within three or four years his firm was regarded as one of San Francisco's leading mercantile and shipping houses. He was active in civic reform, including the so-called "Committee of Vigilance," but like others of his ilk he chose to work behind the scenes for reform rather than running for office. And during all of this he regularly sent remittances and Christmas presents back to his family in New York. At the time of his involvement with SNOW SQUALL he had served two terms as president of the San Francisco Chamber of Commerce and had recently had to cope with nearly ruinous liabilities incurred by his "partner in New York" (possibly Cornelius Comstock), but had weathered the crisis and was very contentedly making long-term investments in drought-ravaged farmland near Los Angeles and Santa Barbara. He died in 1895.[41]

These two men who had to wind up SNOW SQUALL's affairs had very different personalities, yet each had helped shape nine-teenth-century San Francisco: Cazneau with his landmark anchor and militia parades, Dibblee with his meticulous attention to detail. Their task with SNOW SQUALL had two major and interconnected complications. First, Cazneau had to settle what is called "general average." The concept of general average goes back to the Rhodian Law at least and maritime law was further codified in the medieval Laws of Oleron. Without belaboring the point (for many books have been written on the subject), it is perhaps sufficient to quote from an 1859 American compendium, *The Law of Shipping,* to summarize what was involved.

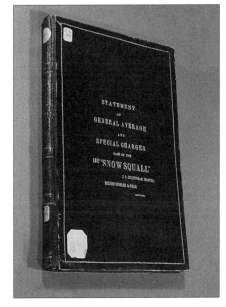

Bound volume of *Statement of General Average and Special Charges, Case of the Ship "Snow Squall."*
ALBERT DIBBLEE PAPERS, BANCROFT LIBRARY, UNIVERSITY OF CALIFORNIA, BERKELEY

WHAT IS GENERAL AVERAGE?
General Average is a contribution by all parties concerned, towards a loss sustained by some of the parties in interest for the common benefit.

*Are* ALL EXTRA CHARGES *incurred for the general good on putting into a foreign port in distress, general average?*

These, together with the warehouse rent and reloading charges of the cargo, are held to be good by general contribution.

But the one which was to cause real contention was this:

*Are the* EXPENSES OF UNLOADING THE CARGO, *either for the purposes of repairing the ship, or for floating her when she accidentally gets aground, general average?*

They are, because the *ship, cargo,* and *freight* are equally interested—the *ship* that she may be repaired, and the *cargo* (in which is the freight) that it may be preserved.[42]

For the next few months there would be much hairsplitting over SNOW SQUALL in San Francisco. Not only did the losses for missing or damaged cargo, and that sold at distress prices by auction in Stanley, have to be settled, but the Thirty-eighth Congress had passed a new law imposing a tax of $2\frac{1}{2}$ percent on freights from eastern ports, effective June 30. Had SNOW SQUALL not met with disaster her cargo would have arrived, and the freight paid on it, well before the end of June, avoiding the tax. Not unexpectedly, this did not sit well with SNOW SQUALL's consignees. In addition, possibly unfortunately for Messrs. Comstock and Green, there was an *additional* tax of 3 percent on the gross receipts—not the profits—of anyone operating an "express business."[43] As to the matter of damaged cargo, Captain Dillingham gave his opinion that "about an equal proportion of the packages were damaged in being removed from the Ship to the Hulk as from the Hulk to the Bark."[44] The New York firm of Johnson and Higgins, "Average Adjusters" (still in business today), tackled the delicate question of just how much of the damage should be included in the general average. "Our proposition and practice (which we have never yet

Hulks at the Falkland Islands Company jetty in Stanley. Photograph taken between 1878 and 1882. Left to right the hulks are the VICAR OF BRAY, the MARGARET, the WILLIAM SHAND, and SNOW SQUALL. SAN FRANCISCO MARITIME NATIONAL HISTORICAL PARK, NEGATIVE NO. P83-135N

had disputed) is this—that the charges and expenses, including the damage to cargo by landing and storing, when a vessel puts into an intermediate port and is condemned after discharge, are to be paid in the general average, the same as if she herself had reladen the cargo and proceeded on the voyage...."[45]

At last, towards the end of February, a resolution seemed to be in sight. On February 21 Dibblee and Hyde telegraphed Green, "AVERAGE NEARLY READY. COMMENCE COLLECTING ABOUT TWENTY-SEVENTH. OWNER'S BALANCE ABOUT TWENTY EIGHT THOUSAND CURRENCY. TELEGRAPH MODE REMITTANCE."[46] On that same day Dibblee and Hyde wrote Green via the steamer SACRAMENTO, that "but for agitation of the question of allowing claims for damaged and short cargo, the adjustor would have had everything closed

Detail enlarged to show SNOW SQUALL's dragon figurehead, which has since disappeared without a trace. Other details such as the sampson post forward are clearly visible. SNOW SQUALL's deck planking is apparently being salvaged using a temporary "gin pole" on the port side. The Falklands' climate, in the rain shadow of South America, is too dry for forests, hence all lumber not salvaged from ships must be imported from Chile.

about 1st January and statement would have been in your hands ere this." They were also prevented from finally closing "by reason of failure of the telegraph."[47] At long last, on March 11, they were able to report to Green that they were sending along the slender volume with the "statement" of general average and a draft of $27,640.48 on Lees and Walter of New York.[48] Fourteen months after SNOW SQUALL had sailed from New York things were settled at last.

Green, of course, had not been idle during all of this. He had purchased two new ships, the 1,078-ton INTREPID, for which he had dickered with the Sewalls of Bath, Maine, and the 1,395-ton BLUE JACKET, built at Greenpoint, Long Island, across the river from his Wall Street office. He gave the command of BLUE JACKET to Captain Dillingham, so obviously there were no hard feelings. Before retiring in 1877 in his late sixties, in 1872 Green bought

Undated photograph, probably the 1920s, of the Falkland Islands Company jetty with a flock of sheep. SNOW SQUALL's after portion is visible to the right of the jetty. The first vessel behind SNOW SQUALL is the Canadian EGERIA, until recently still in use as a storage shed. The masts of a local schooner can be seen beyond the EGERIA.
FALKLAND ISLANDS COMPANY / FALKLAND ISLANDS MUSEUM

one last ship, the 995-ton LADY BLESSINGTON built at Belfast, Maine, in 1855 and named for the late Irish novelist.

Captain Dillingham made several voyages in BLUE JACKET then went into his family's Boston paper business, which owned mills in New Hampshire and Maine. The bank panic of late 1873, with the lawsuits that followed, was followed by the death of his infant daughter in Maine the next year. Then in April 1876 the New Hampshire mill burned "with all its contents." Dillingham resumed his career at sea as master of FLEETFORD and VIGILANT and finally the steamship FINANCE. He died aboard her at age fifty in November 1883 as she was coming up New York Harbor from Rio.

Our young diarist Hubert Taylor went on across the Pacific to China with his San Francisco chum, then came home to New York to end his days as a highly successful banker. He died at eighty-one in 1928, after a career with the First National Bank of

Undated photograph of construction at the Falkland Islands Company jetty over SNOW SQUALL's hull. To the right of the new construction, just above the figure on the lower right, is SNOW SQUALL's starboard-side cargo port, through which items such as railroad rails and long lumber would have been loaded. FALKLAND ISLANDS COMPANY

Brooklyn and as president of the Brooklyn firm of Taylor and Fox, "realty brokers and appraisers." He had won a seat in the New York legislature in 1892 as the only Republican elected from King's County that year. SNOW SQUALL was joined in the Falklands by other hulks abandoned outboard of her in front of the Falkland Islands Company offices. She was cut down to her 'tween-decks when they built a new jetty out over all of them.

In her thirteen-year career, this little Maine-built clipper ship had carried cargoes to and from a remarkable number of ports of call in North and South America, Australia, and the Orient as one of Charles Green's far-flung fleet. It is impossible to say how long she would have continued to earn her keep had she not come to grief. Another five years? Another ten or so? With a couple of exceptions she seems to have had a reasonably fortunate career, though she appears to have been jinxed on the runs out of San Francisco.

Roughly thirty years after the end of SNOW SQUALL's career the last Maine-built wooden square-rigger, Charles Minott's ARYAN of 1892, slid down the ways, ending that chapter of maritime history. The wooden ships and the yards that built them are gone. All that remains are the Percy & Small shipyard and the bow of SNOW SQUALL both at Maine Maritime Museum in Bath, to remind us of the days of "wooden ships and iron men."

# NOTES

[1] *Statement of General Average and Special Charges, Case of the Ship "Snow Squall,"* Albert Dibblee Papers, Bancroft Library, University of California at Berkeley, C-G 180, vol. 41. The *Statement*, a blue leather-bound book, sets forth the circumstances of Snow Squall's stranding and details expenditures and receipts in Port Stanley. Apparently one copy was sent to shipowner Green and the Dibblee copy retained in San Francisco.

[2] New York *Shipping and Commercial List,* November 14, 1863.

[3] Ibid.

[4] *S&CL,* November 21, 1863.

[5] Ibid., vol. C-101, Comstock Family Business Records, Baker Library, Harvard Business School.

[6] Ibid.

[7] Ibid.

[8] *Statement of General Average.* This is the only evidence for crew composition and wages for this voyage as no crew list needed to be filed at New York's customhouse since, technically speaking, the voyage was "coasting," i.e., between two mainland United States ports.

[9] Hubert Taylor Diary. Maine Maritime Museum Library, SM53/3.

[10] James Horsburgh, *The India Directory, or, Directions for sailing to and from the East Indies, China, Australia, and the interjacent ports of Africa and South America: originally compiled from journals of the honourable company's ships, and from* observations and remarks, resulting from the experience of twenty-one years in the navigation of those seas. The original edition was published in two volumes, but the 1855 edition seems to be one.

[11] *Statement of General Average.* The emphasis added in this document consists of underlinings in red ink. It is not Dillingham's marine protest, which would have been sworn to before a United States consul and no such protest has turned up in consular records from the Falklands (if one indeed was ever made).

[12] *Statement of General Average.*

[13] Taylor Diary.

[14] Harbour Master's Office, Stanley.

[15] Dillingham to Pine, March 7, 1864. Falkland Islands Government Archives, vol. H-21 (Misc. Letters to Govt.).

[16] Dillingham to Dibblee and Hyde, December 8, 1864. Dibblee Papers.

[17] *Statement of General Average.*

[18] *Commercial Relations of the United States for the Year Ending September 30, 1860* (Washington: George W. Bowman, 1861), p. 90.

[19] *Statement of General Average.*

[20] Dillingham to Dibblee and Hyde, December 8, 1864. Dibblee Papers, 69/71, Box 6.

[21] Taylor Diary, March 16, 1864.

[22] *The Falkland Islands Company Ltd., 1851–1951* (London: Harley Publishing Co. Ltd., 1951[?], p. 16. This is the F. I. C.'s own

"centenary booklet." Several articles on the company's history appeared in the annual *Falkland Islands Journal,* but in the opinion of Mr. Terry G. Spruce of the F. I. C., contained serious inaccuracies.

23 Dillingham to MacKenzie, April 26, 1864. Falkland Islands Government Archives, vol. H-21.

24 Falkland Islands Company account book, Stanley, May 1864. No date.

25 *Statement of General Average.*

26 R. J. King, Stanley harbor master, letter to author of August 9, 1988.

27 Smyley to Seward, August 18, 1864. National Archives Microfilm Publication T480, Roll 1. General Records of the Department of State, Record Group 59. National Archives, Washington, DC.

28 Ibid.

29 Dillingham to MacKenzie, August 9, 1864. Falkland Islands Government Archives, vol. H-21.

30 MacKenzie to Dillingham, Falkland Islands Government Archives, vol. D-11 (Letters Outward).

31 *Alta California* (San Francisco), July 18, 1864. Taylor Diary, entries for June 13 and July 18, 1864.

32 Ibid. November 6, 1864.

33 Civil War Claims, Record Group 76. National Archives. Dillingham's claim was Number 391, Phinney's Numbers 290 and 291. Case File Number 255 notes that Dillingham's claim was dismissed. (Letter to author of May 21, 1993, David A. Pfeiffer, National Archives, Textual Reference Division.)

34 Ibid., October 18, 1875, p. 274. Docket Books, Entry 19, B 621.

35 Dibblee and Hyde, *Incoming Letter Book,* Bancroft Library, University of California at Berkeley, C-G 180, D543, vol. 260. Green to Dibblee and Hyde, November 22, 1864. Albert Dibblee Papers.

36 Ibid.

37 Dibblee and Hyde, *Incoming Letter Book,* Dillingham to Comstock, December 26, 1864.

38 Green to Dibblee and Hyde, date uncertain. Portland Harbor Museum, Portland, ME.

39 *San Francisco Directory and Business Guide* (San Francisco: Henry G. Langley, 1861–62), p. xii.

40 Information provided by Thomas N. Cazneau's great-great-great-grandson, Patrick Cazneau of Santa Rosa, CA.

41 Adapted from an anonymous typescript biography of Dibblee, almost certainly written by a family member, in the Albert Dibblee Papers.

42 Francis B. Dixon, *The Law of Shipping and Merchants' and Shipmasters' Guide* (New York: Henry Spear, 1859), pp. 480–81.

43 Thirty-Eighth Congress, 1st Session, 1864, Chapter 173, *An Act to Provide Internal Revenue,* Sections 103 and 104.

44 Dibblee Papers, 69/71, Box 6, Dillingham to Dibblee and Hyde, December 8, 1864.

[45] Ibid., Johnson and Higgins to Thomas N. Cazneau, November 25, 1864.

[46] Dibblee Papers, Mss. 761, vol. 202, carton 12. Dibblee and Hyde to Green, February 21, 1865.

[47] Ibid.

[48] Ibid., Dibblee and Hyde to Green, March 11, 1865.

SNOW SQUALL in 1982, just
before Argentina invaded the
Falklands and before a runaway
oil barge smashed the stempost.
In the stempost, just at the
lower strakes of hull planking,
are bronze drifts which may
have secured the lower end of
the dragon figurehead's tail.
NICHOLAS DEAN

# EPILOGUE:
## BACK TO THE FALKLANDS

*David C. Switzer*

Nick has very capably presented SNOW SQUALL's history of a century and a half ago, leaving her deep in the mud and coal dust of Port Stanley in the Falkland Islands. Now we can return to the story I began in the Prologue—the series of expeditions that recovered the bow of the last American clipper ship extant.

*The 1983 Adventure: 23 January – 12 March*
Our first look at SNOW SQUALL on the afternoon we arrived in Port Stanley was a disturbing sight. As Fred wrote in the expedition journal, it was:

> …mortifying. She was deteriorated greatly, and even from a distance one could see that some violent impact had occurred in her starboard bow. The stempost has been ripped out…. The main breasthook (deck hook) has dropped down…. The lesser breasthook underneath is missing. By far the most disturbing damage was on the outside 6 to 15 feet of the starboard bow, where almost half of the outer planks above the high tide line…were ripped out….

Other damage noted was missing frames and some of the 'tween-deck beams. Naturally caused damage was evident in the intertidal zone. There, the plankless frames were badly rotted and quite weak.

We were informed that the damage that Fred Yalouris described had occurred during the Argentine occupation and after the surrender. The most violent damage had occurred as a result of a fierce gale, when SNOW SQUALL was struck by an oil barge moored nearby. Subsequent damage had occurred when boats moored on the clipper's bow rocked and rubbed badly against it due to the wash of the many British military crafts operating in the vicinity. We were informed that the hull had been thoroughly investigated by a British army bomb-disposal squad to make sure there were no explosive devices left behind by Argentine troops. The empty hull, no longer a source of lumber, had become a receptacle for all sorts of junk such as bottles, cable, rusty 55-gallon drums, and other odd bits of metal. As her seams opened, the hull had filled with silt, which gradually covered and hid the lower strata of debris.

Our landlady in Port Stanley was Emma Steen, who owned two guesthouses quite handy to the Falkland Islands Company

SNOW SQUALL as she appeared in 1983.
DAVE SWITZER

(FIC) waterfront complex. Her other "boarders" were a team of Royal Navy clearance divers who were recovering ordnance from HMS ARDENT, which had been sunk during the conflict. Within a few days we were all on close terms. The Royal Navy divers had a heated equipment room on the FIC dock which we were later able to use, and they loaned us a chest for keeping secure what little equipment we brought. Our basic equipment consisted of wetsuits for Sheli and me; drawing equipment; Huston's small tool kit; Nick's assemblage of cameras and film; and, just in case, a High Limb rope-operated chain-saw blade.

Over the years the jetty had been extended over SNOW SQUALL, leaving some 40 feet of the bow exposed to the elements. When our work began on Valentine's Day, we received our first taste of a major feature of the Falklands environment—a constant blustery wind from the west. As we climbed over the bow to begin tagging frames with numbers and establish a centerline, gusts of wind made us unsteady and fearful of slipping and colliding with one of the many exposed rusty spikes.

As we began to familiarize ourselves with the ship's structure, we found a number of initials carved in the waterway. From the looks of the cuts, the initials had been there for some time. Who, we wondered, had carved them, and why? We noted new damage, such as missing pieces of hatch framing, a missing mast partner, deck planking, and the windlass pall seen in earlier photos. Of the damage, most disturbing was a crack that extended through the waterway at frame #12, likely the result of the wartime collision with the oil barge. The discovery of the crack and analysis of its effect on the future stability of the forward bow raised questions as to the future of the SNOW SQUALL Project. If our return to Stanley was delayed for two years, would further degradation, accompanied by another collision, cause the damaged waterway and deckhook section to fall away from the hull and be lost as had, we believed, the outer stem? There could be no assurances that FIC employees could or would rescue the dismembered structure. In the event that the worst-case scenario did occur, what would happen to the remaining bow-section structure when subjected to the force of a severe gale?

When Fred Y suggested that we should consider removing and securing the waterway section and the deckhook now, no one disagreed. The team's assent spawned two more questions: How to safely disengage the two structural elements? And how and where to secure them?

Fred proved to be the consummate "wheeler-dealer." He set off for Government House for a visit with Sir Rex Hunt, the governor general. Appointments were made with the commanding officer of British Forces Falkland Islands, General David Thorne; the Queen's harbor master; and Terry Spruce, managing director of the FIC. Fred's contacts quickly bore fruit. Ladders borrowed from the FIC and the Stanley Public Works Department gave us easier access to the hull. A rowboat belonging to the FIC provided access to the outer sides of the hull.

Our foremost consideration in the process of collecting accurate measurements of the hull structure was the completion of a measured plan view drawing, which required the collection of hundreds of measurements. Indeed, by the end of our first week, nearly five hundred measurements had been collected. These included frame dimensions; intervals between frames; deck beam and plank dimensions; and the dimensions of the timber components of the waterway, stem, and deckhook. Since it was necessary to utilize the process of triangulation to locate the various features of hull structure "in space," as it were, many angles were recorded in addition to the linear measurements.

Added to the various numbers were measured sketches of details such as scarfs and the interesting construction of the deckhook. Finally, in the list of measurements were those called "offsets." These are vertical measurements taken down the hull in a straight line toward the keel, and show the shape of the hull. From these measurements we hoped to get an idea of the fine lines that had put SNOW SQUALL into the class of extreme clippers.

Using scrounged lumber, metal rods, and measuring tapes, Fred Feyling constructed an offset measuring device. It consisted of an 18-foot vertical staff and two horizontal sliding measuring bars. The two Freds held the staff vertical while perched on the frame ends, while Sheli Smith and I collected the offset measurements.

This was our second venture into the water at the FIC complex. The first had been an underwater reconnaissance around the hull, which gave us a chance to examine the Muntz metal sheathing closely. When we rubbed it, the reason for the sobriquet "yellow metal" was apparent. During our tour we came across the lost lower deckhook and buoyed it for later recovery.

Although we had brought our wetsuits, buoyancy compensators, regulators, and fins, we had to borrow weights and rent tanks. SCUBA tank fills were free, thanks to our clearance-diver friends, and their heated storage room gave us a warm place to get suited up. We had been forewarned of the conditions in Stanley Harbor, particularly the sewage that pours in from the

Sheli Smith and Dave Switzer record measurements.
NICHOLAS DEAN

transport vessels, the nearby Sir Tristram, and the town. We had all received hepatitis shots back in the United States, but we reinforced this protection by gargling gin after each dive!

In the meantime Huston Dodge was busy collecting measurements and completing excellent detail drawings. Nick had struck up an acquaintance with an army photographer and had gained access to a darkroom where he could make up contact sheets. All in all, that first week saw a lot accomplished in spite of sharp winds and inclement weather.

During the second week, in anticipation of the need to remove more than the waterway and deckhook, outer hull planks and their supporting frames were tagged with numbers while the deck beams were labeled alphabetically. It was decided that the documentation effort should include the completion of a photo mosaic of the hull on the starboard side. This required that Nick aim his camera while standing somewhat precariously on a narrow ledge that extended along the remains of the English bark William Shand, which lay alongside Snow Squall. Because a tripod could not be set up to ensure that the camera was level, Nick made a simple clinometer and counted on Sheli hanging onto his belt to keep him from falling into the harbor.

Since Sheli was the designated draftsperson, much of her time was spent compiling and making sense of the myriad measurements we collected, and starting the site plan.

We had other archaeological tasks to complete in the Falklands that were unrelated to Snow Squall. On behalf of the New Brunswick, Canada, provincial government we had contracted to complete a survey of the Canadian vessel Egeria, a 1,000-ton bark that was damaged attempting to round Cape Horn in 1872. Like Snow Squall, she headed for Port Stanley for repairs, only to be condemned. Purchased by the FIC, Egeria was razed to below the 'tween-decks forward with her poop remaining largely intact. Roofed over and situated at the head of an extended FIC jetty, Egeria still serves as a storage area for miscellaneous incoming cargo and outward-bound wool.

A second survey performed for the New Brunswick provincial government was carried out by Huston at the site of the remains of another Canadian vessel, the bark ACTAEON. She had arrived at Stanley in 1853 in need of repairs; she, too, was surveyed and condemned. ACTAEON rests inbound of the CHARLES COOPER which, like EGERIA, lies at the head of a jetty and served, as had SNOW SQUALL in early years, as a receiving hulk. The COOPER, a Connecticut-built packet, arrived for a permanent stay in 1866, and, according to John Smith's history, *Condemned at Stanley*, had been the best preserved of the stationary fleet of wooden sailing vessels in Stanley Harbor. At present, however, she is in a serious state of deterioration.

Our second week at Port Stanley coincided with a week-long celebration of a hundred and fifty years of British rule over the islands, and we took the opportunity for a trip to the eastern end of Stanley Harbor to visit the steel bark, LADY ELIZABETH. Launched in 1879 at Sunderland, England, she arrived at Stanley with unrepairable hull damage in 1913. She served as a floating warehouse for the FIC until 1936, when she was beached at her present site in Whalebone Cove. During the Falklands Conflict members of a British Special Air Service Team had hidden on-board and directed air raids on the nearby Argentine airbase.

We made the trip to the LADY ELIZABETH in a jet-propelled military assault boat called a CSB (Combat Support Boat). The craft was made available to us thanks to two new acquaintances, Rob Thomson and Peter Charlesworth, civilians in uniform, serving members of the Royal Fleet Auxiliary (RFA), who "pulled some strings" to put a CSB at our disposal. (In spite of numerous attempts to get Rob and Peter to describe their RFA duties, our questions were always skillfully avoided. We figured that they were "spooks" involved in using high-tech listening devices to monitor the Argentine military air waves.)

The LADY ELIZABETH, with her masts erect and with one sporting a cockbilled yard, was an impressive sight from a distance. Climbing on board was like stepping back into the last days of sail. Fred Feyling directed the survey which was carried out for the World Ship Trust and which involved measurements of the deck area; deckhouses fore and aft; and an evaluation of the condition of the steel plates of her hull. Supplementing the measurements were a series of photographs taken by Nick. Later, back in the states, Fred Y and Fred F completed an extensive report for the World Ship Trust.

We began to wonder how we would ship SNOW SQUALL's deckhook and 19 feet of waterway back to South Portland—and were answered by the fortunes of war. At the time, Port Stanley was overflowing with containers that the Argentine government had used to supply its forces. They were now the spoils of war and officially Crown property. Thanks again to Fred Y's "wheeler-dealer" ability, the harbor master agreed to give us a 20-foot container that had been the property of a firm in Portland, Maine!

But when it was learned that we intended to dismantle some of the forward structure of SNOW SQUALL, there were some Stanleyites who were concerned over the fact that we were removing part of *their* maritime heritage. Their memories of what had happened with FENNIA were still vivid, but we were able to convince them that the salvage would lead to a conservation effort that could not be assured or achieved at Stanley.

Before the removal of the waterway section could take place there were many tasks yet to be completed. The collection of dimensional data had to be completed to ensure that the site plan was accurate. To facilitate the removal of the waterway, a number of previously labeled outer planks had to be removed along with portions of some bow frames.

The disassembly strategy included some preliminary cutting carried out by Huston using a handsaw. The deckhook was the first to go causing a great splash. Then it was floated to the quayside and made fast.

The day set aside for the removal of the waterway with attached dagger knees and ceiling timbers was March 2, when the tide would be the highest for many days. We estimated that the entire assemblage weighed about two tons. The disassembly strategy called for tidal uplift and the use of the High Limb chain saw to sever those elements that were holding the assemblage in place.

On the day before, we lashed empty 55-gallon drums to the waterway to increase its buoyancy at high tide. When we arrived the next morning, the barrels were straining. All that needed to be done was for me to put the chain-saw blade in position and hold it in place while from the oil barge and the WILLIAM SHAND, above, Fred Y and a Royal Navy clearance diver handled the long ropes attached to the saw.

The sawing action began slowly as the blade began to bite into the knee, the last bit of structure keeping the waterway attached to the hull. Soon the blade was whizzing back and forth and sawdust was floating to the surface. Just before the cut was completed, the waterway slipped a few inches jamming the saw. Fred Y set up a come-along but to no avail. We seemed to be stuck.

Then a CSB appeared, skippered by the chief petty officer of the Royal Navy divers who were quartered at Emma's. One nudge and the waterway was free to be towed to the quayside where it joined the deckhook and the once-lost stem piece with a lower breasthook attached to it. The next task was to move the recovered structures to the container to be loaded, which required the loan of a crane and a truck. The British military had come through—a crane and flatbed trailer stood by at the quayside.

Following the disassembly operation, it was necessary to ensure the integrity of SNOW SQUALL's remaining hull structure. Huston, our master carpenter, went to work with more scrounged lumber and shored up the starboard side of the hull to prevent wind- or storm-caused damage. With the shoring in place, the hull minus its forward bow structure presented a rather forlorn sight. A change in the "iffy" Falklands weather brightened the picture with the appearance of a rainbow directly overhead. It seemed a prophetic sign, a signal of the success of what would turn out to be the first of four expeditions to Port Stanley.

The final days of this trip were given over to tidying up: returning borrowed equipment; redepositing the structure in a specially constructed cribwork container situated beneath the jetty; and loading the container. Because it would have made a 12,000-mile trip by the time it reached Boston, the container needed to be loaded so that the contents would not be damaged should rough handling occur during its long journey. With the waterway section already inside, the remaining space was filled with the deckhook and breasthooks, outer hull planking, and frame fragments. The contents of the container were estimated to weigh five tons.

The container made its way to England on board the freighter BALTIC FERRY and, thanks to the generosity of the Ministry of Defence and the shipping company Hogg-Robinson, Ltd., the passage was free. From the Port of Felixstowe, England, to Boston, the container was carried on board the containership TFL DEMOCRACY, which arrived in June 1983 at Boston's Moran terminal. The TFL Shipping Company donated the transportation costs to the project.

Loading the container for shipment to South Portland.
NICHOLAS DEAN

The next stop was South Portland, Maine, where SNOW SQUALL had been launched in 1851 and where the container contents were unloaded at the newly established Spring Point Museum (now called the Portland Harbor Museum). Here, conservation efforts would take over where the archaeology left off and SNOW SQUALL would hopefully become part of a major exhibit.

## The 1984 Adventure: 29 May – 16 June

Before we planned our strategy to bring back a significant portion of SNOW SQUALL's bow, we needed to learn more about the shape of the submerged hull and how deeply the keel rested in the harbor's bottom sediment. We enlisted the help of Bruce Lane who, while employed at Arthur D. Little, had become fascinated with clippers and became a recognized expert with regard to the renowned clipper ship FLYING CLOUD. His knowledge of clipper construction made him an invaluable member of this and subsequent expeditions, as did his engineering "know how." During the early spring of 1984 it was decided that a two-person team, Bruce and I, would travel to the Falklands in May. Our objectives were:

·  Collect more offset measurements of the hull;
·  Acquire wood and metal samples necessary for conservation planning;
·  Trench or probe under the hull;
·  Consider potential logistical and engineering problems;
·  Visit the FIC archives;
·  Continue the survey of the LADY ELIZABETH that was initiated in 1983.

Our trip was originally scheduled for early May; however, a fire at the Stanley hospital necessitated visits by various British government officials who took seats that would have been assigned to Bruce and me on British transport planes. As it turned out, delay after delay caused our departure from RAF Brize-Norton to be postponed nearly a month.

The flight to Ascension Island via Dakar was as previously in an RAF VC30 transport. As we stood on the tarmac while refueling took place, we met M. R. C. "Tim" Parr, an English naval architect and engineer who was en route to Stanley to inspect the wreck of the British East Indiaman JHELUM, whose arrival and condemnation had preceded that of SNOW SQUALL. It turned out that it was to be our good fortune that Tim was bunking at Emma's guesthouse.

After spending a night at Ascension, we flew to Stanley in an RAF C130 Hercules transport. It was a twelve-hour flight with some forty people seated around the cargo. Because this had been the plane that had carried Prime Minister Margaret Thatcher to Stanley at the conclusion of the Falklands War, there was a portable toilet on board near the ramp at the rear. Some of the civilian passengers had been in the United Kingdom for medical treatment and made the trip in litter-type beds. One of them was Madge Biggs, a grand lady whom Bruce and I would later visit at her cottage in Stanley.

Our arrival at Stanley coincided with a military alert at the darkened airport. In addition to squads of soldiers running here and there, a Harrier jet was hovering some twenty feet above the runway displaying its agility by slowly gyrating as its radar scanned the area for intruders. It turned out that the alert was actually a drill that would keep the British Forces Falkland Islands busy for two or three days.

While going through customs we were told, "Wait 'til you see SNOW SQUALL, she's in bad shape." At the time, we thought the comment was a poor attempt at humor.

Upon arrival at Emma's, we dropped off our gear and with flashlights in hand headed for the FIC jetty. When I shone my light in the general direction of the hull and said, "It's right over there, Bruce," there was nothing to be seen, only the high tide lapping against the hull of the WILLIAM SHAND! The remark we heard at customs suddenly rang true.

Gradually our eyes adjusted to the unexpected scene and we could see that the entire upper part of Snow Squall's starboard side was no longer attached to the weakened frames in the intertidal zone. It was now sandwiched between the lower hull remains and the William Shand. It had become detached during a violent storm in February—a southeast gale that blew all day with shuddering gusts. One gust had blown a 20-foot container off the jetty; another, probably occurring at low tide, gave Snow Squall such a buffeting that the upper hull fell away.

The next morning we got a clearer picture of the task that lay before us. In order to gain access to that portion of the hull where we planned to acquire offsets, the dismembered upper hull had to be rescued and moved. That fact presented three questions: How? To where? By whom? The latter question was easy to answer. The task was ours with whatever equipment and labor assistance we could muster.

A snorkel inspection of the lower hull and the separated upper section revealed that the latter rested on the harbor bottom and that just below the surface were deck beams that had been torn from their portside attachments. It was quite obvious that the 12- by 12-inch beams would have to be cut away before any movement of the dislodged hull could take place. The piece of hull including the waterway, lodge knees, outer planking, and inner sheathing measured 36 feet in length by 8 feet, measured from the uppermost strake to the rotted frame ends below. Bruce estimated that it weighed 8 tons. Having a good idea of the task ahead, we spent the rest of the day doing what my journal called "contact business."

Such business included laying on some weights and SCUBA tanks, touching base with the military and FIC officials, and "signing in" at Government House, the office and residence of Governor General Sir Rex Hunt. The "business" began with a visit to the still-under-alert-status military headquarters of British Forces Falkland Islands (BFFI). The commanding officer, General Keith Spacey, already knew something about Snow Squall from files left by his predecessor. He introduced Bruce and me to his adjutant, Major Craig Treebe, and suggested that when we had our needs list made, we should contact Major Treebe. As Government House was on our route back to Emma's and the FIC, we stopped by to sign the guest book. A day or so later we were invited back to Government House for afternoon cocktails with Sir Rex Hunt and Lady Hunt and some of his staff. We told them our story and need for some sort of boat. Lady Hunt called us at Emma's a few days later with a suggestion as to a boat that might be available.

When we returned to BFFI to see Major Treebe, our needs list included: a submersible water pump for operating a yet-to-be-built lance for probing; SCUBA tanks from Royal Navy clearance divers; an inflatable boat for a work craft; a come-along winch; and an underwater saw. Three of the items on SNOW SQUALL's needs list— SCUBA tanks, a saw, and possibly an inflatable boat—were available from the Royal Navy clearance divers. A chain winch-type come-along, called for some reason a "turfer," came from the Stanley Public Works Department located near the FIC. Later, from another Falklands agency, we were able to borrow two submersible water pumps and a length of 3-inch hose.

The Royal Navy Clearance Diver Detachment was now stationed across the harbor at what is called the Camber, the site of a coaling station and pre-World War II naval repair facility. We found their headquarters and were introduced to their commanding officer, Lieutenant Ian Morrison. He had authorized the loan of SCUBA tanks and told us he and his men were eager to put their various underwater cutting devices at our disposal. We did not obtain full use of an inflatable but were promised one on a needs basis.

With all of the equipment needs sorted out, we turned back to the task that lay ahead at the site of SNOW SQUALL. Before we could begin the job of rescuing and moving the dislodged section of hull, we needed to have somewhere to store it until the return of the next expedition. We gave some thought to towing it down the harbor to the hulk CHARLES COOPER. However, an inspection trip made it clear that she was hardly an ideal storage site (but we had a chance to examine and photograph details of her interior and outer hull).

Still with no place to store the hull section, we began the work required to move it. The first step in the removal was to cut the two deck beams about 4 feet from where they partnered with their lodge and hanging knees. The cuts were made on the surface with a handsaw that we had brought down in 1983. The work was easily accomplished. I was surprised to smell the distinct scent of pitch after all the years that SNOW SQUALL had been there.

While we were taking a break to warm up in the office of Billy Morrison, the FIC dockmaster, we told him that we needed to find someplace to store the hull section. Billy pointed to a small slipway across from SNOW SQUALL and suggested we ask permission to store the hull section there; it was owned by the Falkland Islands government.

Bruce Lane adjusts the slip straps as the waterway section is secured in the Falkland Islands government slipway.
DAVE SWITZER

Before getting permission, we took a chance and moved the deck beams to the slipway by hauling them across with long lines. Back at Emma's I phoned the government office to inquire about our use of the slipway. The next morning we found that we had not adequately secured the section. It now floated horizontally with the beam stumps down and outer strakes up. Our new problem was somewhat mitigated by the arrival of a government representative, Alastair Cameron, who gave us permission to use the slipway until 1986.

Now our immediate concern was freeing the beam stump that was caught on the submerged hull remains. By this time we had gotten FIC permission to convert a steel-framed barrel float to a work platform by securing a number of pallets for a floor. By positioning the float directly over the offending beam we were able to dislodge it after much tugging on a line secured to it. It and another piece of the waterway were hauled over to the slipway.

The hull section was now moveable once it was rolled over. Preparations for the "roll over" included positioning the section near the FIC oil barge and securing it until the time for inversion.

Earlier in the day a team of clearance divers had come to do a reconnaissance of the hull area where we believed a hull sample could be cut away. The area was under the FIC jetty where damage to the integrity of the hull would not be a concern. The divers concluded that an underwater circular saw would do the job.

We were now some five days into the project and beginning to realize that we had, perhaps, too much on our plate. There was the hull section to roll over; survey visits to the LADY ELIZABETH to be carried out; a hull sample to be obtained; probing to be done; and—the major reason we were here—offset measurements to collect. We decided to reduce the list by conducting some probes toward the keel to see how deeply the lower portion of SNOW SQUALL's hull was buried and to test the dredge we had brought down.

The probe was actually a "water lance" that we fashioned from half-inch copper tubing and fittings to enable it to be joined to the three-inch hose of the submersible pump. We tried the lance out first, near SNOW SQUALL's stern, now obscured by a sunken barge. The lance worked well, but getting under the barge in pitch-black visibility was a very unpleasant experience. Future probing, as far as I was concerned, would be carried out where the offset measuring would take place, beside the WILLIAM SHAND.

The roll-over of the 37-foot hull section proved to be a less daunting task than we had anticipated, thanks to the help provided by the oil-barge crew and Tim Parr. The strategy was to position the section at the stern of the barge where a block and tackle was secured to a beam stump which acted as a lever. As the barge crew and Tim strained on the tackle, Bruce took a strain on a line running to the opposite side under the section, and it flipped over quite easily. Bruce and Tim then moved to the slipway to prepare for another "long haul." Once at the slipway, the section was made fast on the lower edge of the ramp to await the FIC crane that would move it up the ramp.

On the day of the roll-over the clearance divers returned with an underwater chain saw and circular saw prepared to cut out a 2-foot-square section of hull. Even though the water depth was minimal, the lack of visibility was total. We decided to forego sawing and to rely instead on burning out a section or using a shaped-charge explosive and primer cord.

The divers returned the next day with a Keri Cable, a burning device that heats to 3,000° F. They were confident, but Bruce and I doubted that the long immersed and waterlogged wooden sheathing would be affected. Keri Cable was meant to cut through steel not old wood. Underwater the Keri Cable burned with a brilliant flame but, as we had predicted, there was no evidence that the flame had any effect. By now the divers were very frustrated. Tomorrow, they assured us, would be the day when we would get our sample.

Armed with a shaped-charge explosive, primer cord, and the means to detonate, the divers set to work the next day. First the putty-like explosive was pasted around the area designated for sample removal. Then the primer cord was connected. The explosion, guaranteed by the divers to be minor except on the hull, was to go off at noon while the FIC workers were home at lunch.

Noon came—and the explosion went off, causing a great spume of water as well as a loose jetty plank to rise up through the jetty. When the smoke cleared, a diver inspected the hull's impact area. He reported that the structure suffered some "discontinuity" but no collectable timber sample had been freed. What was collectable was a piece of Muntz metal sheathing, which looked as if it had been cut out with a can opener. The divers were a bit chagrined at their failure. We assured them that the "failure" told us a lot about the strength of the hull below the water. When and if we were to do some cutting ourselves in order to take a part of the bow section home, we would be prepared for the difficult task.

Now the time had come to do what was necessary to collect offset measurements. In 1983 we made do with a very simple device, but now it was important to collect more accurate measurements. Before we left the States, Bruce had begun work on an ingenious method of triangulating points on the hull using a hand-held pointer connected to three stainless-steel wires. Each wire led from the pointer to a device consisting of three take-up reels. The wires leading to the reels were color-coded with thread; they ran along the jetty edge beside a 100-foot tape measure.

When the pointer touched the hull, three measurements along the scale were to be recorded (a different one for each color-coded wire). The recorded measurements would then be combined with a program in Bruce's personal computer, and from this would come points that provided a profile of the hull.

While Bruce completed the topside work of securing lengths of pipe borrowed from the FIC, attaching pulleys, and setting up the other equipment on the jetty, I went to work with the water-lance probe. We had found that the dredge became easily clogged with rocks and mussel shells, but it easily penetrated the seabed. Probing did not positively reach the keel; however, buried timbers were touched. One lay at a right angle to the bow. It could not be identified then. Today I think it may have been a cathead we later recovered in 1987.

Getting everything ready for the underwater aspect of the measuring process was time consuming, difficult, and frustrating. Although seemingly a simple task, the most daunting was threading nearly invisible wire through pulleys the size of Lifesaver candy while wearing dive mitts and making sure you were not snagging the other wires. When we put Bruce's measuring system to work, the temperature was not much above freezing, it was getting dark, and underwater visibility was very limited. I was able to obtain a few "points" at the stem but not without getting entangled in the indicator wires. This trial run told us there had to be some sort of communication between me and Bruce, and we rigged a tether/signal line between us. With the pointer touching the hull, a tug to Bruce said so, and he could record the readings on the measuring tape. A tug from Bruce said to go to the next point-place.

The trial run also told me something about the proper procedure to follow when moving along the hull. Rather than beginning at the stem and working aft, moving from aft toward the bow provided fewer entanglement problems. Before darkness, cold, and a leaking dry suit drove me out of the water, fifty-four points had been recorded in more or less vertical lines along the hull, and when Bruce processed the data upon our return to the States, the fifty-four "hits" provided reliable offset measurements. When we returned to Stanley in 1986, Bruce was to bring an improved version of his device.

We had other tasks remaining, and time had to be taken from setting up stations to attend to those needs. One was acquiring the use of a larger crane. When we found that the FIC crane did not have the lift capacity to move the hull section at the slipway, I called Major Dick Festorazzi of the Royal Engineers to see about getting a large military crane and lifting spreaders to do the job. He came through, and on Saturday, a half-duty day, we had a 10-ton wrecker crane at our disposal for the afternoon. The crane completed the big lift assisted by Bruce and Tim Parr who put their great amount of rigging knowledge to work. By 4:00 PM the section was secured. The cost of the operation was "military currency": a case of beer for the operator. The aft end of the hull section that projected out over the slipway was chocked up in a manner to ensure preservation of the lateral curve of the hull. The upward-thrusting beam ends were capped with plastic to prevent rainwater from seeping into the fresh saw cut and furthering the dry rot attack already well underway. Unknown to us at the time, our RFA friend from 1983, Peter Charlesworth, took it upon himself to visit the slipway to monitor the condition of the hull section during the year that passed before we returned to Stanley.

Earlier, two days of snowstorms and ice buildup on the FIC jetty had interrupted setting up the measuring stations, and we took this opportunity to visit the FIC archives, having gained permission from the managing director, David Britton. There we did some research on SNOW SQUALL and the LADY ELIZABETH. We also visited the Falkland Islands government archives, where we found letters from SNOW SQUALL's Captain James Dillingham to the colonial secretary requesting permission to off-load the gunpowder in her cargo. Another letter to Dillingham from Governor MacKenzie instructed him that landowners living nearby where SNOW SQUALL was to be "stranded" for repairs were to be notified that the "stranding" should not last more than two months!

Our archival research had a social counterpart, thanks to a visit to the FIC jetty and SNOW SQUALL by Madge Biggs, who had been one of the medical passengers on the C130 flight from Ascension Island. She mentioned that she had a suitcase full of picture postcards and photographs that we were welcome to peruse.

We learned a bit about Madge from our landlady, Emma. Madge had been born in Stanley; now she was well into her eighties. The cottage where she lived, a few hundred yards east of the FIC, had been built by her father. During World War II Madge had been very active in the International Red Cross; in recognition of her services she had been awarded the Order of the British Empire by Queen Elizabeth. From Madge we learned that her father had been an amateur photographer and that she and her sister had played on SNOW SQUALL when they were young.

Madge's suitcase held an extraordinary collection of photographic memorabilia. Some of the photos had been taken and developed by her father who, I later learned from Nick Dean, had been employed to punch holes in a piece of copper that was to be used to patch SNOW SQUALL. His photos of SNOW SQUALL included one showing her where she is today and razed to her 'tween-decks. Clearly seen is the deckhook that we recovered in 1983. Madge's collection of postcards proved to be a pictorial history of Stanley before World War II; present-day Stanley must have seemed a very different place to one of Madge's age.

Our last day and a half was given over to many tasks. On the hull remains *in situ* it was necessary to secure loose outer and inner planking. At the slipway we checked to be sure that all exposed endgrain on the recovered hull section was capped with plastic so that rainwater could not penetrate and cause rot. That evening was to see a very low tide. In a foray that lasted from midnight to 2:30 AM, we used the low tide opportunity to measure the angle of the list of the stem using the 1983 vertical offset measurer, which was attached to the stem on the port side. From the top of the staff we tied a weighted string. The angle between the string and the stem measured to be 12 degrees. The low tide also provided our first chance to understand how the stem was constructed, allowing us to examine the outer and three inner stem pieces and the rabbeting that received the butt ends of the outer planking. We were also able to inspect the work of the clearance divers. There was indeed "structural discontinuity"! Near that area we recovered some small wood samples along with some sheathing nails. By the arrival of our last half-day at Stanley things became less frantic as we settled into the final tasks of recovering and storing equipment and extending thanks to Billy Morrison. That thanks was said by way of a handshake and a bottle of Johnny Walker.

By 6:30 AM the next morning, we were at Mount Pleasant Airbase and aboard a C130 Hercules bound for Ascension Island

and a flight to RAF Brize-Norton. When we had arrived two and a half weeks earlier and saw SNOW SQUALL's hull damage, Bruce and I figured we would achieve only a few of our original expedition goals. But, by revising our work schedule—and continually revising the revision—and with the heat of the Raeburn stove in Emma's parlor where wet clothes and a not-so-dry dry suit became toasty warm by the next morning, and with the assistance rendered by all those mentioned above, we were able to bring back most of the information and data we had set out to retrieve. Some of this would add to the historical perspective and technical understanding of SNOW SQUALL; the rest would greatly contribute to the planning required for the "big lift" to take place sometime in the future.

### The 1986 Adventure: 7– 28 January*

The team for our 1986 trip back to SNOW SQUALL was equally divided between four Falkland Islands veterans—Fred Yalouris, Bruce Lane, Nick Dean, and myself—and four "first timers." Two of the latter, Ladd Heldenbrand and Martha (known as Marty) Richardson, had prior SNOW SQUALL experience as Saturday volunteers at the Spring Point Museum where the first elements of rescued structure were being conserved. Ladd had also played a role as a museum fundraiser. Also along was Al Gordon, who can best be described as a very good friend and supporter of the SNOW SQUALL Project. Another newcomer, geologist Bill Marshall, brought expertise with regard to ballast-stone identification, which made him an important team member.

When we set off again to connect with the RAF Air Bridge to the Falklands, we knew that we faced a host of tasks, including:

· Secure a 40-foot container to ship the 36 feet of waterway that Bruce and I rescued in 1984 as well as structural items to be collected during this field season;

*The following draws heavily on an article that Fred Yalouris and I had published in the *Falkland Islands Foundation Newsletter,* and an article of Fred's, "Symbols," that appeared in the *Journal of the Peabody Museum,* Harvard University.

· Carry out preliminary conservation measures and documentation of the above-mentioned structural items, such as knees, a hull section fragment, and miscellaneous timbers;

· Utilize an improved model of Bruce's counterweight measuring system to collect more offset information from the starboard side of the hull;

· Dig test pits through the in-hull overburden in order to better understand what to expect when it came to clearing the hull prior to recovery;

· Carry out a survey of the Liverpool-built East India-man JHELUM for the World Ship Trust, the Falkland Islands Foundation, and the Merseyside Maritime Museum, Liverpool.

When we boarded the RAF Tristar at Brize-Norton Air Base in England, we discovered that David Britton, the managing

Front row, left to right: Bill Marshall, Marty Richardson, Fred Yalouris, Ladd Helden-brand. Back row, left to right: Al Gordon, Bruce Lane, Dave Switzer, Nick Dean.
NICHOLAS DEAN

director of the Falkland Islands Company, was a fellow passenger. Within the first minutes of the flight he brought Fred up-to-date on a new situation that involved the jetty over SNOW SQUALL.

The FIC had strengthened the jetty in 1985 by filling the area directly beneath it with riprap then topping the large boulders with a covering of cement. I recall the look of astonishment on Fred's face as he realized that some significant aspects of SNOW SQUALL's hull were now permanently inaccessible, including the nearly intact starboard section with a main deck beam that Bruce and I had seen and photographed in 1984.

Upon our arrival in Stanley, we found that the tidal environment had been severely altered by the riprap placement. No longer could the tide flow under the jetty when pushed by the prevailing wind. With no tidal flowage, the area had become a repository for bushels of kelp that now completely obscured the hull. Before any work on and around the hull could begin, the kelp had to be "harvested" by loading it into a rowboat and carrying it out past the FIC pier where it was dumped. Until we were able to get a net in place, each workday began with a "kelping" exercise.

Meanwhile we worried about how we were going to ship the 36-foot waterway section back to South Portland. Back in 1984, Royal Engineer Major Dick Festorazzi had told us of the possible availability of 40-foot open containers that had been used to ship prefabricated Brewster houses to Stanley. But because of the additional structure that was to accompany the long hull section, we knew we would need a 40-foot closed steel container, which were few and far between. Back in 1983 our first rescued structure had been carried to the UK on a vessel employed by Hogg-Robinson, Ltd., then the only freight agents employed by the British Ministry of Defence. Fred found out that the company continued to be the only freight carrier for the Ministry.

No longer neophytes at wheeling and dealing, we soon made the acquaintance of Captain Peter Kidd, the Stanley representative of Hogg-Robinson, who pulled many strings so that eventually a 40-foot container was ours for $1,000. The container was delivered and situated in an untrafficked area of the FIC complex. Later, when the time came to move the waterway section from the slipway and load it into the container, we would be charged an hourly rate for a crane and flatbed trailer.

Back at the site, as soon as an anti-kelp net was extended across the bow of SNOW SQUALL, Fred and I got ready to inspect the lower portion of the starboard side. It was important to get an idea of how much silt needed to be removed in order to collect offsets as close to the keel as possible. Fred and I, the only team divers, got ready by donning brand-new bright-orange dry suits over thick underwear. The dry suits were the product of a Norwegian firm, Viking, and were much warmer than a wetsuit or my old not-so-dry suit. During the course of this expedition all of the diving and in-the-water work fell to me. Even after three to four hours in the water, I never experienced being cold.

Our first dive took us along the starboard hull and around the bow. The visibility was uncharacteristically clear, and we got a good idea as to what sort of strategy to employ and the means to do it. Before we surfaced to discuss our findings, I became entangled in the net. If Fred hadn't been nearby I would have had to cut myself free. The entanglement made it quite clear that an untended diver had to be very careful when working near the net.

By now we were going into our fourth day and the topside work routine was picking up. Some of the team were put to work clearing junk from the jetty end of the hull. "Junk" is the proper word, since the hull of SNOW SQUALL had served as a receptacle for anything that needed to be thrown away: rusty 55-gallon drums; old bottles (which gave a hint as to the drinking habits of Stanley residents); and yards of heavy cable that had been wormed and parceled (covered with canvas and heavy lashing) and once may have served as shrouds for a sailing vessel. None of the junk was archaeologically related to SNOW SQUALL. The FIC lent us their crane and an operator, and as some of our team loaded wicker cargo baskets with refuse to be lifted to the jetty and emptied into a trailer, others began the process of collecting structural items.

First to be tagged, removed, and then photographed by Nick Dean were the hanging knees that had lined the port side of the hull and which had supported the 'tween-deck beams. Then the collection activity moved to alongside the port side at low tide, where submerged timbers were found and recovered.

While this work was being carried out a saw team was at work just under the jetty on the port side. There, standing beside a jetty pillar and having escaped the riprap fill, was a very valuable structural item, which came to be known as the "J-Section." In 1983 we had alphabetized the deck beams or beam-support remnants A–J, and the J-Section was the only piece of structure that extended the port side to its original full height to include a bit of main deck and the bulwark. After a lot of effort the section was freed and lifted to the jetty where it provided a better view of hull details above the 'tween-deck.

By now the edge of the jetty was lined with various structural items that had to be cleaned and readied for shipment via

The J-section was the only piece of structure that extended the port side to its original full height to include a bit of main deck and the bulwarks.
DAVE SWITZER

container to South Portland. Timbers that had been submerged or partially so were covered with mussels, kelp, and other weeds. Cleaning by hand proved to be tedious and slow until Ladd Heldenbrand noticed that the nearby Plant and Transport Authority garage had a steam cleaner called, for some reason, a "steam jenny." Ladd convinced the PATA people to lend it to us for a few days, and it proved to be a very effective means of cleaning and "de-sliming." I expect that it was the first time ever that such a method was part of an archaeological conservation procedure.

Following the cleaning, Marty Richardson readied things for shipment, first treating timbers and knees with a fungicide called Con San. The non-polluting chemical was applied using a portable spray pump that we had borrowed from the Agricultural Experiment Station. Following the fungicide treatment certain pieces to be shipped, including the 36-foot waterway section, were treated with polyethylene glycol-400. PEG is a waxy substance, known in Europe as carbo-wax, which when absorbed by wood acts as a preservative and strengthens water-weakened cellular structure.

Meanwhile, with the help of an FIC backhoe, we tested the in-hull overburden by digging a test trench. It would be important to know the consistency of the material that would have to be removed in order to sever the bow section. We also hoped to be able to trench deep enough to reach SNOW SQUALL's inner "backbone," the keelson, which in company with the keel below created the longitudinal strength of the vessel.

The best description of the consistency of the mud was that it was incredibly viscous, and we realized that clearing it away would not be easy. The backhoe shovel could not extend far enough to reach the keelson, but with a probe fashioned out of a piece of rebar, it was possible to penetrate the mud by some four feet. A dull thump told us that the probe was hitting wood; maybe it was the keelson.

When Fred and I inspected the starboard side, we decided that the silt removal necessary to reveal the turn of the bilge—and possibly the keel—would require some heavy-duty suction.

We donned our wheeler-dealer hats and approached a British construction company, Fairclough-Miller, that was rebuilding the fire-damaged hospital. Might we borrow your sludge pump for a few days, we asked. The answer was yes, and the pump was delivered the next day!

We set the pump up on the jetty and connected the 8-inch suction pipe. My job was to direct the pipe as one might operate an airlift or water dredge. I quickly found out that the pipe had a mind of its own. Unlike an airlift or dredge, the section hose was not inert. It thrashed back and forth like a wounded boa constrictor. To quiet the thrashing, I had to ride the hose, holding on with my legs and arms. Once I had my hand too close to the pipe mouth and nearly had it and my arm pulled in. After a few pipe-riding sessions, we decided there had to be a better, safer way to operate our monster; we ended up attaching a long handle to the end of the hose so that a person standing on a float could direct the sucking action. The dredging did clear a lot of silt and harbor sediments from around the hull; however, the writhing/gulping action caused some denting of the Muntz metal sheathing. So, in hopes of penetrating the sediment down to the keel, we borrowed a water pump from the Stanley Fire Brigade and re-rigged our water lance. With the lance it was possible to get a fairly good idea as to the depth of the starboard side of the keel.

The arrival of a crane and a flatbed trailer diverted our attention to the adjacent slipway and the 36-foot waterway section. The crane was so wide that it barely squeezed between the quayside and the building on the other side. Bruce directed the loading of the waterway section onto the trailer, along with the timbers we had stored there. Getting 36 feet of structure into a 40-foot trailer was a bit of a feat. It required altering the sling setup and some very clever maneuvering by the crane operator, who would be paid more than the case of beer that had bought some military crane work in 1984!

Another diversion from hull work came when Billy Morrison, the FIC dockmaster, informed Fred that the FIC supply vessel would be arriving soon. That meant that the jetty had to be completely cleared of the bits and pieces of SNOW SQUALL that had been collected so far. So, by hand and by machine, we moved the pieces to an area near the container where Marty carried out the conservation packing in plastic wrapping.

When the time came to load this material into the container, the Fairclough-Miller people came through again, this time with a Loads-All tractor. When the container was fully loaded, Bruce estimated that 14 tons would be making the trip to South Portland.

By now we had logged two seven-day workweeks. Al Gordon, who was doing so much to make the SNOW SQUALL Project possible, thought we were all a bit mad, given the enormity of our ultimate goal and all that had to be done to reach it. He decided to give our spirits a boost with an invitation to the team to join him for dinner at the Upland Goose, a Stanley hotel known for its fine kitchen. When we all arrived, our host was missing. We knew Al had gone on a boating excursion with the local dive-shop operator, but they were scheduled to return by late afternoon. We waited over a few drinks, and waited some more.

Getting the waterway section into the 40-foot container. DAVE SWITZER

Then we were told that the prepared meal had to be served, so we started—and finished—without our host. It turned out that bad weather had forced them to anchor and wait out the weather overnight, shivering from the cold and nibbling on a few granola bars, while we were enjoying a fine meal.

Fred determined that we should have another break in our routine and arranged to rent two of the Falkland Islanders' vehicle of choice, Land Rovers. Before the conflict with Argentina there were fewer than twenty miles of roads on the island, and in order to visit friends outside of Stanley, one loaded some chain and a plank or two in a Rover and set off across a savannah-like landscape. The chains and planks were on board in case one got stuck in a situation where the four-wheel drive had to be helped by the front-bumper winch with the planks providing additional traction.

With picnic materials provided by Emma, and beer and soft drinks from the FIC store, we went "off road" and headed for a spot on the south side of East Falkland Island near Port Harriet. For those of us who had never been outside of Stanley (all except for Fred and Nick), except to the new air base at Mt. Pleasant, the trip was a delightful experience. En route, following a track, we saw the geologic phenomenon called a "stone run," a stream of boulders seemingly flowing down the mountainous terrain. We asked Bill, our geologist, for an explanation, but he had none and was as baffled by the sight as we were.

Our destination was a beach with surf rolling in. When we arrived we were greeted by a contingent of penguins marching in line. As we lounged about eating lunch, we watched vulture-like birds, called cara-caras, riding thermals. When we ventured away from the lunch site, angry terns screamed and dove at us as they protected their nesting areas. The highlight of our excursion was a visit to a Magellanic penguin rookery swarming with penguin moms, dads, kids, and eggs being tended. In the raucous crowd of birds was one emperor penguin who seemed to have no trouble getting along with his smaller counterparts.

Upon our return to Stanley and our archaeological endeavors, we put Bruce's counterweight measuring device into action to gather offset measurements from the lowermost part of the starboard side. To improve the system's accuracy, Bruce had lengthened the wire system so that it extended the *entire* length of the jetty. But with the impending arrival of the FIC supply vessel, there was no room on the jetty, so instead we created "Bruce's Lane," a catwalk fashioned from scrounged pieces of lumber, disassembled pallets, and lengths of pipe. For the FIC dockworkers, here was another example of American madness.

When we began our measurements, fierce wind conditions caused frustrating backlashes of the wires around the pulley wheels on the jetty. Having figured out the underwater procedure on my 1984 trip, I found my work with the pointer was easier than for those topside as they worked to undo snarls and record readings. Despite the problems, it was possible to record twice as many points as were collected in 1984, giving us an accurate profile of the starboard side. Such a profile would be an important feature of the planning that would precede the recovery of the bow in 1987 or 1988.

On January 28, as planned, Fred, Marty, Bruce, and Ladd left for the UK leaving Bill, Nick, and me to complete last-minute details that included disassembling "Bruce's Lane," storing our equipment, and filling out, with the help of Peter Kidd, the paperwork necessary for the shipment of the container to England and thence to Boston. (It was during this time that our scrounging ability was lauded by an FIC dockworker who remarked, "If one didn't watch out, those Yanks would pick up your spit!")

Of the three who stayed on, I was the first to leave in order to be back in time for the beginning of the spring semester at Plymouth State College. Nick stayed a week or so longer; he was hired by the Falkland Islands Development Corporation to serve as a tour guide for BBC Producer Anthony Burton, who had come to East Falkland to view the various vessel remains outside of Stanley. Bill Marshall spent a few extra days to do a bit of exploring.

The container with the waterway section and eighty-one various timbers arrived at the Spring Point Museum on April 19 with the carefully packed contents in excellent condition. Holding tanks for the timbers had been constructed in advance. Unloading the waterway structure required the use of a backhoe and cargo slings. To get the structure into that part of the laboratory where its forward counterpart, rescued in 1983, was stored, required a come-along and rollers.

As the Saturday volunteers at the Spring Point Museum went to work on the various timbers and knees that had returned in the container, casual planning for the recovery of the bow got underway. That event was slated to take place in 1987. By July the casual planning became increasingly formalized. No longer could we travel to Stanley and count on a military presence for assistance. The final and most daunting part of our project would require us to be as self-sufficient as possible.

## The 1987 Adventure: The "Big Lift"

Present at the summer planning meetings in 1986 was newcomer Dick Swete who was recruited to oversee the underwater work necessary to prepare SNOW SQUALL for her final voyage. Dick, a Texas A & M graduate, was an experienced nautical archaeologist who had been a field-school student on the DEFENCE Project. Since then he had been a member of Clive Cussler's NUMA Team and was currently working on a nautical archaeology project in the harbor of Plymouth, Massachusetts. Dick's experience with regard to lifting or moving large structural components of sunken vessels would prove to be invaluable.

Also present at the meetings was Bruce Lane, by now an old SNOW SQUALL hand. Bruce's engineering responsibilities were twofold: one was to design a framework assemblage that would support and protect the exhumed bow section on its 11,000-mile journey to the Spring Point Museum; the second involved putting together a "Manual of Methods and Procedures" for the final SNOW SQUALL expedition in January 1987.

As we came into fall, the planning meetings took place during the Saturday volunteer sessions at the Spring Point Museum. Involved now in the planning, in addition to equipment needs, were conservation requirements. This aspect of the planning brought Betty Seifert into the picture. Once the conservator at the Maine State Museum who was responsible for the conservation of artifacts retrieved from the Revolutionary War privateer, DEFENCE, Betty was now head conservator at the Spring Point Museum where she and Marty Richardson took care of the structural materials and artifacts recovered from SNOW SQUALL in 1986. These were kept wet in a number of holding tanks that had been constructed by volunteer Gary Carbonneau, a contractor from New Hampshire who was also a very-much-respected underwater photographer. Gary introduced another volunteer, dive buddy John Tomasi, to the SNOW SQUALL Project. Our equipment collection was facilitated by the late Armand Giraurod, a Saturday volunteer with family connections to a national hardware-store chain.

During the fall, Bruce Lane's plans for a 40-ton-capacity steel lifting/transport frame were being transformed into reality at a local steel-fabrication facility. With the help of professional engineer Bob Ware, Bruce supervised the trial construction and disassembly of the frame in preparation for shipment to Port Stanley.

In addition to readying the frame for shipment, attention was focused on assembling the procured and donated equipment which included the frame components (6 tons), diving gear, giant lift bags (once helicopter-transported fuel bags from the Vietnam War), pumps, compressors, tool kits, and spare parts. To be sure that all of the equipment reached Port Stanley on schedule, plans were set in motion for shipment by November 2. We would be reusing the 20-foot container in which we shipped the first recovered items in 1983.

Back in 1986 Fred had made it quite clear to the manager of the FIC, Terry Spruce, that our intention was to rescue a significant section of SNOW SQUALL's bow, and by now we were seen by Stanleyites as a group of dedicated archaeologists. Manager Spruce gave his okay for the recovery/rescue to take place.

The "Big Lift Operation" got underway on December 22, 1986, when team members Dick Swete, Bill Marshall, John

Tomasi, Marty Richardson, and Raymond Liddell arrived at Emma's boardinghouse in Stanley. As a surprise had awaited Bruce and me when we arrived in 1984, so, too, did a surprise await the visit of the advance team to the SNOW SQUALL site. This surprise, however, proved to be very pleasant.

Where the oil barge once had been moored was a different vessel. It was an ex-Argentine offshore supply boat, a 130-foot-long prize of war once registered in Buenos Aires. Formally named YAHUIN, the boat had been purchased by the Falklands Island Company in order to drain and sell the hundreds of gallons of diesel fuel in her tanks. Quickly the name YAHUIN was dropped in favor of what seemed a more appropriate name, BLACK PIG!

The advance team immediately realized that the PIG's presence would be extremely advantageous for the work that was to be carried out. Her length and height provided shelter from the nearly constant blustery west wind; her spacious decks provided plenty of room for equipment stowage and conservation tanks; and her multistory pilothouse provided expedition "office space" for the conservators and those keeping the expedition journal.

Within a day or so of its arrival the advance team was deeply involved in setting the scene for work on-site. A kelping operation similar to that of 1986 was begun; a kelp net was extended from the bow of the PIG to the quayside; and Bill Marshall made a number of "duty calls" to announce the expedition's presence, ranging from the Government House to Director Terry Spruce of the FIC to military and port administration personnel. The team also reasserted our now renowned scrounge expertise by securing a work float and situating it beside the WILLIAM SHAND. The float, serving as a dive and equipment platform, greatly facilitated the recovery operation.

Bruce and I, accompanied by Gary Carbonneau, arrived on December 30, and after leaving our bags at Emma's, we set off to see the subject of our attention for the next month. Stanley was experiencing some very low tides; at dead low tide the bow section was extremely accessible. The low tides also revealed the mess of timbers and other structural elements that we would have to deal with before the work of hull clearance got underway.

That work began the next day as soon as we received permission to deploy a davit on the PIG as a lifting boom. With a two-block tackle setup, the boom made removal of timbers a relatively easy task. We began to tag frame ends along the port side so that we'd have provenance references when archaeologically important items came to light in the hull.

In 1986 we had noticed that the bow section had been reduced in height by the recovery and rescue of the starboard-side structure, and now underwater visibility had deteriorated as more sedimentation found its way into the hull. The lack of current due to the riprap placement didn't help, either.

By the time Fred, Nick, and Betty arrived, to be followed by Al Gordon a bit later, things were in full swing; however, we were already behind schedule due to the completely unexpected contents of the hull and the silt overburden. The test pits that we had dug near the jetty in 1986 did not prepare us for what our dredges were encountering: wooden packing-case fragments; huge lumps of coal; and ballast stones. Lack of underwater visibility was compounded by cold weather and clogged pumps. It was getting more and more difficult for our divers to jump into that miserable water two or three times a day.

During our planning sessions we had talked a lot about how the bow section was to be detached from the aft section that extended under the FIC jetty. The optimum tool, we agreed, would be a hydraulic underwater chain saw, a machine that none of us had any experience operating. It would require a large compressor to provide the air power, and we weren't sure if such a compressor would be available in Stanley. So, mainly in the interest of keeping fingers and feet intact, we decided the cutting would be carried out using large cross cut saws. We had brought two saws with us so that one could be sharpened while the other was in use.

I began the sawing on the starboard side some 30 feet aft of the stem. To ensure that the cutting line on the port side was exactly in line with its starboard counterpart, we used a triangulation process to locate the cutting line.

The sawing progressed quite easily at first with no trouble cutting through the Muntz metal sheathing. By the time the cut extended down 3 feet, all of the sawing was being done in a total blackout situation. Upon reaching the 12- by 12-inch rider keelson the sawing process began to slow down. We decided to cut out a piece of the keelson to check the condition of the timber. When cut free a 1-foot section of keelson floated to the surface emitting a distinct odor of hard-yellow-pine pitch! Bruce, who was estimating the weight of the section to be recovered, was quite surprised but happy that there was less waterlogged material than anticipated.

Meanwhile, we heard that the container ship ASIFI, which was to carry our bow section to Maine, had arrived at the military port facility two miles down the coast. Our anxiety about meeting our schedule went up a notch, but it turned out that ASIFI had another Falklands port of call and wouldn't return for a week or so. This also made it possible for us to use the military port

Bruce Lane hands Bill Marshall one of the crosscut saws used to "disconnect" some 30 feet of SNOW SQUALL's bow from the hull section under the jetty. DAVE SWITZER

facility's wharf space to begin assembling the lifting/transport frame that had arrived in our container in early January. It fell to Bruce Lane to supervise the assembly and to string the heavy cod net that would serve as a "hammock." Without assistance from a detachment of Royal Engineers the assembly of the frame on schedule would have been impossible.

We also received valuable assistance from a number of professional and amateur divers who heard about what we were do-

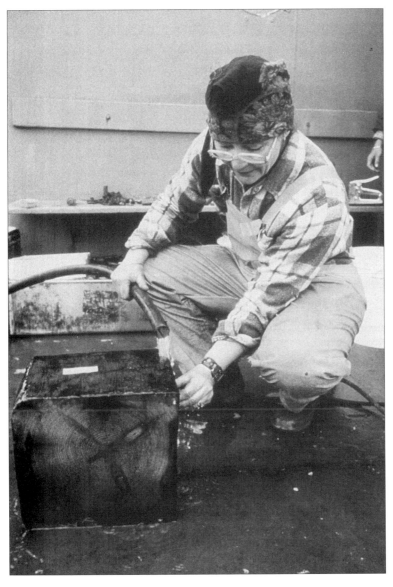

Conservator Betty Seifert with a sample cut from the keelson. When cut free, this piece of southern hard pine had floated to the surface and still had a strong aroma of pitch.
DAVE SWITZER

ing and showed up at SNOW SQUALL to help. We called contacts in the U.S. and England to find a pneumatic chain saw and a skilled diver to operate it, and on February 1 diver Tony Graham arrived with his equipment and was in the water within an hour! He did two weeks' work in two days. The week before Tony's arrival, Dick Swete and the diving team had finished tunneling and had placed lifting chains under the hull about eight feet aft of the stem and four feet forward of the cut line. The tunneling was a daunting,

The team looks down upon the object of its affection.
DAVE SWITZER

dangerous task performed by our divers, military volunteer divers, and Stella LaBlanc, a New Hampshire native and professional photographer living in Stanley. The digging began on the port side using a dredge and a balanced nozzle (a water jet designed so that there was no recoil). The goal of the tunnel teams was to get under the keel then push the nozzle up along the starboard side. When bubbles or turbulence were noted, the dredge would be worked down to meet the tunnel and a line could be passed through.

In addition to being wary of silt slides, the tunnelers had to deal with the sharp edges of Muntz metal sheathing. Finally, after many setbacks, the aft tunnel was ready for the moment of unification—port side to starboard. Dick Swete wormed his way past the keel and Stella headed down from the starboard side. They touched hands! A line was passed, and soon the first fire hose-enclosed lifting chain was in place. Our four giant lifting bags (each having a lifting capacity of 20,000 lbs.) were placed in the water and hooked up to the chains.

With the lift bags in place, the "Big Lift" begins.
BETTY SEIFERT

On February 2 the bags were inflated to their maximum load, but except for a few creaks and groans, nothing happened. The next day the four lift bags were deflated and filled with water so that they would be easier to sink. Gary Carbonneau worked furiously with the airlift to remove mud and reduce suction on the port side of the hull. Tony Graham resumed cutting on the interior of the hull, but encountered many obstructions and ruined five chain-saw blades. He had one blade left.

Raymond Liddell noted in the log book for that day: "A final challenge to the expedition's character, perseverance, and good humor was made by whatever forces or spirits hold old wooden ships on the bottom of the ocean in their muddy, slimy embrace." Almost simultaneously, the rain began to beat down with fury, the chain saw seized up and refused to cut, the underwater communication system shorted out, and with an eerie wail, the supply hose for the hookah breathing apparatus burst. We were forced to suspend diving operations for the day while we set to repairing equipment. High tide was expected at about 11:00 AM on the next day, and we decided that we would make our second try then.

On the morning of February 4, we undertook our work with determination, hoping that the hull had been severed completely and the bags would work. Fred did a final-inspection dive, the bags were inflated, and we waited. A diver was sent down with the underwater communication gear to report on progress. At about 11:22 AM we heard through the speaker system, "We have separation!" A multitude of cheers came from the team and the many onlookers who had gathered on the jetty for the occasion. The bow came up very slowly, in a quiet and stately manner—first the stem broke the surface, then the after portions. After years of groping blindly underwater we would finally get a look at the structure. The sheathing was of a shining golden hue, and we all marveled at the sharp, concave lines of the bow.

A local tug slowly towed the bow section two miles east to the other end of Stanley Harbor to the military port facility for the lift onto the ASIFI. The frame had been lifted on board several days before and was now picked up by the two giant cranes and gently lowered into the water, the bow was floated over it, and two large nylon lifting straps were passed under the hull to take up slack (using the ship's cranes) so that the chains and lift bags could be removed. It took several hours to maneuver the hull into position on the frame.

By mid afternoon everything was in place, and the signal was given to begin the lift. As the whole assembly broke the surface, all seemed well until it got about a third of the way out of the water, when the steel frame began to bend inwards at the top and a number of bolts sheared, sounding like rifle fire. Obviously, the bow section weighed more than we had figured, and was probably carrying 10 to 15 tons of mud and water. Although the frame was badly bent, it was still intact, and if we didn't continue at this point, we might have to abandon the whole project. Fred gave the go ahead and slowly the bow rose again. The frame had bent as

The bow section rests in the lifting/transport frame in a hammock of heavy cod net. The frame bent under the load, but remained intact.
BETTY SEIFERT

much as it was going to, and the cod net was not tearing, so the whole contraption held. There was a collective sigh of relief as the two cranes gently lowered the giant artifact onto the deck of the container ship ASIFI, where it was nestled between tiers of containers piled three high. A specially designed heavy-canvas covering would shield the top and four sides of the bow section as ASIFI plowed north through the South Atlantic. We spent the next day packing our own container with our equipment and the prepared loose timbers and artifacts and then it was loaded onto ASIFI.

Since there remained a substantial amount of mud, silt, and coal in the bow section, it made a lot of sense to have someone use the steaming time to Portland, Maine, to clean it out. This would also make the U.S. Department of Agriculture happier at our port of entry. Nick Dean volunteered to be the SNOW SQUALL supercargo and spent the month-long voyage spraying the bow section with salt water to keep it wet and mucking out the residual culch

SNOW SQUALL's bow is lifted up to the deck of the ship, to its spot between tiers of containers.
BETTY SEIFERT

between soakings. With the dead mussels, sewage-soaked Port Stanley mud, and fungicide applications, it was not pleasant work. His most interesting find was a belaying pin, perhaps last used when they took down the SNOW SQUALL's rigging in 1864. Gale-force winds seemed determined to shred the canvas cover, but even as the ASIFI bucked into heavy seas, the frame and lift net kept the bow section secure.

Late in the afternoon of March 11, the ASIFI picked up Pilot Granville Smith and headed into Portland past Portland Head Light. Granville brought that day's newspaper with him and announced that there would be quite a welcome. When the Moran tugs came alongside to ease the ASIFI into the Bath Iron Works pier, the Portland fireboat provided an escort, its plumes of water making rainbows in the sunshine. Just as the expedition had enjoyed a lot of local assistance back in Stanley, so, too, Portlanders and South Portlanders turned to. In a carefully planned and coordinated operation, the bow section was transferred to a Cianbro barge and then placed on a Merrill Industries lowbed trailer using cranes supplied by Fred I. Merrill and W. H. Green and Sons for the last leg of its trip to the Spring Point Museum.

## The Final Adventure: An Archaeological Epilogue, 1987–93

The final adventure provided very different thrills than the field operations in Stanley. We knew that a successful conservation strategy and an effective campaign to set the strategy in place was absolutely necessary to the ultimate goal of the SNOW SQUALL Project: a meaningful interpretive exhibit.

The person who took on the conservation challenge was Betty Seifert, who came to the project from the Maine State Museum where she had been introduced to the science of conserving waterlogged artifacts. She oversaw the transformation of what had been a welding classroom at the Southern Maine Vocational Technical Institute into a sophisticated and well-equipped facility. As the laboratory facilities grew so did the numbers of Saturday volunteers who hailed from South Portland and surrounding communities.

When the 1986 container shipment arrived, in addition to the rescued waterway section, it was jam-packed with various timbers that had been retrieved from in and around the hull. Most had been wet-wrapped in burlap, treated with a fungicide, and packaged in polypropylene. The longer timbers, six to eight feet plus in length, had been treated with a fungicide, but were not packaged.

Unloading the container had required a crane and a front-end loader. Once the timbers were outside the container, they had to be carried into the conservation lab. In some instances a hand

The bow section at the stem shows the characteristic sharp entrance and fine lines of a clipper.
DAVE SWITZER

truck could be used; most often, however, what was required to move the timbers was plain old-fashioned heavy lifting. The longer timbers required as many as four to six lifters. The last item out of the container was the 36-foot waterway section. It was "snaked" out using a crane and placed by a wide doorway leading into the lab extension where the first recovered waterway section and the deckhooks were stored along with wind-dried planking. To move the hull section into the building took, as I recall, an entire Saturday. Bruce and I and Fred Yalouris labored like pyramid builders moving stone blocks.

Subsequent Saturday work sessions focused on cataloging the recovered timbers, a task which necessitated recording dimensions, completing a rough sketch, and adding comments relative to tool marks and possible function. At this stage the cataloging effort was rather old-fashioned as it was all accomplished without the benefit of a computer.

With Saturday volunteers busy with steel brushes, scalpels, and picks, slowly but surely the timbers and other ship parts were

The disassembly crew poses with the bow section before removing it from its lifting/transport frame.
DAVE SWITZER

cleaned and de-nailed or de-spiked. Betty Seifert had created and now supervised an amazingly conscientious group of workers. When the bow and accompanying structure arrived in 1987, Betty and her assistant, Marty Richardson, having been on hand at Stanley during the bow recovery, were extremely ready to take on the major conservation tasks ahead.

The first job was to protect SNOW SQUALL's bow from the elements and provide a situation whereby the bow could be kept wet. Once more the volunteers came through, and within a couple of volunteer work Saturdays, SNOW SQUALL was secure in its "ship house." Until we had an automated sprinkler system, Dick Reimschneider volunteered to turn on the sprinkler for a period of time every evening.

The "ship house" was only partially adequate to the conservation needs that Betty Seifert envisioned which included spraying the hull with a mixture of fresh water and polyethylene glycol (PEG) and with fungicide to terminate wood-eating fungal growth. Until the museum had a facility that could comply with various environmental-protection statutes that required secure drainage and a reuse reservoir to receive the treated water, PEG and fungicide could only be applied topically.

Our next task was to remove the supporting netting. Before it could be cut away, specially designed screw jacks had to be set in place to support and level the bow. Once the jacks were installed by Bob Ware, the net came down. The bow of SNOW SQUALL, now unobscured, was an even more impressive sight and we began to get to "know" SNOW SQUALL and better understand what had gone into her construction. For instance, the shape of the deckhook recovered in 1983 confirms what Nick writes about the use of lumber at the Butler yard when SNOW SQUALL was built. On its exterior the deckhook's shape and dimensions are symmetrical, but such is not the case with the internal dimensions. Clearly, the Butler shipwright was ingeniously using timber stock on hand for its construction.

One of the first items that we studied was the foremast step, which had been felt underwater but had never been seen until the

"Big Lift." By touch, the step didn't fit our mind's-eye picture of a maststep. Instead of a mortise in the keelson into which the heel of the foremast would have been stepped, this maststep was un-mortised. Our best guess was that the mast was fashioned in such a way as to straddle the "step."

Such a maststep seemed rather unique until we had a visit from a wooden shipbuilder, Jim Stevens of Boothbay. Jim said that steps such as this "clothespin" step were quite common. Such a step, he explained, would not catch water that could rot the keel-son and mast heel. (A few years later, when the Wiscasset land-mark schooners, HESPER and LUTHER LITTLE, were demolished, Nick Dean was on hand to photo-record structural features in-cluding a "clothespin"-cut mast segment and its step.)

The weight of SNOW SQUALL's foremast had left an imprint of the octagonal shape of the below-deck portion where it strad-dled the keelson. Beside the step on the starboard side was part of a limber board which, when removed, provided access to floor timbers of the frames.

When marine surveyor Bob Cartwright visited the museum, he commented on the massiveness of the construction seen in the keelson assemblage, considering SNOW SQUALL's tonnage of 742 tons. He was also impressed by the formidable number of metal fastenings in the form of iron spikes and drifts.

Up forward in the "eyes" of the bow, wedge-shaped timbers were found packed athwartship on either side of the keelson and extending to the inner sheathing or ceiling. We had felt these tim-bers during our dives at Stanley and thought they might have com-prised an anchor-chain locker. But now our visual examination of the timbers and the area forward of them gave no hint of the wear marks one would expect to find that would have been caused by a pile of anchor chain. I think they may have served as "stiffeners" at the bow and were set in place possibly late in SNOW SQUALL's career. One of the timbers was fashioned from mahogany, which suggests that it had been set in place during one of the clipper's voyages to the Orient. Allied with the so-called stiffeners were structural features that had been installed during the building process. These were forward-pointing dagger knees found in the waterway and reinforced with cast-iron knees. The dagger knees were meant to prevent the hogging or sagging of the bow as age overtook the clipper ship.

A noticeable feature of the hull exterior was the garboard strake, which stands proud of the hull by at least two inches. Was that sort of construction unique? We thought it might be, until I came upon an example in a 1997 publication, *The American-Built Clipper Ship*. The author, William Crothers, describes such a feature as a Lang Safety Keel, a British innovation.

With the support net removed, we could measure the angle of deadrise—that is, the angle between horizontal and the turn of the bilge. In clipper ships the amount of deadrise differentiated between extreme and medium clippers, with the greater deadrise being an indicator of the extreme variety. SNOW SQUALL's deadrise of 30 degrees confirmed her classification as an extreme clipper, as did her fine and concave entrance at the bow. When standing facing the leading edge of the stem, one was struck by her fine

Mylar gauges were fashioned as movement indicators during the preservation process.
DAVE SWITZER

features and the hollowness extending aft for ten or so feet. She clearly knifed—rather than plowed—her way through the seas.

Next, we turned our attention to the Muntz metal sheathing that protected Snow Squall's underside below the waterline. Close examination of the sheathing revealed that two different weights had been installed—the heavier 24-oz sheets encased the bow and ran aft some twenty feet where they met lighter 22-oz sheathing. On the section left behind in Stanley, an even lighter sheathing protected the stern. The sheathing weight was indicated by stamps. What we were looking at was probably the third application of sheathing in Snow Squall's career. For a vessel to remain in top condition for insurance purposes, Muntz metal sheathing had to be replaced every thirty-six to forty months.

During the sheathing inspection, Bruce Lane discovered that there was an ongoing problem with "bronze disease," the scourge of bronze subject to saltwater contact. The bronze nails holding the Muntz metal sheathing in place were corroding due to an electrolytic reaction with the various iron nails and drifts used as fastenings in the hull.

The task ahead seemed daunting. Removing a single sheet of sheathing meant that seventy-five clenched nails had to be pulled from each 48- by 14-inch piece of sheathing. First we numbered each sheathing plate and then made a one-to-one tracing on Mylar. Then with a special tool designed by Bruce Lane, we experimented with the removal process—each nail that was pulled was set in a template so that its original position could be recorded. The idea was that the sheathing would be replaced with each nail going back into its original hole! More than once as I drove back to Plymouth, New Hampshire, I wondered if we weren't on the verge of being archaeologically anal! As it turned out, the sheathing removal did not have to take place due to a bold conservation strategy that would occur in 1993.

By now Betty Seifert had left to become the chief conservator at the Maryland Archaeological Conservation Laboratory at St. Leonard. For a time we got along by ourselves, then the position of full-time conservator was renewed with the arrival of Molly Horvath. She had served as Betty's understudy and had gone on to the University of Maine at Orono to study wood technology and, importantly, to become introduced to new approaches to the treatment of waterlogged wood. With Molly Horvath's arrival (soon to be Molly Carlson), a new conservation era began at the Spring Point Museum.

Like Betty Seifert, Molly was a very effective organizer of volunteers. Under her direction the museum became more education oriented through the hosting of various school groups. She also initiated the process of converting the old catalog data to a computerized database! When completed, the catalog record of the artifact collection associated with the bow structure listed an astounding total of 1,473 items of wood, glass, metal, textile, ceramic, bone, and leather. The number of items and the variety of composition that had to be effectively treated spoke to the fact that from a nascent stage the Spring Point Museum conservation laboratory under the leadership of Betty Seifert and Molly Carlson had become one of the largest of its kind east of the Hudson River.

Under Molly's direction, analysis of wood types found in SNOW SQUALL began. The results were revealing and, indeed, surprising. While in the Falklands we had been able to identify the outer hull planking, inner hull planking, and the keelson as having been fashioned out of southern hard pine or yellow pine. As far as other species employed in SNOW SQUALL's construction we guessed that the knees were oak or hackmatack, and that the frames were probably oak. That is what the standard references to nineteenth-century American shipbuilding suggest, although the late William Avery Baker, in his multivolume *Maritime History of Bath,* does speak of alternative species of timber being adopted as the forest sources of traditional wood species in Maine became more and more sparse.

When the opportunity was presented to do a "hands-on" analysis, Molly corroborated the hard-pine structural entities, e.g., the keelson assemblage, the inner and outer hull sheathing, plus the stern. The keel turned out to be rock maple; that rock maple was commonly used in clipper-ship construction was confirmed by William Crothers' analysis of construction material found in American-built clippers. When Molly completed her analysis, she had recorded eleven species of wood ranging from beech to mahogany. Later, more structural irregularities were recorded during SNOW SQUALL's last days at the Spring Point Museum.

During the summer of 1992 the SNOW SQUALL Project took a new turn, one that veered away from sprinklers, chemicals, and cleaning. We began work documenting the bow structure under a long-range program of the National Park Service U.S. Department of the Interior designed to document the engineering, industrial, and maritime heritage of the United States. The aspect of the program or project to be carried out at the Spring Point Museum is known as the Historic American Building Record (HABR), which was administered by the Historic American Building Survey/Historic American Engineering Record (HABS/HAER). Bill Bayreuther, executive director of the museum, applied to receive an architect intern through the Sally Kress Tompkins Maritime Internship Program funded by HAER and the American Council of Museums. Upon receipt of information that the museum had been awarded the first Sally Kress Tompkins internship, additional funding was received from a number of Maine-based foundations.

The first-ever Sally Kress Tompkins intern was Karl Bodenseik, a student at Roger Williams College. As his major focused on historic preservation, Karl's architectural experience was oriented toward documenting historic houses. He was a bit taken aback when he stepped into the "ship house" and saw what he would be documenting. Indeed, he and his supervisor, Dale Waldron of the Rhode Island School of Design, appeared to be dazed by the task they had taken on. It was up to Molly and me to provide assistance and encouragement.

It dawned on me that with no experience with naval architecture, Karl and Dale would have difficulty seeing SNOW SQUALL as a naval architect would. Early in the morning of the day after their arrival, Molly and I employed a strategy to "open their eyes." It involved attaching lines of red surveyor's tape on the outside of the hull at the site of every third or fourth frame. The tape strips created the effect of emphasizing the curve and hollow of the bow section. The previous evening Karl and Dale had pored over the HABS/HAER instructions regarding the taking off of lines. That information coupled with the visual enhancement got them started. Gradually, measurements via tape measure and angles gained through the use of a transit and measuring staff material-ized into a set of plans including an outboard profile, an axometric view, a below-deck plan and section, a 'tween-deck plan, plus sheer, half-breadth, and body plans, and finally a table of offsets.

The finished drawings or plans were, at the time, believed to be not only important to the archaeological record and interpreta-tion of the structure, but also to the re-assembly of the bow re-mains slated to take place in the planned new wing of the museum. There had been ongoing discussions about changes at the museum, and an architect had been hired who came up with views of a cou-ple of possible extension scenarios. Each included a conservation area in which SNOW SQUALL would sit prominently. Drains and holding tanks were included so that proper spraying with PEG and fungicide could occur. A gallery would enable the public to watch the conservators at work. When our stabilization efforts were com-plete, the conservation area would become an exhibit area. A bene-factor who wished to remain anonymous had issued a challenge to the museum: "Raise a million dollars and I will equal it."

The need to apply a fungicide was made immediate by the presence of a voracious wood-eating fungus in a number of places on the bow. A well-known destroyer of wood, haephae basidio-mycetes earns its name through the consumption of cellulose. The fungus attack presented what Molly termed "a conservation crisis." The daunting question was whether an environmentally permissible means might be found to counter the attack?

But while Molly searched for answers to that question, another reality loomed during the summer of 1992. The museum had encountered a funding deficiency, and the planned expansion had to be put on hold. It was suggested that a new home be found for the bow remains and other material recovered from the Falkland Islands.

What if we couldn't find a new home? What would we do with the bow section that had awed us each time we opened the door to the "ship house?" One suggestion was to bury it, another was to sink it. I recall that museum volunteer Bob Bent and I laughed about returning the bow and allied structure to Port Stanley. But there was nothing funny about the situation. Fred Yalouris had since stepped down as the SNOW SQUALL Project's director; I had been asked to take over. It was rather like being asked to take command of the TITANIC after she rammed the iceberg!

In the search for a new home, Dr. Stephen Williams, the recently retired director of Harvard's Peabody Museum, was of great assistance, making contacts and evaluating the conservation methods necessary to stabilize the hull. Three museums were approached: Penobscot Marine Museum in Searsport, Maine; Maine Maritime Museum in Bath, Maine; and Mystic Seaport Museum in Mystic, Connecticut. Even though the transfer of SNOW SQUALL was to be accompanied by a generous dowry that would support continuing conservation efforts, none of the institutions was prepared to take on the responsibility of the care and maintenance of a 60-ton artifact.

We were getting scared, time was running out, and pressure was mounting to make some decisions. Then Nick Dean had a brainstorm that saved the day. He called me one evening and asked what I thought about going back to the museums we had approached and asking them how much they wanted or what they could accept of the remains. I think Nick used the metaphor, "If they don't want the whole sausage, maybe they'd like a piece of it."

Bob Webb, then curator at Maine Maritime Museum, was approached first with the question, "How much?" His reply was that Maine Maritime Museum would be pleased to receive 17 feet of the bow aft of the stem plus the foremast step assemblage. It was understood that the conservation dowry would be generous.

Suddenly the word was out. A bit later we received a call from the San Francisco Maritime National Historical Park; a curator there told me that they would be happy to take away a section of hull aft of the portion going to the Maine Maritime Museum. I faxed him one of the HABS/HAER plans on which I had drawn to scale the section they had requested, and we had a deal. Eventually, the South Street Seaport Museum in New York City came into the picture, agreeing to take the 36-foot waterway section. The Spring Point Museum (now the Portland Harbor Museum) retained the deckhooks and the J-Section, which have since been incorporated into a unique reconstruction that provides a hands-on opportunity to understand various features of ship structure.

While it was a bit troubling to be the director of the disassembly of the object of our attention since 1983, it was a far better solution than burial or redeposition. Regarding the latter, any structure that was not disbursed was documented and buried in a marine clay environment. Such an environment would keep the timber in good condition in the event of exhumation.

We still needed to do something immediately about the fungi. Molly Carlson began to think about a radical, hitherto unheard of maritime conservation procedure. After consulting with Dr. R. W. Rice, a wood-physics specialist at the University of Maine at Orono, her confidence in the success of the untried procedure increased to the point where she and Dr. Rice made arrangements with the Old Town Lumber Company in Old Town, Maine, to use a lumber-drying kiln to dry the bow section that was to go to Maine Maritime Museum. If the procedure was successful, the museum would receive a stabilized, conserved, and fungi-free bow and conservation history would be made. We didn't think about the possible failure of the procedure.

In October 1993 the disassembly process got underway. Engineer Bob Ware and his men tore down the "ship house," exposing SNOW SQUALL to sunlight and rain for the first time since 1987. Molly and I, assisted by Nick Dean and Bruce Lane, supervised the cutting process.

After working to choose a saw path that would, hopefully, avoid the many spikes and drifts in the hull, I marked the path by stapling surveyor's tape along the route. Using chain saws, Bob's men began the disassembly while a representative of the San Francisco Maritime NHP looked on. The 17-foot mark on the bow section headed to Bath did not reach the maststep assemblage, which was cut out separately. When the bow was in the "ship house" the maststep assemblage had been braced to prevent it from toppling over if the iron fastenings gave way. As the cutting out of the maststep was about to get underway, I was straddling the keelson in preparation for moving to the starboard side. Just as I stepped over, the whole assemblage came crashing down! Had I delayed my position shift for a minute, both of my legs would have been broken!

By the end of the first day good progress had been made; however, the presence of unseen drifts in the keel ruined the chain-saw blades and required cutting by a Sawsall. Day two saw the arrival of the flatbed trailer hired to haul the hull section to San Francisco and the continuation of the disassembly. In some instances the route of the saw path became so confined that only a crosscut saw could do the job.

On the third day Bob Ware was busy constructing a bracing system in the bow section to prevent its collapse. The same was accomplished on the San Francisco-bound hull section. A crane arrived to lift hull portions onto waiting flatbed trailers. The last act at this stage was to haul the long waterway section out of the lab extension and position it so that it could easily be loaded for shipment to New York and the South Street Seaport Museum.

On the last day of the disassembly, I arrived early to see the bow section, accompanied by Molly Carlson, on its way to the kiln at Old Town. The remaining task at the ex-"ship house" site was to examine the structural features that had been designated for burial. These were the sections of hull that stood on either side of where the maststep assemblage had been extracted.

The examination yielded some more information about the

intricacies that were a part of SNOW SQUALL's construction. Between some of the frames we found what are known as salt stops, blocks of wood that kept in place the wood-preserving rock salt that had been poured into the frame spaces. We noted, too, that the dimensions of the futtocks that comprised some of the frames differed from their adjoining partners—one was approximately half the size of its neighbor. The shipwright had used a misshapen timber to fashion this futtock.

In December 1993 the drying of the bow section was complete after sixty days in the kiln. During that period Dr. Rice monitored the heat, the water withdrawal, and the condition of the bow. The drying process began at a low temperature with a resulting low evaporation rate. As the temperature was gradually increased, the evaporation rate increased. Upon the completion of the drying process, the bow section was found to have given off 10,000 pounds of water! The chemical treatment that had preceded its entrance into the kiln—an application of boric acid/ sodium borate, PEG, and a fungicide—produced a well-stabilized and fungi-free oversized marine artifact. Fears that the dryness might cause severe checking and shrinkage proved to be groundless. The Muntz metal sheathing, which we once considered removing, survived the kiln treatment unscathed and was now out of danger of electrolysis-caused deterioration.

When the bow section and maststep were delivered to Maine Maritime Museum in December, the museum had acquired a maritime archaeological conservation first. As compared to traditional conservation processes carried out on hull fragments of similar size, Molly's approach was relatively instantaneous—sixty days versus one, two, or three or more years.

Currently the bow is in visible storage as it rests in a specially constructed "ship house." An interpretive display utilizing the HABS/HAER plans that Karl Bodenseik produced tells viewers a bit about what I used to call "the elephant." During October 2000 a Saturday visit to the museum by the project benefactor set some wheels in motion. A grant has been made to further guarantee that the last American clipper will be an integral and highly visible part of the museum's exhibit on the history of commercial sail.

It is hard to believe that eighteen years have gone by since Fred Yalouris and Nick Dean took the first steps toward this archaeological adventure. For those of us whose lives were shaped (or sometimes bent) as a result of years of involvement with SNOW SQUALL, there is a comfortable feeling that, all in all, we did the right thing. Four museums in places that figured prominently on SNOW SQUALL's sailing career—Maine, her birthplace, and New York and San Francisco, her ports of call—now each hold a piece of the only surviving representative of the clipper era.

# EXPEDITION MEMBERS AND SUPPORTERS

The story of our archaeological adventure is dedicated to Dick Swete, whose expertise made the eventual recovery of the bow possible. Dick passed away in November 2000 in Madagascar, a victim of malaria. He was there pursuing a dream, locating and excavating the SERAPIS, John Paul Jones's famous prize.

1983
Fred Yalouris, Director
Nick Dean, Photographer/Historian
Dave Switzer, Nautical Archaeologist
Sheli Smith, Nautical Archaeologist/Draftsperson
Fred Feyling, Engineer
Huston Dodge, Master Carpenter

1984
Dave Switzer, Field Director and Diver/Archaeologist
Bruce Lane, Engineer/Offset Recorder

1986
Fred Yalouris, Director/Nautical Archaeologist
Dave Switzer, Nautical Archaeologist
Bruce Lane, Engineer/Offset Recorder
Nick Dean, Photographer/Historian
Ladd Heldenbrand, Conservator Assistant/General Topside
    Assistant
Martha (Marty) Richardson, Conservator
Al Gordon, Overseer/Expedition Supporter
Bill Marshall, Geologist

1987
Fred Yalouris, Director/Nautical Archaeologist

Dave Switzer, Assistant Director/Nautical Archaeologist

Nick Dean, Photographer/Historian

Bruce Lane, Engineer

Dick Swete, Nautical Archaeologist/"Big Lift" Coordinator

Betty Seifert, Conservator

Marty Richardson, Assistant Coordinator

Raymond Liddell, Cinematographer

Al Gordon, Overseer/Expedition Supporter

Bill Marshall, Geologist/Diver

Gary Carbonneau, Underwater Photographer/Diver

John Tomasi, Diver

During the trips to Stanley we were fortunate to have been supported in a number of ways by the following people:

The late EMMA STEEN, whose bed and board included huge breakfasts, heavy-duty lunches, and sumptuous dinners of upland goose and mutton.

DAVID BRITTON, managing director of the Falkland Islands Company, who supported our archaeological efforts, and who granted permission to bring SNOW SQUALL back to South Portland.

TERRY and JOAN SPRUCE—Terry for his support as director of the Falkland Islands Company; Joan for her hospitality and keen historical interests.

JOHN and VERONICA FOWLER, for their hospitality by providing, in 1983, the use of their washing machine and dryer and for providing a domestic change of venue.

The late MADGE BIGGS, OBE, who shared her collection of early Stanley photos and graced us with marvelous stories.

JOHN SMITH, historian and museum director, who lured Nick with the question, "What are you Mainers going to do about SNOW SQUALL?"

BILLY MORRISON, Falkland Islands Company dockmaster, a provider of good advice—with a blind eye to our scrounging activities.

GEORGE BETTS, master of the Falkland Islands Company vessel MV MONSUNEN, who lent us weights, and who provided much-needed hacksaw blades for the disassembly of the lower deck hook.

LES HALLIDAY, Stanley harbor master and immigration officer, who facilitated our entrances and exits.

DAVE EYNON, dive shop proprietor from whom we rented SCUBA tanks, and who took Al Gordon and Ladd Heldenbrand on their great adventure on the schooner PELICAN.

STELLA LEBLANC, photographer and diver, who provided valuable assistance leading up to the "big lift" in 1987.

COMMANDING GENERALS of British Forces Falkland Islands, who authorized various aspects of assistance from the military.

ROYAL NAVY CLEARANCE DIVERS, who contributed to the success of the 1983 and 1984 field seasons.

ROYAL ENGINEERS, without whose assistance we never would have been able to assemble the lift/transport frame.

MILITARY PERSONNEL from various branches, who, when their duty day was over, volunteered to help with the arduous task of clearing the bow of debris before the "Big Lift."

PHOTOGRAPHER ASSISTANCE, through the use of a military darkroom and that of photographer Peter Gilding. Nick Dean's darkroom skills made it possible to snap photos and see the results almost immediately.

THE PEOPLE OF STANLEY, who made us feel welcome after they realized that their town was making a significant contribution to American maritime history.

# SNOW SQUALL PLANS AND LINES

On the following pages are drawings of the ship's construction details and shape made by the Clipper Ship SNOW SQUALL Bow Recording Project, which is part of the Historic American Engineering Record (HAER), a long-range program to document the engineering, industrial, and maritime heritage of the United States. As part of the National Park Service, U.S. Department of the Interior, the HAER program is administrated by the Historic American Building Survey/Historic American Engineering Record Division (HABS/HAER), Dr. Robert J. Kapsch, chief.

The Clipper Ship SNOW SQUALL Bow Recording Project was sponsored during the summer of 1992 by the Spring Point Museum, William A. Bayreuther, executive director. This project was awarded the first Sally Kress Tompkins Maritime Intern, jointly funded by HABS/HAER and the Council of American Maritime Museums, Peter Neill, president. It also received grant funding from the Davis Family Foundation, the Joan Whitney and Charles Shipman Payson Charitable Foundation, and the Odiorne Fund of the Maine State Archives, plus in-kind support from Southern Maine Technical College.

The field work and measured drawings were prepared under the project management of Robbyn L. Jackson, HAER staff architect. The recording team consisted of Dale O. Waldron, architect supervisor (Rhode Island School of Design), and Karl N. Bodensiek, Sally Kress Tompkins Maritime Intern (Roger Williams College), with assistance from David C. Switzer (SNOW SQUALL Project director) and Molly J. Horvath (Spring Point Museum conservator). The draftsmen were Karl N. Bodensiek, Dale O. Waldron, and Todd A. Croteau.

# TABLE OF HULL MEASUREMENTS

*All dimensions below are to outer surface of hull and are given in feet, inches and eighths of an inch (see note B).*

## STATIONS — STARBOARD

| | | 1 | 2 | 3 | 4 | 5 | 6 | 7 | 8 | 9 | 10 | 11 | 12 | End Cut |
|---|---|---|---|---|---|---|---|---|---|---|---|---|---|---|
| Heights Above Base | 9' Butt | | | | | | | | | | | | 2-11-2 | 2-6-2 |
| | 8' Butt | | | | | | | | | | | | 2-4-2 | 1-11-0 |
| | 7' Butt | | | | | | | | | | | 3-2-6 | 1-10-0 | 1-5-0 |
| | 6' Butt | | | | | | | | | | 4-0-0 | 2-6-2 | 1-5-0 | 1-0-6 |
| | 5' Butt | | | | | | | | 5-2-6 | 4-3-6 | 3-1-2 | 1-11-4 | 1-1-4 | 0-9-6 |
| | 4' Butt | | | | | | | | 3-11-4 | 3-3-0 | 2-5-2 | 1-6-6 | 0-10-4 | 0-7-4 |
| | 3' Butt | | | | | | 4-8-2 | 3-4-0 | 2-10-4 | 2-4-4 | 1-10-2 | 1-2-6 | 0-8-6 | 0-6-0 |
| | 2' Butt | | | | 5-10-6 | 3-6-4 | 2-9-6 | 2-3-0 | 1-11-4 | 1-8-4 | 1-5-0 | 0-11-6 | 0-7-6 | 0-5-2 |
| | 1' Butt | | 7-0-2 | 3-2-0 | 2-5-4 | 1-10-4 | 1-6-2 | 1-3-4 | 1-2-0 | 1-0-6 | 0-10-4 | 0-8-0 | 0-4-6 | 0-2-6 |
| Half-Breadths | 9'-6"WL | 0-9-4 | | | | | | | | | | | | |
| | 8'-6"WL | 0-8-6 | 1-2-6 | | | | | | | | | | | |
| | 7'-6"WL | 0-8-0 | 1-1-0 | 1-10-2 | 2-3-2 | | | | | | | | | |
| | 6'-6"WL | 0-7-2 | 0-11-0 | 1-8-6 | 2-1-4 | 3-1-2 | | | | | | | | |
| | 5'-6"WL | 0-6-4 | 0-9-4 | 1-6-6 | 1-11-0 | 2-9-4 | | | | | | | | |
| | 4'-6"WL | 0-5-4 | 0-8-0 | 1-4-2 | 1-8-4 | 2-5-2 | 2-11-0 | | 4-5-4 | 5-2-0 | 6-6-0 | | | |
| | 3'-6"WL | 0-4-6 | 0-6-6 | 1-1-2 | 1-4-4 | 1-11-6 | 2-5-2 | 3-1-4 | 3-6-6 | 4-3-2 | 5-5-4 | 7-4-2 | | |
| | 2'-6"WL | 0-4-0 | 0-5-6 | 1-9-6 | 1-0-2 | 1-5-0 | 1-9-2 | 2-3-0 | 2-7-2 | 3-1-4 | 4-1-2 | 5-11-4 | 8-3-4 | 8-11-2 |
| Diagonals | A | 0-11-4 | 1-7-0 | 2-5-2 | 2-11-0 | | | | 6-6-4 | 7-1-4 | 8-2-2 | 9-6-0 | 11-0-0 | 11-4-2 |
| | B | 0-8-6 | 1-1-0 | 1-11-4 | 2-4-2 | 3-1-6 | 3-7-2 | 4-3-4 | 4-8-2 | 5-2-0 | 5-10-2 | 6-10-4 | 7-11-0 | 8-4-2 |
| | C | 0-6-0 | 0-8-2 | 1-2-2 | 1-4-6 | 1-9-2 | 2-0-4 | 2-3-6 | 2-6-0 | 2-8-4 | 3-0-2 | 3-6-6 | 4-2-2 | 4-6-0 |

## PORT

| | | 1 | 2 | 3 | 4 | 5 | 6 | 7 | 8 | 9 | 10 | 11 | 12 | End Cut |
|---|---|---|---|---|---|---|---|---|---|---|---|---|---|---|
| Heights Above Base | 10' Butt | | | | | | | | | | | | 13-1-6 | 11-9-4 |
| | 9' Butt | | | | | | | | | | | 10-11-4 | 9-9-6 | 8-8-4 |
| | 8' Butt | | | | | | | | | | 9-8-6 | 8-1-4 | 7-4-0 | 6-8-0 |
| | 7' Butt | | | | | | | | | | 7-5-4 | 6-2-6 | 5-6-4 | 5-1-4 |
| | 6' Butt | | | | | | | | | | 5-8-4 | 4-10-0 | 4-3-6 | 4-0-2 |
| | 5' Butt | | | | | | | | 5-6-4 | | 4-4-6 | 3-9-6 | 3-4-6 | 3-2-0 |
| | 4' Butt | | | | | 8-9-0 | 6-1-4 | 5-0-0 | 4-1-6 | | 3-4-2 | 2-11-4 | 2-8-0 | 2-5-4 |
| | 3' Butt | | | | 8-10-4 | 5-10-0 | 4-3-6 | 3-7-4 | 3-0-4 | | 2-6-0 | 2-2-6 | 2-0-4 | 1-10-2 |
| | 2' Butt | | | 8-0-2 | 5-3-0 | 3-8-0 | 2-10-6 | 2-6-2 | 2-2-0 | | 1-10-2 | 1-8-0 | 1-5-4 | 1-3-6 |
| | 1' Butt | | 7-4-2 | 3-7-6 | 2-7-4 | 2-0-6 | 1-9-0 | 1-6-0 | 1-4-2 | | 1-1-4 | 0-11-4 | 0-9-4 | 0-8-0 |
| Half-Breadths | 12'-6"WL | | | | | | | | | | 8-10-2 | 9-4-4 | 9-9-6 | 8-8-4 |
| | 11'-0"WL | | | | | | | | | | 8-5-6 | 9-0-0 | 9-4-2 | 9-9-4 |
| | 9'-6"WL | 0-11-6 | | | | | | | | | 7-10-6 | 8-6-2 | 8-10-6 | 9-3-4 |
| | 8'-6"WL | 0-9-2 | 1-2-2 | 2-1-0 | 2-10-6 | 3-10-0 | 4-11-4 | | | | 7-5-4 | 8-2-6 | 8-6-0 | 8-10-6 |
| | 7'-6"WL | 0-8-0 | 1-0-2 | 1-10-4 | 2-7-6 | 3-7-2 | 4-7-0 | | | | 7-0-0 | 7-8-2 | 8-0-6 | 8-5-2 |
| | 6'-6"WL | 0-7-2 | 0-10-4 | 1-8-0 | 2-4-4 | 3-3-0 | 4-2-0 | 4-10-6 | 5-6-4 | | 6-5-4 | 7-1-6 | 7-6-4 | 7-10-4 |
| | 5'-6"WL | 0-6-2 | 0-8-6 | 1-5-2 | 2-0-6 | 2-10-2 | 3-8-2 | 4-4-0 | 4-11-4 | | 5-10-2 | 6-6-0 | 6-9-6 | 7-3-4 |
| | 4'-6"WL | 0-5-4 | 0-7-4 | 1-2-6 | 1-9-0 | 2-5-0 | 3-1-2 | 3-8-2 | 4-3-2 | | 5-1-2 | 5-8-2 | 6-2-0 | 6-5-4 |
| | 3'-6"WL | 0-4-6 | 0-6-4 | 0-11-4 | 1-4-4 | 1-10-6 | 2-5-2 | 2-10-6 | 3-5-4 | | 4-1-6 | 4-8-0 | 5-1-4 | 5-4-6 |
| | 2'-6"WL | 0-4-2 | 0-5-6 | 0-9-0 | 0-11-4 | 1-3-6 | 1-8-0 | 1-11-6 | 2-4-6 | | 2-11-6 | 3-4-6 | 3-9-0 | 4-0-6 |
| Diagonals | A | 1-0-0 | 1-6-2 | 2-6-2 | 3-4-0 | 4-3-4 | 5-2-2 | 5-9-6 | 6-4-4 | | 7-1-2 | 7-7-0 | 7-11-4 | 8-2-0 |
| | B | 0-8-2 | 0-11-6 | 1-9-4 | 2-5-0 | 3-1-2 | 3-8-2 | 4-1-2 | 4-6-4 | | 5-0-2 | 5-4-2 | 5-7-4 | 5-9-6 |
| | C | 0-6-0 | 0-8-0 | 1-0-6 | 1-3-6 | 1-8-0 | 1-11-2 | 2-1-4 | 2-3-6 | | 2-7-2 | 2-9-0 | 2-11-2 | 3-1-0 |

# BODY PLAN

Lines are to outside of hull.

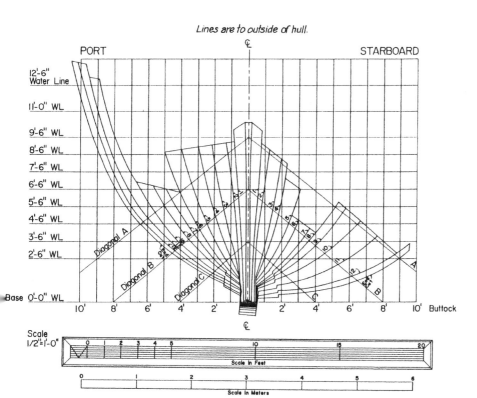

Notes:

A. SNOW SQUALL's lines were taken with the bow fragment lying on a metal cradle and supported by blocking and jacks. The hull lies listing to port, with the keel running lower as it goes aft. Due to the condition of the hull and lack of symmetry, both port and starboard lines were lifted. Stations were established on the starboard side at intervals along the hull where it was deemed necessary and free of obstruction. The stations were then squared to the keel and marked with survey flagging tape. The starboard stations were transferred to the port side under the keel and marked. At station 1 points for measurement were established at intervals of one - and-a-half feet, and subsequently transferred to each station using a water level. A ten-foot staff with measured one-foot increments was used to triangulate to these points, thus producing the data necessary for the drawings.

B. Example: 13-6-6 = 13' 6-3/4" (the numerals indicate feet-inches · 1/8 inches). Measurements were scaled from the Sheer and Half-breadth Plans.

C. The lines depict the hull "as is" (1992) and are not an attempt to recreate "as built" lines.

D. All offsets are to the outside of the Muntz Metal sheathing or the outside of the hull planking.

E. Station 9 on the port side was found to be inaccessible due to blocking employed to support the hull.

F. While the accuracy of most field measurements is estimated to be +/- 1/2", plots inevitably introduce larger errors due to the smaller scale of the drawings.

DELINEATED BY: Dale O. Waldron, 1992   Todd A. Croteau, 1993

CLIPPER SHIP "SNOW SQUALL" BOW RECORDING PROJECT
UNITED STATES NATIONAL PARK SERVICE DEPARTMENT OF THE INTERIOR

SOUTH PORTLAND

CLIPPER SHIP "SNOW SQUALL" (1851)
SPRING POINT MUSEUM
CUMBERLAND COUNTY

MAINE

SHEET 2 OF 10

HISTORIC AMERICAN ENGINEERING RECORD
ME - 7

IF REPRODUCED, PLEASE CREDIT: HISTORIC AMERICAN ENGINEERING RECORD, NATIONAL PARK SERVICE, NAME OF DELINEATOR, DATE OF THE DRAWING

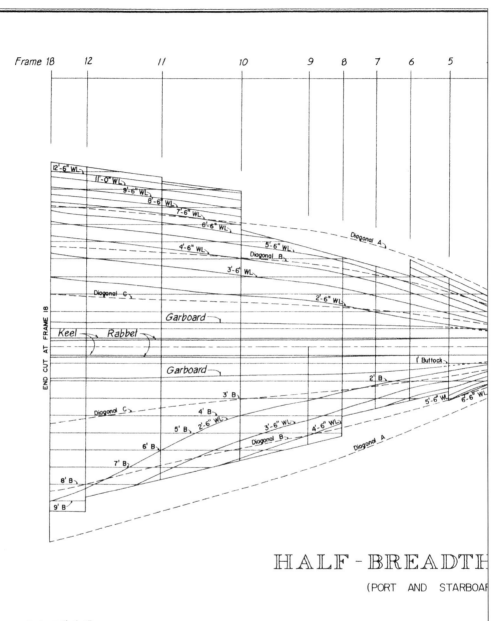

Frame 18    12       11         10      9  8  7  6  5

12'-6" WL
11'-0" WL
9'-6" WL
8'-6" WL
7'-6" WL
6'-6" WL
Diagonal A
4'-6" WL
5'-6" WL
Diagonal B
3'-6" WL
Diagonal C
2'-6" WL

END CUT AT FRAME 18

Garboard

Keel — Rabbel

Garboard

1' Buttock

2' B
3' B
Diagonal C
4' B
5' B  2'-6" WL
5'-6" WL
6'-6" WL
3'-6" WL
6' B
Diagonal B  4'-6" WL
7' B
Diagonal A
8' B
9' B

# HALF-BREADTH

(PORT AND STARBOAR

Scale: 1/2" = 1'- 0"

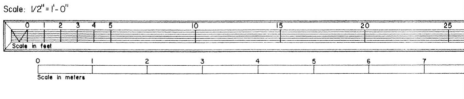

Scale in feet
0  1  2  3  4  5        10        15        20       25

Scale in meters
0    1    2    3    4    5    6    7

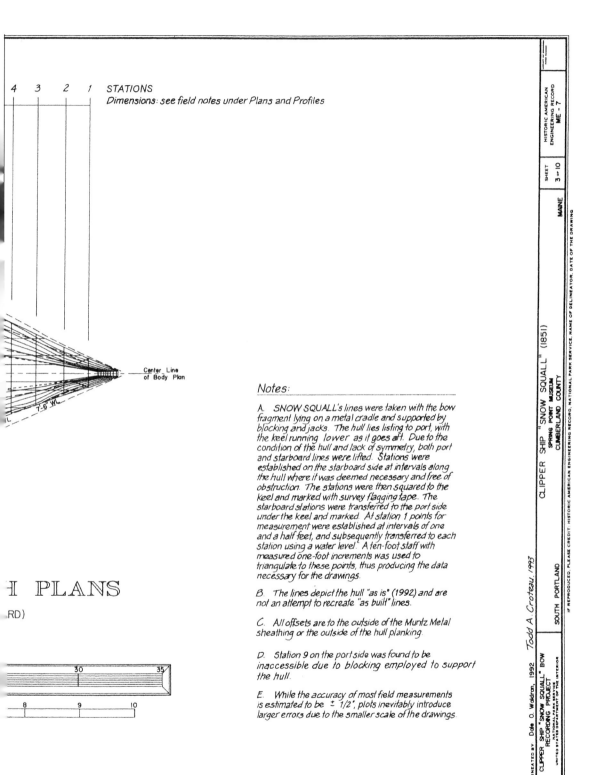

4   3   2   1    STATIONS
                 *Dimensions: see field notes under Plans and Profiles*

Center Line
of Body Plan

7-6 WL

Notes:

A.   SNOW SQUALL's lines were taken with the bow fragment lying on a metal cradle and supported by blocking and jacks. The hull lies listing to port, with the keel running lower as it goes aft. Due to the condition of the hull and lack of symmetry, both port and starboard lines were lifted. Stations were established on the starboard side at intervals along the hull where it was deemed necessary and free of obstruction. The stations were then squared to the keel and marked with survey flagging tape. The starboard stations were transferred to the port side under the keel and marked. At station 1 points for measurement were established at intervals of one and a half feet, and subsequently transferred to each station using a water level. A ten-foot staff with measured one-foot increments was used to triangulate to these points, thus producing the data necessary for the drawings.

B.   The lines depict the hull "as is" (1992) and are not an attempt to recreate "as built" lines.

C.   All offsets are to the outside of the Muntz Metal sheathing or the outside of the hull planking.

D.   Station 9 on the port side was found to be inaccessible due to blocking employed to support the hull.

E.   While the accuracy of most field measurements is estimated to be ± 1/2", plots inevitably introduce larger errors due to the smaller scale of the drawings.

H PLANS

RD)

30          35

8      9      10

DELINEATED BY Dale O. Waldron, 1992   Todd A. Croteau, 1993

CLIPPER SHIP "SNOW SQUALL" BOW
RECORDING PROJECT
UNITED STATES DEPARTMENT OF THE INTERIOR
NATIONAL PARK SERVICE

SOUTH PORTLAND

CLIPPER SHIP "SNOW SQUALL" (1851)
SPRING POINT MUSEUM
CUMBERLAND COUNTY

MAINE

SHEET
3 OF 10

HISTORIC AMERICAN
ENGINEERING RECORD
ME - 7

IF REPRODUCED, PLEASE CREDIT: HISTORIC AMERICAN ENGINEERING RECORD, NATIONAL PARK SERVICE, NAME OF DELINEATOR, DATE OF THE DRAWING

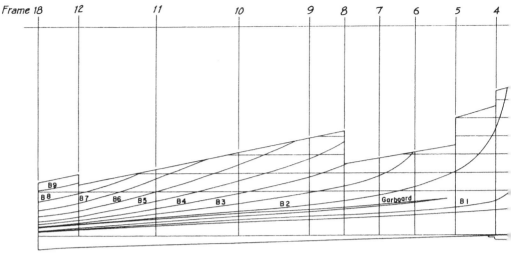

Frame 18   12      11      10      9  8  7  6  5  4

B 9
B 8   B 7   B 6   B 5   B 4   B 3   B 2   Garboard   B 1

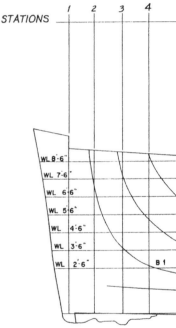

STATIONS        1   2   3   4

WL 8'-6"
WL 7'-6"
WL 6'-6"
WL 5'-6"
WL 4'-6"
WL 3'-6"
WL 2'-6"                    B 1

## Notes:

A.  SNOW SQUALL's lines were taken with the bow
fragment lying on a metal cradle and supported by
blocking and jacks. The hull lies listing to port, with
the keel running lower as it goes aft. Due to the
condition of the hull and lack of symmetry, both port
and starboard lines were lifted. Stations were
established on the starboard side at intervals along
the hull where it was deemed necessary and free of
obstruction. The stations were then squared to the
keel and marked with survey flagging tape. The
starboard stations were transferred to the port side
under the keel and marked. At station 1 points for
measurement were established at intervals of one
and a half feet, and subsequently transferred to each
station using a water level. A ten-foot staff with
measured one-foot increments was used to
triangulate to these points, thus producing the data
necessary for the drawings.

B.  The lines depict the hull "as is" (1992) and are
not an attempt to recreate "as built" lines.

C.  All offsets are to the outside of the Muntz Metal
sheathing or the outside of the hull planking.

D.  Station 9 on the port side was found to be
inaccessible due to blocking employed to support
the hull.

E.  While the accuracy of most field measurements
is estimated to be +/- 1/2", plots inevitably introduce
larger errors due to the smaller scale of the drawings.

Scale:  1/2"= 1'- O"

0   1   2   3   4   5
Scale in feet

0          1          2
Scale in meters

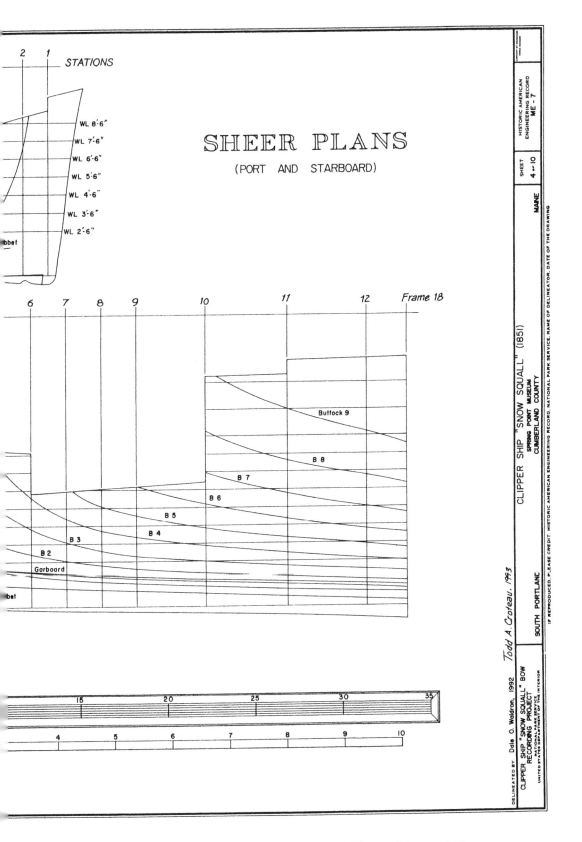

STATIONS

WL 8'-6"
WL 7'-6"
WL 6'-6"
WL 5'-6"
WL 4'-6"
WL 3'-6"
WL 2'-6"

bbet

# SHEER PLANS

(PORT AND STARBOARD)

2  1

6  7  8  9  10  11  12  Frame 18

Buttock 9

B 8

B 7

B 6

B 5

B 4

B 3

B 2

Garboard

bet

15  20  25  30  35

4  5  6  7  8  9  10

DELINEATED BY Dale O. Waldron, 1992    Todd A. Croteau. 1993

CLIPPER SHIP "SNOW SQUALL" BOW
RECORDING PROJECT
NATIONAL PARK SERVICE
UNITED STATES DEPARTMENT OF THE INTERIOR

CLIPPER SHIP "SNOW SQUALL" (1851)
SPRING POINT MUSEUM
CUMBERLAND COUNTY

SOUTH PORTLAND    MAINE

HISTORIC AMERICAN
ENGINEERING RECORD
ME - 7

SHEET
4 of 10

IF REPRODUCED, PLEASE CREDIT: HISTORIC AMERICAN ENGINEERING RECORD, NATIONAL PARK SERVICE, NAME OF DELINEATOR, DATE OF THE DRAWING

# BELOW DECKS PLAN & SECTION

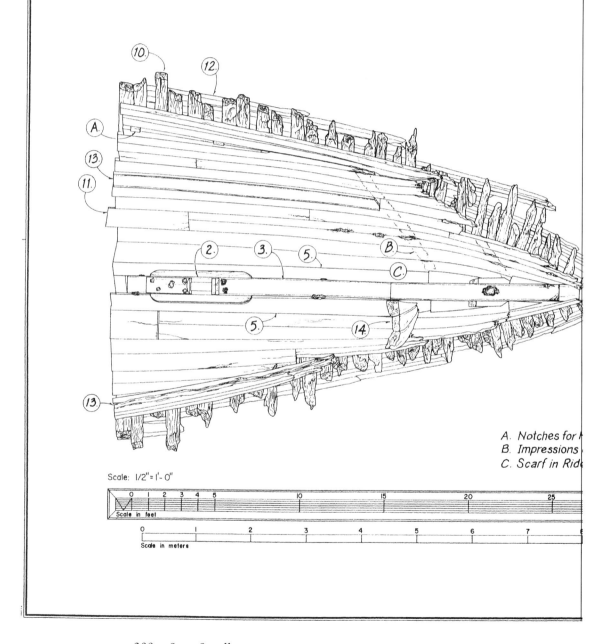

A. Notches for
B. Impressions
C. Scarf in Rid

Scale: 1/2" = 1'- 0"

0  1  2  3  4  5      10      15      20      25
Scale in feet

0      1      2      3      4      5      6      7
Scale in meters

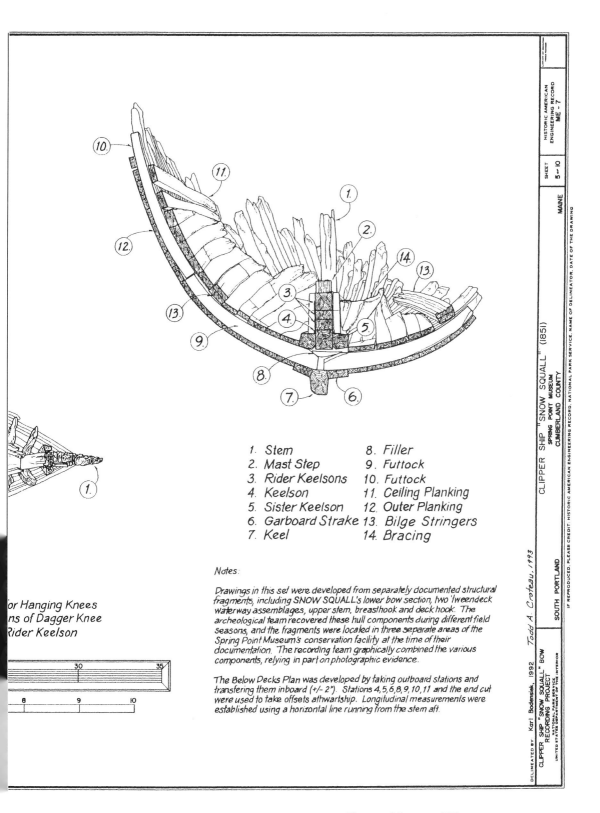

1. Stem
2. Mast Step
3. Rider Keelsons
4. Keelson
5. Sister Keelson
6. Garboard Strake
7. Keel
8. Filler
9. Futtock
10. Futtock
11. Ceiling Planking
12. Outer Planking
13. Bilge Stringers
14. Bracing

or Hanging Knees
ns of Dagger Knee
Rider Keelson

Notes:

Drawings in this set were developed from separately documented structural fragments, including SNOW SQUALL's lower bow section, two 'tweendeck waterway assemblages, upper stem, breasthook and deck hook. The archeological team recovered these hull components during different field seasons, and the fragments were located in three separate areas of the Spring Point Museum's conservation facility at the time of their documentation. The recording team graphically combined the various components, relying in part on photographic evidence.

The Below Decks Plan was developed by taking outboard stations and transfering them inboard (+/- 2"). Stations 4,5,6,8,9,10,11 and the end cut were used to take offsets athwartship. Longitudinal measurements were established using a horizontal line running from the stem aft.

DELINEATED BY: Karl Bodensiek, 1992   Todd A. Croteau, 1993

CLIPPER SHIP "SNOW SQUALL" BOW
RECORDING PROJECT
UNITED STATES DEPARTMENT OF THE INTERIOR
NATIONAL PARK SERVICE

SOUTH PORTLAND

CLIPPER SHIP "SNOW SQUALL" (1851)
SPRING POINT MUSEUM
CUMBERLAND COUNTY

MAINE

SHEET
5 OF 10

HISTORIC AMERICAN
ENGINEERING RECORD
ME - 7

IF REPRODUCED, PLEASE CREDIT: HISTORIC AMERICAN ENGINEERING RECORD, NATIONAL PARK SERVICE, NAME OF DELINEATOR, DATE OF THE DRAWING

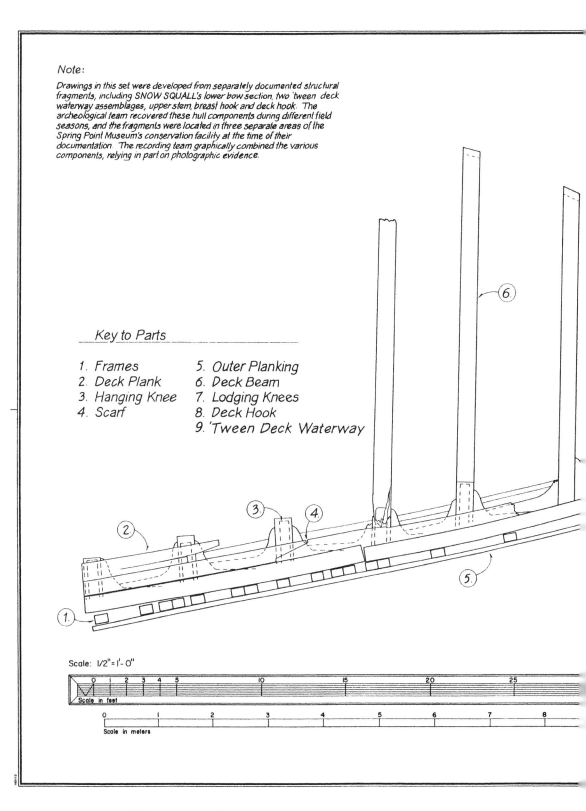

Note:

Drawings in this set were developed from separately documented structural fragments, including SNOW SQUALL's lower bow section, two 'tween deck waterway assemblages, upper stem, breast hook and deck hook. The archeological team recovered these hull components during different field seasons, and the fragments were located in three separate areas of the Spring Point Museum's conservation facility at the time of their documentation. The recording team graphically combined the various components, relying in part on photographic evidence.

## Key to Parts

1. Frames
2. Deck Plank
3. Hanging Knee
4. Scarf

5. Outer Planking
6. Deck Beam
7. Lodging Knees
8. Deck Hook
9. 'Tween Deck Waterway

Scale: 1/2"= 1'- 0"

Scale in feet

Scale in meters

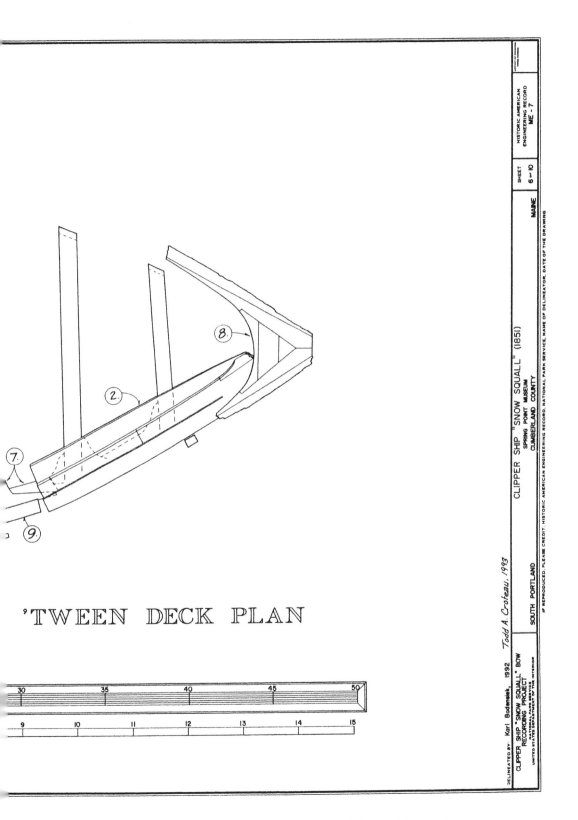

'TWEEN DECK PLAN

DELINEATED BY Karl Bodensiek, 1992    Todd A. Croteau, 1993

CLIPPER SHIP "SNOW SQUALL" (1851)
SPRING POINT MUSEUM
CUMBERLAND COUNTY

CLIPPER SHIP "SNOW SQUALL" BOW
RECORDING PROJECT
NATIONAL PARK SERVICE
UNITED STATES DEPARTMENT OF THE INTERIOR

SOUTH PORTLAND                    MAINE

SHEET
6 OF 10

HISTORIC AMERICAN
ENGINEERING RECORD
ME - 7

IF REPRODUCED, PLEASE CREDIT: HISTORIC AMERICAN ENGINEERING RECORD, NATIONAL PARK SERVICE, NAME OF DELINEATOR, DATE OF THE DRAWING

* *Waterway Assemblage produced from 'Tween Deck Plan and Inboard Profile.*
  *Planking and Frames scaled from 1982 and 1983 photographs.*

## *Waterway Assemblage* *

*'Tween Deck Stanchion*

*Rider Keelson*

*Mast Step*

## *Lower Bow Section*

Notes:

Drawings in this set were developed from separately documented structural
fragments, including SNOW SQUALL's lower bow section, two 'tweendeck
waterway assemblages, upper stem, breasthook and deck hook. The
archeological team recovered these hull components during different field
seasons, and the fragments were located in three separate areas of the
Spring Point Museum's conservation facility at the time of their
documentation. The recording team graphically combined the various
components, relying in part on photographic evidence.

Scale: 1/2" = 1'- 0"

```
  0  1  2  3  4  5         10        15        20        25
Scale in feet
```

```
  0        1        2        3        4        5        6        7        8
Scale in meters
```

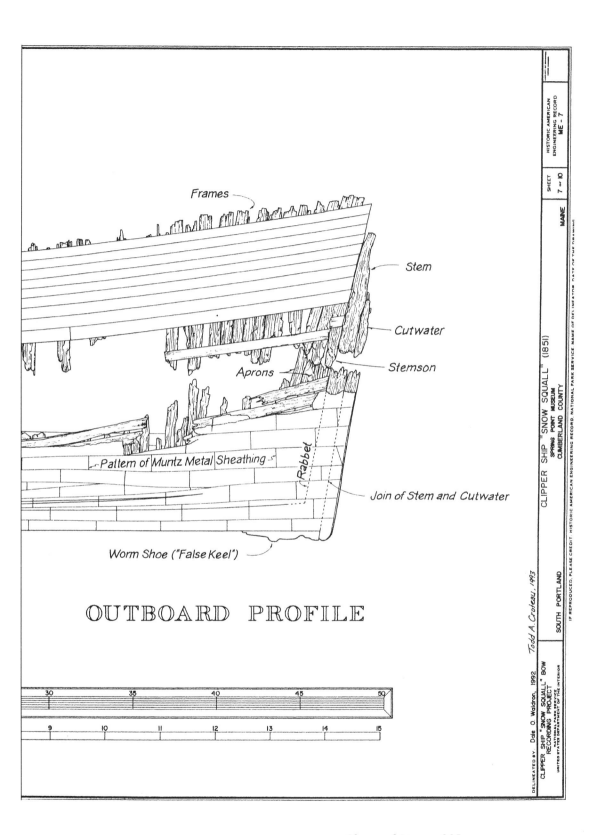

Frames

Stem

Cutwater

Aprons

Stemson

*Pattern of Muntz Metal Sheathing*

*Rabbet*

*Join of Stem and Cutwater*

*Worm Shoe ("False Keel")*

OUTBOARD PROFILE

DELINEATED BY Dale O. Waldron, 1992    Todd A. Croteau, 1993

CLIPPER SHIP "SNOW SQUALL" BOW
RECORDING PROJECT
NATIONAL PARK SERVICE
UNITED STATES DEPARTMENT OF THE INTERIOR

SOUTH PORTLAND

CLIPPER SHIP "SNOW SQUALL" (1851)
SPRING POINT MUSEUM
CUMBERLAND COUNTY

MAINE

SHEET
7 OF 10

HISTORIC AMERICAN
ENGINEERING RECORD
ME - 7

IF REPRODUCED, PLEASE CREDIT: HISTORIC AMERICAN ENGINEERING RECORD, NATIONAL PARK SERVICE, NAME OF DELINEATOR, DATE OF THE DRAWING

30    35    40    45    50

9    10    11    12    13    14    15

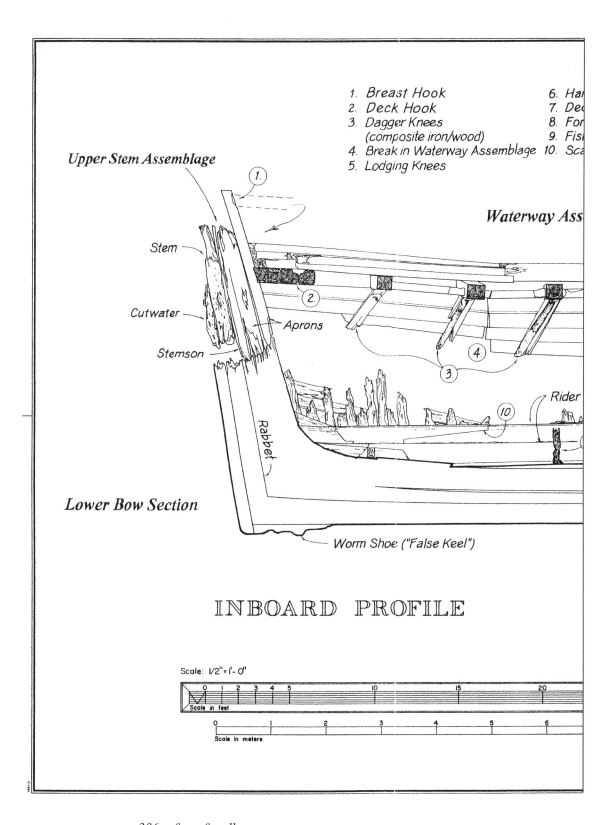

1. Breast Hook
2. Deck Hook
3. Dagger Knees
   (composite iron/wood)
4. Break in Waterway Assemblage
5. Lodging Knees

6. Ha~
7. Dec
8. For
9. Fisl
10. Sc~

Upper Stem Assemblage

Waterway Ass

Stem

Cutwater

Aprons

Stemson

Rider

Rabbet

Lower Bow Section

Worm Shoe ("False Keel")

INBOARD PROFILE

Scale: 1/2" = 1'- 0"

0  1  2  3  4  5        10       15       20
Scale in feet

0      1      2      3      4      5      6
Scale in meters

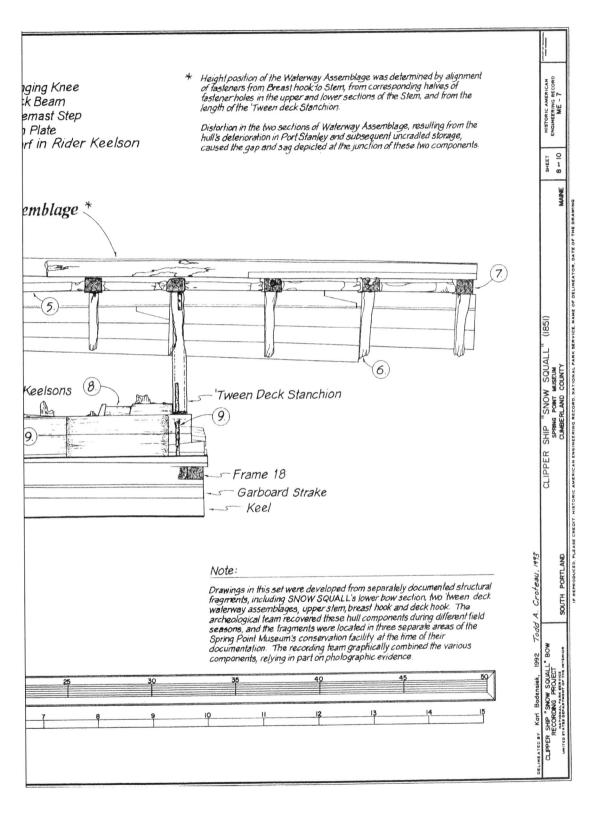

ging Knee
k Beam
mast Step
Plate
rf in Rider Keelson

\* Height position of the Waterway Assemblage was determined by alignment of fasteners from Breast hook to Stem, from corresponding halves of fastener holes in the upper and lower sections of the Stem, and from the length of the 'Tween deck Stanchion.

Distortion in the two sections of Waterway Assemblage, resulting from the hull's deterioration in Port Stanley and subsequent uncradled storage, caused the gap and sag depicted at the junction of these two components.

emblage \*

Keelsons

'Tween Deck Stanchion

Frame 18
Garboard Strake
Keel

Note:

Drawings in this set were developed from separately documented structural fragments, including SNOW SQUALL's lower bow section, two 'tween deck waterway assemblages, upper stem, breast hook and deck hook. The archeological team recovered these hull components during different field seasons, and the fragments were located in three separate areas of the Spring Point Museum's conservation facility at the time of their documentation. The recording team graphically combined the various components, relying in part on photographic evidence.

CLIPPER SHIP "SNOW SQUALL" (1851)
SPRING POINT MUSEUM
CUMBERLAND COUNTY
MAINE

HISTORIC AMERICAN ENGINEERING RECORD
ME - 7
SHEET 8 of 10

SOUTH PORTLAND

DELINEATED BY Karl Bodensiek, 1992. Todd A. Croteau, 1993
CLIPPER SHIP "SNOW SQUALL" BOW
RECORDING PROJECT

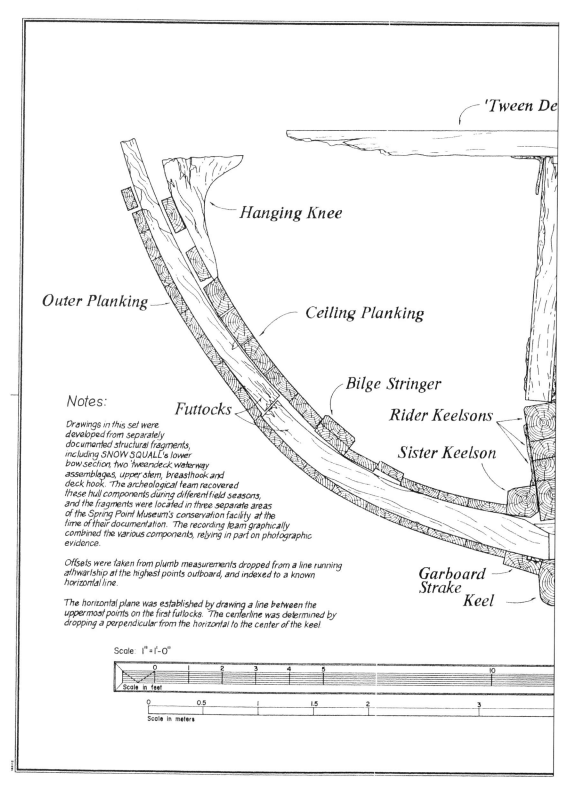

Notes:

Drawings in this set were developed from separately documented structural fragments, including SNOW SQUALL's lower bow section, two 'tweendeck waterway assemblages, upper stem, breasthook and deck hook. The archeological team recovered these hull components during different field seasons, and the fragments were located in three separate areas of the Spring Point Museum's conservation facility at the time of their documentation. The recording team graphically combined the various components, relying in part on photographic evidence.

Offsets were taken from plumb measurements dropped from a line running athwartship at the highest points outboard, and indexed to a known horizontal line.

The horizontal plane was established by drawing a line between the uppermost points on the first futtocks. The centerline was determined by dropping a perpendicular from the horizontal to the center of the keel.

Scale: 1" = 1'-0"

Scale in feet

Scale in meters

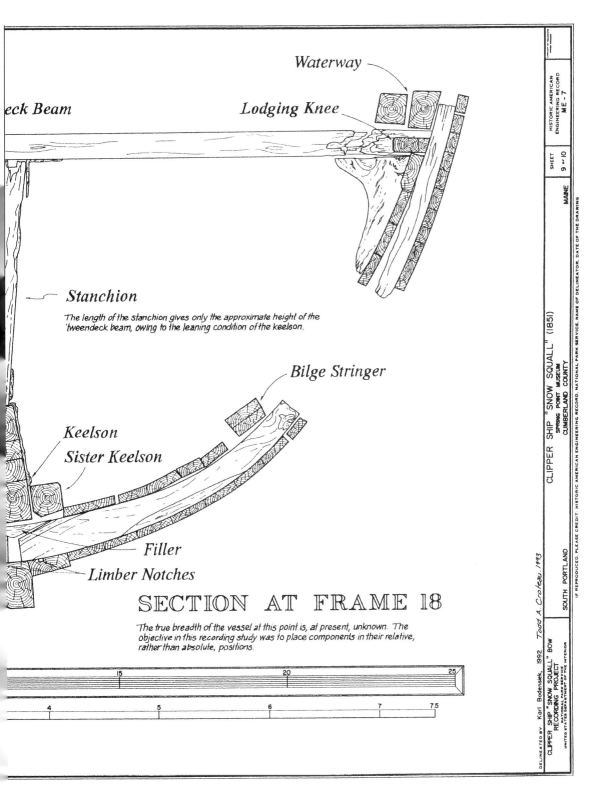

Waterway

Lodging Knee

eck Beam

Stanchion

The length of the stanchion gives only the approximate height of the 'tweendeck beam, owing to the leaning condition of the keelson.

Bilge Stringer

Keelson

Sister Keelson

Filler

Limber Notches

## SECTION AT FRAME 18

The true breadth of the vessel at this point is, at present, unknown. The objective in this recording study was to place components in their relative, rather than absolute, positions.

15   20   25

4   5   6   7   7.5

DELINEATED BY: Karl Bodensiek, 1992  Todd A. Croteau, 1993

CLIPPER SHIP "SNOW SQUALL" BOW RECORDING PROJECT

NATIONAL PARK SERVICE UNITED STATES DEPARTMENT OF THE INTERIOR

SOUTH PORTLAND

CLIPPER SHIP "SNOW SQUALL" (1851)

SPRING POINT MUSEUM

CUMBERLAND COUNTY

MAINE

SHEET 9 of 10

HISTORIC AMERICAN ENGINEERING RECORD ME - 7

IF REPRODUCED, PLEASE CREDIT: HISTORIC AMERICAN ENGINEERING RECORD, NATIONAL PARK SERVICE, NAME OF DELINEATOR, NATIONAL PARK SERVICE, NAME OF DELINEATOR, DATE OF THE DRAWING

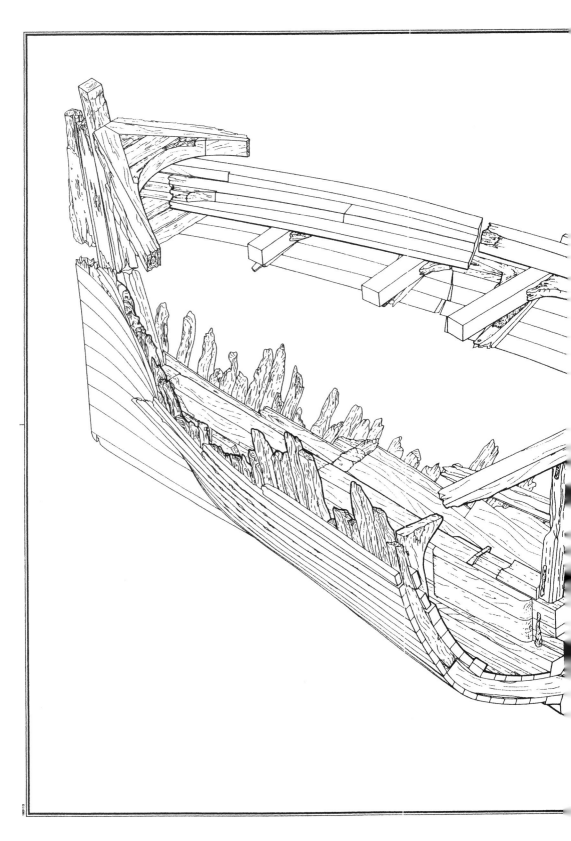

# AXONOMETRIC

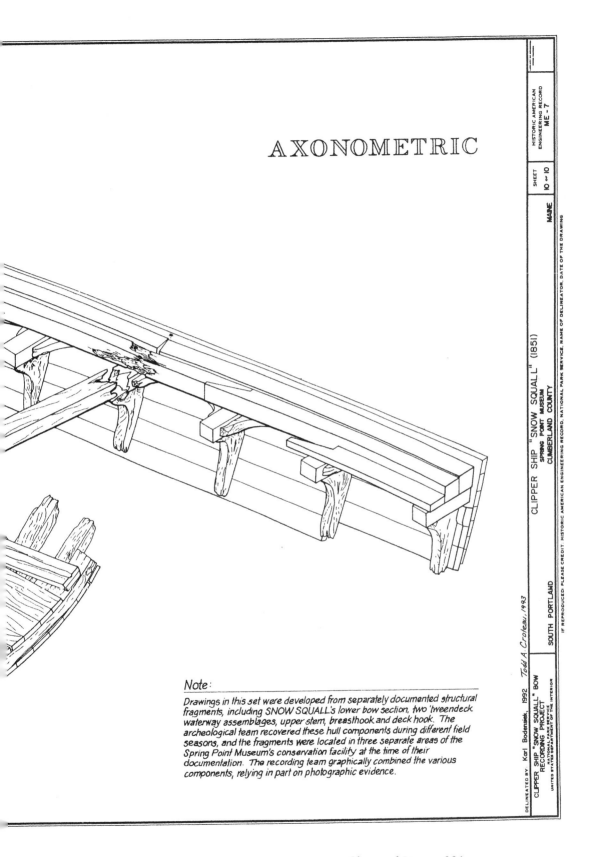

CLIPPER SHIP "SNOW SQUALL" (1851)
SPRING POINT MUSEUM
CUMBERLAND COUNTY
MAINE

HISTORIC AMERICAN
ENGINEERING RECORD
ME - 7

SHEET
10 of 10

IF REPRODUCED PLEASE CREDIT: HISTORIC AMERICAN ENGINEERING RECORD, NATIONAL PARK SERVICE, NAME OF DELINEATOR, DATE OF THE DRAWING

DELINEATED BY Karl Bodensiek, 1992    Todd A. Croteau/1993

CLIPPER SHIP "SNOW SQUALL" BOW
RECORDING PROJECT
NATIONAL PARK SERVICE
UNITED STATES DEPARTMENT OF THE INTERIOR

SOUTH PORTLAND

Note:

Drawings in this set were developed from separately documented structural
fragments, including SNOW SQUALL's lower bow section, two 'tweendeck
waterway assemblages, upper stem, breasthook and deck hook. The
archeological team recovered these hull components during different field
seasons, and the fragments were located in three separate areas of the
Spring Point Museum's conservation facility at the time of their
documentation. The recording team graphically combined the various
components, relying in part on photographic evidence.

Over the course of research for this book a number of potential sources of information were consulted, some of them, like certain New York and Boston newspapers, rather difficult for a non-New England reader to come by. While these have, of course, been identified in the notes, they have not been included here. What follows may be considered suggestions for further reading.

The American Clipper Ships

Clark, Capt. Arthur H. *The Clipper Ship Era.* New York: G. P. Putnam's Sons, 1920.

Crothers, William L. *The American-Built Clipper Ship.* Camden, ME: International Marine, 1997.

Cutler, Carl C. *Greyhounds of the Sea.* New York: Halcyon House, 1930.

Howe, Octavius, and Frederick C. Matthews. *American Clipper Ships.* 2 vols. Salem, MA: Marine Research Society, 1927.

Clark writes from a retired captain's experience, limiting himself to so-called "California clippers," while Cutler takes a broader view of things. Howe and Matthews give brief "biographies" of a number of clippers (including Snow Squall). Their book is available in a paperback reprint from Dover. Cutler's meticulous file-card notes are at the G. W. Blunt White Library at Mystic Seaport Museum. Crothers's book deals primarily with the design and layout of American clippers.

Archival Resources

For American vessels such as Snow Squall there is a wealth of information at the United States National Archives in Washington, DC, and College Park, MD. The principal sources of information are Record Group 36, Records of the Bureau of Customs (crew lists), Record Group 41, Records of the Bureau of Marine Inspection and Navigation (vessel documentation), Record Group 59, General Records of the Department of State (correspondence), and Record Group 84, Records of Foreign Service Posts of the Department of State (captains' protests, vessel arrivals and departures, etc.).

Manuscripts:

Bancroft Library, University of California, Berkeley
    Albert Dibblee Papers
Maine Maritime Museum
    Sewall Family Papers, MS 22
    Hubert Taylor Diary, SM 53/3
Steven J. Nitch Collection
    Edmund Rice Papers


## SUGGESTIONS FOR FURTHER READING

Albion, Robert G. *The Rise of New York Port.* New York: Charles Scribner's Sons, 1939.

Clark, Manning. *A Short History of Australia.* Melbourne: William Heinemann, 1969.

Dana, Richard Henry. *The Seaman's Friend.* Boston: Thomas Groom & Co., 1841. A wealth of detail on nineteenth-century American shipboard customs and practices.

Decker, Peter R. *Fortunes and Failures: White-Collar Mobility in Nineteenth-Century San Francisco.* Cambridge, MA: Harvard University Press, 1978. An excellent analysis of the rewards and hazards of San Francisco business.

Duncan, Roger F. *Coastal Maine, A Maritime History.* New York: W. W. Norton & Co., 1992.

Johnson, Linda Cooke. *Shanghai—From Market Town to Treaty Port, 1074–1858.* Stanford, CA: Stanford University Press, 1995.

Lockwood, Stephen C. *Augustine Heard and Company, 1858–1862, American Merchants in China.* Cambridge, MA: Harvard University Press, 1971.

May, Ernest R. and John K. Fairbank, eds. *America's China Trade in Historical Perspective.* Cambridge, MA: Harvard University Press, 1986.

Morison, Samuel E. *The Maritime History of Massachusetts.* Boston: Houghton Mifflin Company, 1921.

Paine, Lincoln P. *Down East, A Maritime History of Maine.* Portland, ME: OpSail Maine 2000; and Gardiner, ME: Tilbury House, Publishers, 2000. A short, readable history.

Rowe, William Hutchinson. *Shipbuilding Days in Casco Bay, 1727–1890.* Yarmouth, ME: published by the author, 1929.

Scontras, Charles A. *Cooperative Efforts Among Maine Workers: Beginnings and Foundations, 1820–1880.* Orono, ME: Bureau of Labor Education, 1994. Analysis of the Portland labor scene, unfortunately lacking an index.

Strange, Ian J. *The Falkland Islands.* London and Pomfret, VT: David & Charles, 1981.